The Danish Army of the Napoleonic Wars 1801–1814, Organisation, Uniforms and Equipment

Volume 1: High Command, Line and Light Infantry

David Wilson

Helion & Company Ltd

Helion & Company Limited
Unit 8 Amherst Business Centre
Budbrooke Road
Warwick
CV34 5WE
England
Tel. 01926 499619
Email: info@helion.co.uk
Website: www.helion.co.uk
Twitter: @helionbooks
Visit our blog at https://helionbooks.wordpress.com/

Published by Helion & Company 2020
Designed and typeset by Farr Out Publications, Wokingham, Berkshire
Cover designed by Paul Hewitt, Battlefield Design (www.battlefield-design.co.uk)

Text © David Wilson 2020
Plates © David Wilson 2020
Cover: Frederik VI, King of Denmark, original artwork by David Wilson

Every reasonable effort has been made to trace copyright holders and to obtain their permission for the use of copyright material. The author and publisher apologise for any errors or omissions in this work, and would be grateful if notified of any corrections that should be incorporated in future reprints or editions of this book.

ISBN 978-1-913118-91-4

British Library Cataloguing-in-Publication Data.

A catalogue record for this book is available from the British Library.
All rights reserved. No part of this publication may be reproduced, stored in a retrieval system, or transmitted, in any form, or by any means, electronic, mechanical, photocopying, recording or otherwise, without the express written consent of Helion & Company Limited.
For details of other military history titles published by Helion & Company Limited, contact the above address, or visit our website: http://www.helion.co.uk
We always welcome receiving book proposals from prospective authors.

Dedications

To my wife Josette for many years of patience

To Teddy Suren for his original inspiration and 'joie de vivre'

To Jean François Blanc for his constant encouragement.

In memoriam of my dear friend, Lieutenant Colonel Anders Lindström,
Late of the Royal Swedish Army and of Tradition of Scandinavia.
14 October 1941–3 September 2014

Contents

Foreword	vii
Introduction	ix
1 The Historical Background	11
2 Recruitment and Service	17
3 The Generals and the High Command, including the Guides	21
4 The Livgarden til Fods	31
5 The Line Infantry Organisation, Basic Tactics and Uniforms	41
6 The Jægerkorps and the Light Infantry Battalions	76
7 The Infantry Colours	90

Appendices

I	The Soldier's Personal Equipment 1808–1814, the Official List	116
II	Danish Ranks and British equivalents	117
III	Danish Military Music	118
IV	The Development of Danish Muskets and Locks	119
V	Danish Food and Rations	121
VI	The Battle of Køge, 29 August 1807	123
VII	The Orders of Battle and Actions of the Danish Auxiliary Corps of the Grande Armée	125
VIII	Known Military paintings by C.A. Lorentzen 1749–1828	128

Bibliography and Sources	129

List of Plates

Plate 1. Generals and Senior Officers	22
Plate 2. The Guide Corpset	28
Plate 3. Livgarden til Fods I	32
Plate 4. Livgarden til Fods II	36
Plate 5. The Danish Cadets	38
Plate 6. Danish Line Infantry Musketeers	42
Plate 7. Danish Line Infantry Grenadiers and Jægers	44
Plate 8. Danish Hats and Legwear	50
Plate 9. Danish Infantry Equipment	52
Plate 10. Danish Bearskins	55
Plate 11. Danish Line Infantry Officers 1805–1814	60
Plate 12. Danish Line Infantry Drummers and Hornists 1805–1814	63
Plate 13. Musical Instruments	64
Plate 14. Danish Line Sapper c.1813 of the Prince Christian-Frederiks Regiment	66
Plate 15. Danish Line Infantry Regimental Distinctions c.1808	68
Plate 16. Danish Rank Distinctions: Officers and NCOs' Epaulettes 1801–1812	72
Plate 17. Danish Line Rank Distinctions 1812–1815	74
Plate 18. Danish Jægere I, 1806–1810	78
Plate 19. Danish Jægere II, 1810–1814	80
Plate 20. The Light Infantry/Sharpshooters.	82
Plate 21. Danish Infantry Weapons	84
Plate 22. Danish Firearm Locks	86
Plate 23. Danish Officers' Shabraques	88
Danish Colours I Livgarde til Fods	94
Danish Colours II Cadets and Grenadiers	95
Danish Colours III Danske Livregiment	96
Danish Colours IV Norske Livregiments	97
Danish Colours V. 3rd and 4th Battalions	99
Danish Colours VI Royal Regiments	100
Danish Colours VII Queen's Regiment	101
Danish Colours VIII Queen's Regiment	102
Danish Colours IX Arveprins Frederiks Regiment	103
Danish Colours X Fynske Regiment	104
Danish Colours XI 1st & 2nd Jyske	105
Danish Colours XII 3rd Jyske	106
Danish Colours XIII Oldenborg	107
Danish Colours XIV Slesvigske	108
Danish Colours XV Holstein	110
Danish Colours XVI Fanions	111
Danish Colours XVII Fanions	112
Danish Colours XVIII Marine and Københavns Regiments	113
Danish Colours XIX Landvaernet	114

Foreword

David Alan Wilson, who took the artist's name of Jacdaw, has placed on the table his first volume in a planned extensive work on *The Danish Army of the Napoleonic Wars 1801–1814*. This is a remarkable and beneficial achievement. Together with his early education in the history of art and his dedication to historical re-enactment and production of figurines combined with his profound interest in the Ancien Régime has paved his way into writing and painting about this fascinating period of political and military turmoil within the dual monarchy of Denmark and Norway. Further, being a member of the French *La Sabretache; Société d'Etudes d'Histoire Militaire* has definitely added to his dedication and qualifications for military dress.

An obvious Danish contribution to this publication has been given by Jørgen Koefoed Larsen, Member of Danish Military Historical Society – who *sine qua non* has contributed generously with his vast and reliable knowledge of every area of research on this subject.

The value of portraying this particular subject in the English language is considerable further to the fact that only a few keen readers outside of Scandinavia have dived deeply into detail in this field due to its intricate terminology, which is not accessible in one of the main languages. For such a task a master is required – and Jacdaw was available and has here thoroughly transmitted his knowledge.

The military uniforms are spectacular. Their use is obvious as they must fulfil the purpose of both identifying on the field of conflict the nationality of the wearer as well as being a source of inspiration in times of peace. Basically, the study of the uniforms of the Napoleonic wars requires both the consideration of the conditions of life in the field and to the government's need to signal its own splendour – and thus its military power.

Throughout the first centuries of Danish-Norwegian uniforms they were conspicuously influenced by the victorious military nations. When absolute monarchy was introduced in 1660, French principles of dress codes became universal. The Danish-Norwegian armies experienced a reorganisation in 1761, and simultaneously the Prussian model became the example to follow. Subsequently in the fields of military operations and tactics, inspiration was deduced from leading Danish officers experiences during the Seven Years War (1756–1763), the American War of Independence (1775–1783), the Russian-Swedish War (1788–1790), and from the early French Revolutionary Wars (1792–1801).

Around the opening of the new century a couple of new trends became increasingly evident. Firstly, with effect from 1803 the regulation of conscription made the armed forces in principle entirely national. Secondly, the appearance of the enrolled subjects was cared for in elaborate detail by Crown Prince Frederik, who from 1784 ruled as prince regent, and became king in 1808. Over the years he developed a well-informed knowledge in military matters, and as head of the dual monarchy he avoided a long and bloody war until 1807. He was advised how to benefit from the armed neutrality, and he gained time to prepare by strengthening the efficiency and the self-respect of his armed forces. So, also for uniforms for the army of Denmark and the duchies as well as for the army of Norway he issued numerous and meticulous instructions.

The uniform colours for the two life regiments remained stable in the royal colours of red and yellow. However, whenever needed, a constant stream of changes floated from the royal hand. For uniforms and equipment, he distanced himself from France, Sweden and partly from Great Britain, as they were his most likely enemies, and found instead inspiration from the closest ally until 1811 – Russia – and in addition from Austria, Prussia and other German states – in particular Hesse-Cassel.

Already as prince regent he made it clear that Denmark and Norway would not just copy, but rather design everything for their own military use and in their style, forming the best possible functioning and well cared for army to defend the kingdoms. So, his armed forces became armies of their own in both colour and design. This unique appearance – due to direct royal influence during the Napoleonic Wars – makes the armed forces of the dual monarchies a fascinating study.

In order to produce fully reliable results within this field, a qualified use of authentic historical sources remains a must. Thus, only a study of the normative sources, and how regulations would be applied according the King's approvals and to his directives, is insufficient, as these sources will not depict *wie es eigentlich gewesen*. Contemporary artists, who depicted the very appearance of the soldiers, take on an important role – because their paintings were visible for comparison at the same time as the uniforms and equipment were actually being in service. Although very few uniforms have survived, the few which have are very important, especially if they remain conserved unaltered.

Jacdaw's use of these three very different sources of information is balanced, critical and thus reliable.

So, the method used is a solid way of approaching the interesting but difficult theme, and it makes the final result invaluable. Through the fascination of this colourful edition disposing of it immediately becomes apparent and beneficial.

Hans Christian Wolter
President of Danish Military Historical Society

Introduction

This book is one of the first books written in English covering this extremely loyal and dignified nation and its colourful and interesting army of the Napoleonic period. I have tried to cover as much ground as possible, including their army, the militia as well as the naval troops who served ashore. I have divided the book into two basic parts, the first covering the Danish army and the second covering the Norwegian army, each of these two parts have been sub-divided into the infantry, including their arms and colours, the cavalry, including their arms and standards, the artillery, including the principal pieces of ordnance and equipment, and lastly the different units of militia. The part which covers Norway follows the same presentation, but concentrates principally on the differences rather than the similitudes in the two armies. Originally, I only intended to write a one-volume work, but confronted with so much original material it has now grown to three.

For primary sources, I have used as many contemporary sources as possible, including the von Brockdorff collection, and a vast number of watercolours spanning most of the period, the work of the artist Johannes Senn (1778–1861), who painted a number of watercolours of the uniforms in use at the time – seen by the highly uniform-interested Frederik VI.

Von Brockdorf (born in 1810) married in 1837 the illegitimate daughter of Frederik VI, Caroline Augusta Dannemand. She and her family had received several gifts from the King, and inherited several artefacts when the King died in 1839, which was later were enlarged by further inheritances and became the Brockdorff family collection, which piece by piece was eventually presented to different museums. Part of this collection consisted of books, some of which were given to the Military Archives; among these were apparently two copies of *The Danish Army 1804*. That is how the name 'Von Brockdorff' became to be noted on the registration cards – the family was the donor and not the author. Further research carried out by Jørgen Koefoed Larsen has shown that it is more than likely that the real artist who painted the plates of the *The Danish Army 1804* was the young D.W.H. Voigt, who was then a *Feldjaeger* (later corporal when his unit became the Guide Corpset). He definitely painted the plates of 1817, and no doubt he painted both those in 1804 and a lot of the uniform plates of the period as well.

Senn's paintings were commissioned by the King for his mistress, known as Mrs Dannemand. She had only received two finished paintings when Senn painted a realistic portrait of the King showing him with the queen stumbling due to an infirmity. The painting was removed from the exhibition, so the artist just went home and made a copy. The King then withdrew his commission and the third painting was never completely finished, nor was it given to the mistress.

Senn's Revuerne (1808–1810) gives authentic information in particular on how the *Kongelige Livgarde til Hest* was dressed, amongst others, when his Majesty reviewed them. Senn also wrote a book called *Danske Klædedragter* [Dress in Denmark] 1806–1808 and *Klædedragter i København* [Dress in Copenhagen] circa 1808–1812, which besides showing civilian dress of all classes, also shows a lot of highly detailed uniforms in use, a natural part of society. Senn collaborated with Eckersberg, Heuer and Rieter, all well known for their uniform paintings and sketches as well. Nor should we forget the Suhr brothers with their illustrations of the Danish army in Hamburg circa 1812–1814. Another contemporary artist whose work is of a major interest is C.A. Lorentzen, little known outside of Denmark. His paintings show the subjects in natural settings and he painted most of his subjects from life, not in the studio, so he shows details otherwise unknown. Another detail to note is that he usually portrayed himself as a civilian somewhere in the painting.

I must add that as both the Danish and Norwegian language, both ancient and modern, are not the easiest of languages for a non-native to understand, so please excuse any errors which I may have made. I have followed period names as much as possible, but the names frequently have different spellings as they are written differently today, along with some German in the region of Holstein.

This study started over five years ago as a simple fascicule for some friends who wished to paint some Danish Napoleonic model soldiers. They they did not have any information on the subject, but they knew that, thanks to my late friend Lieutenant Colonel Anders Lindström, I had a couple of books on the subject and could I write them a few lines and make a couple of sketches. This is where the adventure started. One thing led to another and I became fascinated by all the aspects of this army, but I discovered that there was very little written on the subject in English, so I decided to write a little more and I wanted it to be as accurate as possible as I have seen so many people, myself included, led astray by books which have had little or no research, being simply copied from a preceding book and perpetuating myths and wasting valuable time and effort for all concerned. I must mention Alan Perry of Perry Miniatures who was responsible for putting me in contact with Jørgen Koefoed Larsen who has been my guide through this book.

This book is my humble attempt to write a good working document which is as accurate as possible; covering the uniforms of both the Danish and Norwegian armies of the Napoleonic Wars. As this is principally a uniform book there is just enough historical information to place the details in their context. This first volume covers the Infantry uniforms, their arms and equipment and their colours including the Jægers and light infantry.

Obviously, I cannot be dogmatic about all that I have written and I am sure some errors may have crept in, but where I have come across conflicting information, I have given pride of place to the closest contemporary source. Any other 'interpretations' are my own, based on Danish usages and customs of the time, along with a little bit of logic and a lot of help from friends in both Denmark and Norway.

There is sometimes a little confusion with contemporary and modern texts due to changes in the Danish language which can be difficult for one who is not a native Danish researcher. For example the use of C has in many cases been replaced with a K, so that Compani has become Kompani, the town of Corsöer is now Kørsor and Corps has become Korps. In certain areas place names have been modified Jydske has lost the D and is now Jyske, not forgetting Copenhagen, or København as it was once known.

Another problem concerned weapons. The once very complete collection of small arms which was on display at the Tøjhusmuseet has been dispersed, swords in particular, to a number of other smaller museums throughout the country. So, to inspect these arms in sequence is now quite complicated. Fortunately, I own a copy of their inventory published by Kay Nielsen (although some are misnamed) and Jørgen Koefoed Larsen has supplied the rest from his private archives. Nor must I forget Trond Wikkborg of Norway with his help on arms used in Norway.

A special mention must be made of Jørgen Koefoed Larsen, without whose precious help this work would not have achieved the degree of authenticity that it has. I must also mention his patience with my very poor Danish and his supplying me with many extraordinary documents and putting them into their context and correcting my errors along the way.

Also, I would like to extend my thanks to the following researchers for their kind and irreplaceable help and encouragement that they have given me over the years on Danish and Norwegian uniforms: Torstein Snorrason, for his kindness and patience with me and his gift of rare books; Knut Erik Strøm, who has helped me with the least-known aspects of one of the least-known armies of this period and for his personal work on the Norwegian militia and volunteers; Erik C. Aagaard, who pointed my research in the right direction and provided a vast number of documents on the Norwegian colours.

I must also mention Ola Jonsgaard Moen and Trond Bækkevold, who helped me to start this project; Dr Peter Bunde who has supplied me with examples of all of his own research on this army; Karsten Sjold Petersen, senior researcher of Tøjhusmuseet in Copenhagen.

Thank you all so much.

1

The Historical Background

Denmark was drawn into the Napoleonic Wars against its will as the country had other problems to deal with. As a maritime power, foreign trade was essential to the survival of the country and it needed to trade to be able to import foodstuffs as although the majority of Danish territory was fairly average agricultural ground, along with other areas it was still recovering from effects of the Icelandic volcano of 1784. At this time, agriculture and the structure of farming as a whole was undergoing major reforms. These reforms were not completed until after the end of the Napoleonic Wars. Normally Denmark traded foodstuffs with Norway in exchange for wood and metal ores. Unfortunately, most of the raw materials for a modern industry (and for building a modern army) had to be imported. Although not a rich country, Denmark was earning good money with its large merchant fleet transporting merchandise throughout Europe, to and from the colonies, as well as transporting goods for other countries.

At the beginning of the Napoleonic era, Denmark was rules by Christian VII, King of Denmark and Norway as well as the Duke of Schleswig and Holstein. In theory he was an absolute monarch, but due to his health, as he was clearly becoming more and more insane with age, he controlled less and less the country. Different parties and groups at court took the power and ruled in his name. The most famous was his personal physician, Struensee, in consort with the Queen, Caroline Matilda of Great Britain, but Struensee's rather liberal and erratic ruling made him a lot of enemies, which in the end it cost him the power and his head. Then a more conservative group around Frederik V's Dowager Queen, Juliane Marie (she was the late Frederik V's second wife) took power, exiling the young queen. The infant Crown Prince Frederik (1768–1839) was put under trusted 'guard' and out of sight. His apparently 'weak condition' as a child was observed (the harsh treatment the Crown Prince received at the hands of Struensee, for example letting him wander around half naked with bare feet, probably improved his health and it was administered as a cure, not mistreatment as it was interpreted at the time) and many hoped he would either die young or become an easy puppet. However, helped by his trusted teacher von Bülow, in true Hamlet style, he apparently at first accepted this secondary role, but in secret he laid plans for the future.

In 1784, just after his confirmation, aided by group of more liberal-minded helpers, he staged a bloodless palace revolution. From then on, he was the de facto ruler in his father's name, known as the Prince Regent. He became king in 1808 upon the death of his father under the name of Frederik VI.

Denmark, traditionally an ally of the Russian Empire, attempted to maintain its neutrality and did so until 1807, but also tried to continue to maintain free trade. This led Denmark to side with Russia, Sweden and Prussia in a union of Armed Neutrality in 1801. This was a consequence of the weakening of French naval power in the ongoing war with England. This led to growing number French privateer attacks against neutral shipping, and also growing number of North African and Turkish pirate attacks. Denmark then created a strong convoy system, convoying over 800 ships with success until 1801. However, French-owned shipping and Dutch merchants sometimes used the Danish convoys for protection as well, and as the Danish king's instructions (in fact the Prince Regent's) were not to let anybody (in effect the British Navy) stop and inspect or 'press' crews into their service, in Danish-led convoys. Thus, in the end Denmark inevitably collided with the Royal Navy in three separate 'incidents'. This made Denmark seek help from its closest ally, Russia, and the subsequent forming of the pact of Armed Neutrality, but soon Denmark found itself drawn into unexpected troubles.

The Russian Czar, Paul I, was, unknown to Denmark, siding more and more with the French, against Danish wishes; this was the consequence of Britain having taken Malta and subsequently failed return it to the Knights of Saint John, of which the Russian Czar was the Grand Master. This Paul took as a personal insult. Denmark was now forced to oblige, as withdrawing from the treaty would have meant war with a unified Sweden, Russia, and possibly France as well. Denmark's main asset in the alliance with Russia was that Denmark, as the strongest Baltic navy, controlled all traffic into the Baltic sea, and that the Danish fleet in effect was 'Russia's Front Door', to the Baltic Sea.

For Denmark this was a major problem. With the British fleet under Admiral Sir Hyde Parker, with Vice Admiral Nelson as second in command, now at the head of the Danish straits leading into the Baltic Sea they knew they would receive the first blow. The British, fearing that Russia would side with the French and also take Sweden, Prussia, and Denmark with them, decided to act strongly. In 1801 the British sent their fleet to threaten Copenhagen and finished by fighting a major sea battle on 2 April 1801 against the Danish fleet. Both fleets fought hard with doggedness and a great deal of courage was displayed by both sides, but in the end the Royal Navy prevailed and took out many of the older ships of the Danish fleet laying in the straits of Copenhagen as blockships without masts or rigging. After Nelson's personal account it was 'the hardest battle he had ever fought'. In the end they saw fit to sign an armistice, as pacifying Denmark was only the first step in a longer campaign where Saint Petersburg was the main target. So an Armistice came as a blessing for both sides, as both had sustained heavy casualties.

What Nelson did was to send a letter saying he would be forced to burn all Danish prisoners on all captured Danish ships, if the Danish did not stop firing, and let the British pass. The Danes did not call for a truce either, but accepted one as the battle appeared to be lost, and to save their prisoners from being burned alive. Nelson, the perfect gentleman, then gracefully refrained from burning his Danish prisoners. Although the British claimed many ships as taken, they were only able to claim one ship as a prize, as the rest were too damaged so they were sunk or were burnt. Denmark, having been informed secretly of the murder of the Russian Czar during the negotiations, now felt free to sign an armistice, allowing the British fleet to sail through Danish waters to attack the Russians. Only later did the British realise that the new Russian Czar Alexander and his government were also willing to sign a treaty, so the British fleet sailed back to England with matters settled for the moment, but they used much of their time during the return voyage mapping the Danish straits in case of further action. In 1804 Britain also made an alliance with Denmark's arch-rival, Sweden, for the use of Swedish Pomerania in the war on the Continent, and so also now had a secure presence in the Baltic, on both sides of the Danish straits. Also, Sweden began plotting against Denmark, leading to growing British suspicions against Denmark.

Following this battle Denmark strengthened the seaward defenses of Copenhagen, built new ships and further modernised its army, but as it did not have the economic resources it was unable to strengthen its landward defences as well or the permanent garrison of Copenhagen, which would have dire consequences later on.

However, one has to understand, the de facto ruler of Denmark, the Prince Regent, feared and hated the French Revolution, and admired the British. He was himself half British by his mother, who was British, and his paternal grandmother was also British. So he saw the new Napoleonic France as his most likely enemy and Britain as his natural ally, never as a potential enemy. He even went so far as to make a major reduction of the Danish high sea fleet in his plans for the Danish fleet of 1806, and would instead concentrate on an inshore fleet of smaller vessels and gun boats. Also, he secretly told the British government 'Denmark will never be a Enemy of Britain, but will in case of a French attack on its border, see itself as natural ally of Britain'. This, the British Government underhandedly also accepted.

With Napoleon having defeated first Prussia in 1806 and then Russia in 1807, Denmark now strongly feared French attacks against its borders, so they deployed nearly all of their army, under the personal command of the regent, Prince Fredrik, along the Holstein border. In reality, Denmark was prepared to join the Prussians in 1806–1807 if they had been able to beat, or at least resist, the French, and Napoleon was fully aware of this. After some border clashes, a truce was agreed to, but Denmark still feared the worst, and stayed on the alert focusing on the border, facing the French. What eventually happened was totally unexpected.

Understanding of what really happened in Denmark has for years been clouded by a massive myth and probable cover-up of the real truth, but today with the declassification of the papers and letters by the British Foreign Minister George Canning and the 2007 publication of Thomas Munch Petersen's *Defying Napoleon, How Britain Bombarded Copenhagen and seized The Danish Fleet in 1807*, it is possible to obtain a clearer picture.

The story is as follows. In May 1807 George Canning became foreign minister of Great Britain, and in reality, the leader of the government as the prime minister the Duke of Portland, was weak and sick. Canning no doubt had a clever brain, but he was also a man beset with the idea, that God the almighty had made him the one to quell the French Revolution. Further, he was a man not to take advice from others, and for whom the result justified the means. In 1806–07, Britain was suffering defeats on all fronts from South America, on the Baltic coast to the Dardanelles. Only at sea had Britain had strongly beaten the French. All of their Allies on the continent: Austria, Prussia, Saxony, Sweden and Russia had also been defeated in the 3rd and 4th Coalitions. As a result, a considerable British army now found it themselves under siege in Swedish Pomerania. The idea of an attack on Denmark and the neutralisation of the Danish Fleet ('Russia's front door to the Baltic sea') followed Russia's final defeat at the Battle of Friedland on 14 June 1807 was becoming more and more accepted by the British parliament. This was helped by a massive use of what we today would call 'Fake News' concerning how close Denmark was to joining Napoleon. So, in a secret council meeting held on 10 July, in London, the decision was made: 'To make a Demonstration against Copenhagen'. By 17 July it specified the objective as; 'To Secure possession of the Danish Fleet … ' At the same time it was stressed that it should 'send a strong message to the Russians'.

British history has always claimed that the Danish rejected going to war alongside the British, and cites its 'aggressive convoying' and (unfounded and false) rumors of the Danish fleet being made ready for action against Britain, as it was the last important fleet left in Europe following the defeat of the Franco-Spanish fleets at the Battle of Trafalgar. The British by this logic had the right to fear that the Danish fleet would be used to reinforce the French fleet in their project of an invasion of England, and that these were justifiable reasons for a preemptive attack. This was false and Denmark had no 'aggressive convoying'; when the British attacked there was only one tiny 20-gun corvette on convoy duty outside of Denmark, but over 2,000 defenceless Danish Merchantmen were taken as prizes, by British ships even before the British attack. The ships perceived to be equipping for action against the British were in fact just 16 gunboats, one frigate, and a ship of the line being made ready for normal patrolling and to guard against a potential French attack.

Denmark had concentrated all of its forces to defend the country against French attacks. This Canning knew, having received information about these preparations on 7 July. The attack was confirmed on 31 July without informing Denmark. France had also heard rumours of a British fleet bound for Denmark and also wished to be prepared, in case Denmark joined with the British. For British plans it would be fine to let Denmark fend for itself against France, but what it really wanted was an open access to the Baltic, as a mean to influence Russia and secure supreme control of the Baltic. Great Britain had no strategic interest in Denmark's soil, only its (open) straits. With Sweden as an ally, Øresund would be secure anyhow.

Also, a persistent myth has arisen, even accepted by most Danish historians, that Great Britain acted over some secret information gathered by successful British spies at the meeting at Tilsit. This is nothing but a myth. As we now know from all Canning's letters and papers, the British had no real information and no spies at Tilsit. The famous 'Spy Rapport Direct from Tilsit' received 21/22 July 1807 was in fact a fabricated letter made in England by the comte d'Antraigues, a French royalist émigré resident in London and based mainly on rumors and lies gathered in Germany. It earned d'Antraigues both a pension and refuge in England.

Napoleon and the Russian Czar Alexander had met on 7 and 9 July 1807 and drawn up the Treaty of Tilsit. It has been claimed that Napoleon sought to establish the Continental Blockade, and that in a secret clause, the Czar Alexander promised to use his influence at a later date to force Denmark to agree also and force Denmark to close its ports to trade with England as well. In reality, there was no such 'secret clause'. What Napoleon wanted was for Russia to use its influence to make England agree to a peace agreement with France, and if Britain rejected this, ' … Russia to use its influence to make Denmark and Sweden to become allies against the British, until the British agreed to make peace'. At the end of July, the Russian diplomatic mission in Britain informed Canning that the Czar was preparing a peace suggestion on behalf of the French, and were politely told ' … that he would consider it when he received the text from Tilsit'. So what Canning was preparing was not a peace, but a continuation of the war by actively forcing all the remaining neutrals into the war. Additionally, Canning wanted to ' … stun Russia into her senses again'. This also gave the British the opportunity and reason to 'take out' the last neutral maritime nation left in Europe; that they could take over its shipping and thus gain control of its colonies may also have been a temptation. This would mean that Britain would so gain an absolute control of the sea, both militarily and economically; this may also have been a reason, though not officially stated. Whatever the reasons, the British reacted in August 1807. This was not so difficult, as they already had a large army retreating from Swedish Pomerania, which had been allied with Sweden, but was now being overrun by the French. Reinforcements had long since been made ready in British ports, but were now officially diverted for an attack on Denmark and they set sail on 30 July.

A three-pronged attack was now planned, one fleet from the North Sea, which passed the Kronborg, with both sides politely saluting each other; another fleet from the south, and lastly a fleet in the Storebælt to make sure that no help could cross the straits. Denmark was simply told that it had to surrender its entire fleet, unconditionally, only to be returned to them after the war, and agree to an alliance on purely British terms; or take the consequences. The British diplomacy was so high handed and insulting, that Denmark, which otherwise would eventually have sided with England, because of the strong French threats, now felt that it had no other choice than to oppose the British, as Denmark could not exist without the control of its own fleet. War was declared, but having only a few regular troops in Zeeland as the rest of the army was still deployed along the frontier in Holstein against the French, and so relying mainly on town militias with a few regular troops and the rural *Landeværn* of often badly organised, ill-equipped and ill-led soldiers, Copenhagen stood no chance. The Danish still tried to counterattack and reinforce the fortress on several occasions, but without success against the might of the British army. The most notable battle was the Battle of Køge on 29 August 1807, when the quickly assembled Danish militia tried to relieve the besieged capital. They were brave men, but they had no chance as they faced an equal number of veteran British and Hanoverian forces led by the future Field Marshal Wellington.

The British answer to Danish resistance was a terror bombardment principally carried out by the Royal Navy and aimed at the population, killing hundreds of civilians and forcing the commander, Ernst Peymann, to agree to parley. As he did not have clear orders from the Prince Regent and the High Command, he agreed to a truce and was obliged to hand over the Danish fleet for good and save the city.

At the same time the British managed to persuade nearly 1,000 soldiers from the Danish regular 'foreign' Marine regiment, which was composed mainly of Hanoverians and Germans, former professional soldiers who had enlisted in the Danish army, to desert and join the King's German Legion. When compulsory military service for all Danish nationals was introduced in Denmark in 1803, this had ended all official 'foreign' enlistment in the Danish army. Those enlisted foreign men still having time left to serve were assembled in the Marine Regiment to serve on the Danish fleet, when needed and to always have a defence force ready, but they were also thereby kept under strict control behind the walls of Copenhagen. They had shown not much will or ability to fight during the siege, but those who joined the KGL later served with distinction in Spain. What was not so well known until quite recently is that when the British left, 987 deserters and stragglers from British and KGL regiments were rounded up on Zeeland and, although most ended up as prisoners of war, some chose to join the Marine Regiment also. The British and KGL uniforms and weapons were confiscated and put into store as they were not standard issue, but some of them were modified and later reused as the Danes rarely wasted anything.

Upon the ending of the operation against Copenhagen, Canning wrote on 2 October 1807: 'We are hated throughout Europe and that hate must be cured by fear … '

Left with little choice and with much (justified) bitterness towards Britain, this attack pushed Denmark in to an alliance with Napoleon, and they remained French allies more or less until 1814. Having no high sea fleet meant that supplying Norway and the control of the Straits was difficult, at best. However, a decision by the Crown Prince in 1806 to begin a major enlargement of the 'inshore fleet' (mainly gunboats) and to build more coastal batteries was a good one, being the basis for the future defence. Denmark was thereby able to defend its coast and even some parts of the straights. Even so, the supply route to Norway remained risky at best, and easily cut by the British Navy.

A privateer war was then fought against British shipping; it was often successful and a large number of prizes were taken. There were a number of other naval actions (again often successful) in the Baltic Sea between Danish gunboats and brigs and British warships. The Danes built a large number of these smaller ships, heavily influenced by a Swedish naval architect Fredrik Henrik af Chapman. Swedish-born of British parents, Chapman (1721–1808) was the author of a major work, *Architectura Navalis Mercatoria* (1768) and several other shipbuilding-related works. His *Tractat om Skepps-Byggeriet* [*A Treatise on Shipbuilding*] published in 1775 was a groundbreaking work in modern naval architecture. He pioneered the prefabrication in shipyards, the first shipbuilder in Northern Europe to do so and managed to produce several series of ships in record time. Although he never worked directly for Denmark, the Danes had studied his work on smaller gunboats and gun-brigs for the Baltic and this heavily influenced their designs. Along with these warships the Danes developed new tactics and gave the British as well as the Swedes a run for their money, but the details of this part of the war are outside the scope of this book. Norway in reality had to fight a war on their own, due to the difficulty to receive supplies and reinforcements from Denmark.

At the same time, because of their treaty with England and the Russian attacks on Finland, the Swedes were pushed into attacking Norway, where they were regularly outmanoeuvred and beaten by the Danish-Norwegian troops under the command of Prince Christian August, a fine tactician as well as a clever politician, in a number of battles, small by the standards of other Napoleonic battles, but important by Scandinavian standards. Throughout the year of 1808, there was a fair amount of skirmishing until well into 1809, with the Danish-Norwegian army using ski troops with success until an armistice was drawn up between the two countries. Both adversaries were now exhausted, the Danes due to the British blockade and disease and Sweden through disease and defeat on all fronts.

Denmark, now under the overall rule of the new king, Frederik VI, had assembled an army for an invasion of the southern Sweden province of Scania, but hesitated. Both Napoleon and Czar Alexander had promised military help (Napoleon a Franco-Spanish army corps) and both promised: 'that everything the Danish could conquer, they would be allowed to keep'. However, Frederik VI did not trust Russia, and the French 'support' was both expensive, and slow to arrive. The corps of Spanish soldiers which finally arrived soon rebelled and were brought off and returned to Spain on British ships, giving no help at all! Yet the true reason for Frederik not acting was probably that he knew that if Sweden lost Finland to Russia, Russia would have no interest in helping Denmark keep Norway. In the end, the indifferently-led and badly-supplied Swedish army eventually lost Finland to Russia, and the Swedes deposed their absolutist king, Gustav IV Adolf. When this happened, Frederik now hoped that he might be able to keep his hold on Norway, by a political campaign of becoming king of Sweden himself. It soon became clear that he had played his cards badly (he was never a good politician, being far too honest!), and that Sweden would not in any way accept a Danish king for many different reasons. So, in the end, Frederik accepted that his cousin Christian August, a Danish Prince of Holstein, more German than Danish (who had secretly deployed all his political abilities) was accepted by all the parties concerned, to take the crown instead. Christian August was adopted by the new, but ailing and childless, king of Sweden, Charles XIII.

Frederik had hoped that this would make Sweden an ally, and thereby gaining an alternative supply route for Norway. However, Christian August's sudden death from a stroke in 1810, and the sudden candidacy of the French Marshal Bernadotte as crown prince (he was crowned king of Sweden in 1818 under the name of Karl XIV Johan), backed by heavy bribing of the Swedish nobles, (false) promises of recapturing Finland, (false) promises of peace and friendship with Denmark, and (also false) claims of being backed by Napoleon, destroyed this hope. Napoleon had accepted this unexpected move, against Danish wishes or knowledge, to get rid of the ever-troublesome Bernadotte (even claiming that this was an alternative to having him shot!) and probably hoped to gain some direct influence in Sweden. However, Bernadotte's plan clearly was to use the Swedish crown as his chance to getting revenge on Napoleon. At once he started to plot with the Russian Czar and Great Britain, to get Norway to please his Swedish backers and thereby get himself a power base, which he hoped would eventually gain him the French throne.

Towards the end of 1811 and early 1812 Bernadotte and the Czar made secret plans to assemble an army in Scania and together attack Zeeland with British help. However, the deteriorating relations between France and Russia and the subsequent threat to the Russian borders in 1812 made the Russians stay at home. The Swedish Army did not dare attack on its own. Through their spies Denmark had found out about the treaty and assembled the main part of its army on Zeeland ready to defend it. A 'Mobile Corps' of around 13,000 men and 40 cannon was also formed to defend the Danish border around Hamburg-Lübeck and, together with French forces, to secure the French flank and rear during the French invasion of Russia.

Because of the changed situation after the French defeat in Russia 1812, Denmark actively sought a way to join the alliance against Napoleon. Danish forces even helped defend Hamburg against the French, but Britain, backed by Russia on the behalf of Sweden, would only accept if Denmark agreed to turn Norway over to Sweden (to be compensated by receiving parts of Westphalia!). This was totally unacceptable for Denmark, so again Denmark was forced into the war on the French side.

Between 1813 and 1814, the Danish 'Auxiliary Corps', although small (in fact the size of a strong division), put up a good fight, frequently beating their direct adversaries. The French 'Iron Marshal' Davout, who was at first suspicious of this corps of unknown value thrust upon him for his defence of Hamburg in 1813, after seeing the Danish corps in action declared to Prince Frederik of Hessen 'Now that I know your Corps, I march as happily with them as I would with any French Veterans!' Even their small cavalry arm surprised the enemy cavalry and both the Prussians and the Russians learned to have a healthy respect for them, coming off worst on more than one occasion when fighting against the Danes. Nevertheless, the Danish were eventually beaten, being both outnumbered and outflanked. In December they were forced to make peace with the Allies and turn Norway over to Sweden by the Treaty of Kiel, 14 January 1814. Following the defeat of Napoleon in 1814 Denmark was left weakened and their traditional enemy, Sweden, now governed by Bernadotte as Crown Prince, ever covetous, invaded and annexed Norway following a national revolt against the treaties of 1814.

By the time of the Treaty of Kiel in 1814, Denmark was bankrupt and had been stripped of many of its territories to the general indifference of the other European states, both friends and foes alike. In 1807, the country's principal territories had consisted of Norway, the islands of Zeeland – where the capital of Copenhagen is located – Funen, and the mainland between the Jutland peninsula and the Duchy of Schleswig-Holstein as well as Iceland, Greenland, the Faroe Islands and two colonies in the West Indies, together with some small possessions in India and West Africa. Nor should be forgetting the fortress of Christiansø, east of the island of Bornholm, still Denmark's most eastward possession to this day. This dispersed geography, combined with one of the most extended coastlines in Europe in relation to the size of the country, meant that the Danish army was by necessity divided into numerous different corps, each one defending a different part of the realm and rendering the concentration of the army extremely difficult if not nigh impossible, especially if not supported by a strong active fleet.

During the war, both Norway and the isle of Helgoland were lost forever. Yet by cleverly allying himself with the Austrian Emperor during the Vienna congress, King Frederik managed to receive a small compensation, in the form of the German Duchy of Lauenburg, and some much-needed money from Sweden and political acceptance in Europe.

Contrary to normal myth, Frederik VI had no wish to show off, to command everything to show himself to be a famous general, or in any way idolise Napoleon. Frederik VI did not see himself like this in any way, but as an absolute monarch, he felt it necessary to 'Be his own minister of War' and this was the role he played during the Napoleonic Wars. The fighting he left to the best of his generals and did his best to support them. Neither did Frederik VI idolise Napoleon. Until 1807 he clearly saw him as his most likely enemy, and did his best to prepare to fight him, but in 1808–14 Napoleon was now his strongest ally and his only hope of keeping Norway. As Napoleon always treated him with respect, so Frederik respected him also and acknowledged him as a fellow monarch and successful general. Still, he also saw his faults and stayed on his guard. The English had virtually raped Denmark in 1807 and the Russians and Bernadotte (again with British help), had stabbed Denmark in the back in 1809–1814, so Frederik probably ended up by respecting Napoleon as a man who was no worse than the rest!

2

Recruitment and Service

The Danish kingdom was divided into several regions with different forms of military service and defence organisations. Zeeland, with the capital of Copenhagen, was the main fortress and the principal naval base; it was seen as the most important place to defend and for long time Denmark kept a professional army for its direct defense recruited mainly from Germans. This was expensive, and in the end was not found to be very effective.

Denmark's main sources of income came from its maritime trading and its agriculture, but because of the often-conservative land ruling nobility, a rather obsolete and unproductive farming system was maintained. The peasantry and small farmers were normally uneducated and forced to work for the landed nobility, who generally saw soldiering as a punishment. When the Crown Prince became Regent, together with the influence of some more broadminded noblemen, like von Rewentlow and his tutor in military matters, General von Huth, a movement was started in 1789 to totally reform the agricultural system, resulting in bringing much more land under the plough and forming a class of free and better educated independent farmers. However, in exchange for these new rights and a chance of wealth, the crown now expected that all male peasants would be counted, and by lot, all those found to be able, would in the future perform military service, through the conscription of all Danish subjects, thereby forming the first national army. Although there was some resistance from several parties, most notably the formal army commander Prince Karl of Hessen (an advocate of a Prussian-inspired professional army) and the ever-poor economy, this system was enforced step by step.

By 1802, Denmark had finally changed its system of recruitment for good. From then on, with only a few exceptions, it was now based on national conscription from the rural classes with service for two years, followed by six more in the army reserve. Those living in the towns and cities were exempted from formal service, but they were obliged to form local defense units trained to defend their towns against attack, and to perform 'police duties'. Because of its special status, the Duchy of Holstein had reclaimed, amongst other exceptions, special rights to lower the numbers of recruits drawn from its population, which was accepted. This meant that more troops from Schleswig and Jutland were obliged to serve in Holstein instead. Danish nationals were also allowed to enlist voluntarily in some of the specialist units such as the Guides, the Altonaiske Jæger Grenadier Kompani, or the artillery.

The age of service was first set at 20 years of age, it was then raised to 22 years; finally, in 1808, and it was again lowered to 20 years. The time of service was set at two years for the basic training period. The soldiers were kept on the rolls for eight to 12 years after that, but furloughed home, liable to be recalled for service at the state's pleasure; in peace this was normally only 14 days a year for field exercises. For the 'veterans' who were aged between 28 to 34 years old, normally service was only in case of emergency or war.

The average height for soldiers was between 165–170 cm and the minimum acceptable height allowed until 1808 was 160cm. The best recruits of between 160 and 170cm would normally be taken for the light infantry, jægers, hussars or light dragons if they were found fit and able. The best recruits over 170cm would be taken for the grenadiers or, if they were used to horses, the Ryttere (heavy cavalry), again if found fit and able. Recruits over the height of 170 cm, again if found strong, able and maybe having some kind of artisanal background or education, were chosen for the artillery or engineer corps. The best, strongest and most able, over 170 centimetres in height and from any part of the Danish kingdom, could be chosen to serve in the Royal Lifeguards, but here good looks counted as well. For example, nobody with red hair was to be accepted! (Red hair was regarded as uncouth in Denmark at the time).

All the remaining recruits formed the Line Infantry. From 1801–1807, a *Landeværn* (home guard) made up of soldiers having already performed their service, were also formed. However, as the new recruitment system had first started in 1802, these new recruits could only be expected to join in in 1808. Therefore, only a small number of former national recruits, who had served alongside the professional army, and former professionals, were really available to join. This had the effect that the *Landeværn* was only of half the strength planned (400 soldiers to a battalion instead of the planned 800), and both NCOs and officers also were lacking. In 1808, they finally received the soldiers trained 1802–1808, and as a consequence, the *Landeværn* was converted into *Annekterede* (reserve) battalions, becoming the third and fourth battalions of the foot regiments. The minimum height for the recruits was lowered to 157cms, and those of the right age (20–24 years old), not previously acceptable because of their height, were now allowed to join the regimental jæger companies in the *Annekterede* battalions. As a consequence, they received specially shortened muskets. The same was also done to form a fifth company in the *Annekterede* battalions of the Jægers, so that they now also had five companies as well.

Although full national conscription had been introduced in Denmark in 1802, there were still a number of old enlisted or *Geworbne* soldiers who continued to serve out their contracts until well after 1815. After 1802, the older types of enlisted men, mostly German foreigners, were gathered into a specific unit, the Marine Regiment, and later on the remainder was transferred to the Marine Battalion of the Copenhagen Infantry Regiment.

Partly due to its geography, Norway had a home guard system based around a few fortresses and major towns, often the same place. As their only enemy would be Sweden and as the terrain did not allow large armies to be assembled, their defence system dated back to the Vikings or possibly even earlier, but all the same it was still quite well adapted to the situation. Norway had been allowed special rights and lower taxes, and in many ways the Norwegian army must be seen as an army in its own right. However, in Norway there were a few regular paid soldiers and specialists, but the majority of the troops there were conscripts whom the communities paid and equipped, their numbers calculated according to the population The conscripts had to train every Sunday for nine years and take part in manoeuvres 12 days a year.

In Norway, the conscription was not based on population, but on the taxation class of farms. For example, one very rich farm = one dragoon, four poor farms = one infantryman (broadly speaking). There were quite a large number of young men liable for service. City dwellers were not exempt, but had to serve in the city militias or yeomanry. The community did not pay for the equipment as such, but they had to maintain the horses and necessaries like the knapsacks, tenting equipment, and such like. Sunday training had been abolished for all but the rawest recruits before 1800; thereafter there were a number of either regimental, battalion or company gatherings/exercises every year.

One must remember that both in Denmark and Norway, a number of the enlisted personnel were not really full time servicemen, but conscripts who had agreed to a longer contractual period of service in the garrisons, in exchange for a shorter period on the active service rolls.

They were usually furloughed in peacetime, but were liable for exercises, state work on fortresses or on the roads, as needed.

The same system, but with a few local modifications, was also used for the defence of the island of Bornholm. With the exception of a few regular officers and artillerymen, all the soldiering in various units was carried out by the islanders themselves, bolstered by some regular units after 1808 – the 2nd battalion of the Dronningens Regiment in particular.

Arms

During the Napoleonic Wars, weapons and tactics were changing and this influenced the way an army would be armed and equipped. New weapons were invented and more precise firearms were produced as a result. This also happened in Denmark, and although at the start the Danes were slow to adjust to the new tactical doctrines and modern production methods they soon adjusted themselves and caught up with their allies and enemies, even surpassing some.

From the first reorganisation of the *Kronborgs Geværfabrik* (Kronborg Gun factory) producing muskets and side arms in Hellebæk between 1750 and 1760, to the construction of a modern arms factory, producing cannons and side arms around Frederiksværk, a real modernisation and standardising of arms was partly achieved. However, Norwegian iron ores were not of a very good quality, and, as a consequence, Denmark had to import iron ore from Sweden and Germany, making arms production both relatively more expensive and difficult. Also, such items as bronze and sword and sabre blades had to be imported, mainly from Germany. As Denmark was slow in adjusting to new doctrines, mainly due to their economic situation than anything else, quite a number of old weapons were modified to meet the changing demands of the army. It was the policy of the Danish army that every firearm in the arsenals was to be used, meaning that several of the older models had to be repaired or upgraded, and as a consequence the army was never really able to adopt a standard musket.

In theory all the muskets used by the line infantry were to be of the same model. This was achieved by 1808 in Denmark by the general issue of the modern Musket M1794. But those of the *Annekterede* battalions were more mixed, with new and older models in same unit. Many of them had been modified from older models, so the quality varied depending on the age and usage; this situation was again down to economical obligations. Units in Norway and Bornholm also employed a mix of older and new weapons. Developments included the adoption of the Kyhls internal lock (used from 1807), similar to the British Nock internal lock, together with the use of conical touch holes from the 1790s to help speedier loading.

For the most part, except for a few models made especially for the *Landeværn* 1801–1807, the muskets were made using new materials and parts and old barrels were not reused. However, some older cavalry carbines and pistols were shorted from 1798, and at the same time those barrels declared to be fit were reused. New barrels were made for the remainder. Some older muskets (M1774, M1785, M1789 and M1791) were also refurbished and repaired, but they were mainly shipped to Norway and to local defence militias. A few workers had left the *Kronborgs Geværfabrik* for Russian service before 1807, but with the declaration of war this was then strictly forbidden until 1814. The new locks had fewer parts, and so the pay for each lock fell, but as one only produced one lock for each musket, it was not possible to earn more earn more by making more, 50,000 had be made of the old type for M1794, but only 20,000 were ever made of new model for M1807. This led to complaints from the craftsmen, and in the end some compensations, as everybody knew that prices rose between 1807 and 1814.

Unfortunately, the lack of raw materials and their excessive price lowered their general quality especially in 1812–14. This mainly led to delays or halts in production.

The production of firearms and other weapons for the army had until 1800 had been made at the *Kronborgs Geværfabrik*. Due to the ever-rising threat of armed conflict the production of weapons was increased to meet forthcoming demands. The production of close-quarter weapons (swords, sabres, lances and so forth) was transferred to Frederiksværk, which meant that *Kronborgs Geværfabrik* would limit its production to firearms only. The factory at Frederiksværk was named *Kniv og Sabelfabrikken* (Knife and Sabre Factory). The cannon foundry was also here and all cannons made during the war came from this factory, as did most of the carriages. These two factories supplied the Danish army from 1807 to 1814.

As with arms, Denmark was also organising its own production of uniform cloth. The cloth was produced centrally in Copenhagen, but the uniforms were normally tailored by the regiments or by local contractors. The uniforms can be classed under three major periods; 1800–1807, the end of the 18th-century uniforms; 1808–1812, the years of silver and gold, when they still had some resources; and 1813–1815, the years of iron and wool, when austerity was the byword.

All of these transitions of uniform took place under Frederik VI, starting whilst he was acting as regent for his insane father Christian VII. After he succeeded his father to the throne in 1808 he continued the modernisation of the uniforms. This process had begun in 1789/90 and was followed up in 1796, 1802 and 1808, and partly in 1812–1814, when, due to the blockade and general rise of prices of imports, resulting in a general lack of supplies and finance, a series of economic measures had to be made, which eliminated a lot of the finery and concentrated on the essentials. The 1796 and 1802 changes were minor modifications to this uniform model/system. The 1808 uniform change was a major one, changing both the style and the whole concept of uniforms. The changes in the uniform made them both more comfortable, permitted greater mobility and improved the protection of the individual soldier from both the weather and the enemy. In 1810, grey uniforms were approved for the light infantry. The 1812 changes were mainly about removing or reducing the silver and gold lace: officers' epaulettes were removed as economy measures and to modernise the uniforms, also trousers became grey or white instead of blue, again both practical and cheaper.

Drill and Tactics

Although in many ways Scandinavia in general was regarded as among the poorest areas of Europe of the time, Denmark and Norway applied military regulations and practices that were often surprisingly progressive, especially with regards to light infantry, drill regulations and field craft.

The Dano-Norwegian officers were, at least theoretically, very much up to date. Scharnhorst's theories (influenced by having read Johan von Ewald's works) was one of the main subjects taught in the Danish and Norwegian Cadet Academies before 1808.

Danish tactics and fighting styles were formed by its either broken or highly cultivated terrain. A string of highly experienced, competent, and even in some cases exceptional officers, mainly of German birth (principally Hessians), formed a surprisingly modern and quite effective army for a state of its size and its limited finance.

One of the foremost generals was Heinrich Wilhelm von Huth, a veteran of the wars of Frederick the Great, who reformed the artillery from 1766, firstly along Prussian lines but later incorporating his knowledge and experience of French and Austrian innovations and tactics as well. The Danish school of artillery cadets was soon one of the best of its kind. From his privileged position, at the Danish court – at first, he had been the military teacher of the Crown Prince, later the Prince Regent and finally King Frederik VI – he also influenced infantry tactics and was helped by probably one of the foremost and most influential light infantry tacticians of his time, General von Ewald. Huth also was one of the major forces behind the Reforms of Danish Army between 1789 and 1803, which effectively helped to create a national army. The Prince Regent must be given credit for the modern army which was created due to his deep involvement and firm backing.

After von Huth's death in 1806, the Prince Regent personally took over the reins of the reforms and furthered the formation of a modern army. Although he was never a great general, he was a good organiser, and had clear mind and practical sense, but not only this; he was also a man who knew his own limitations, something quite out of character for the time. Although he was the formal supreme commander, he never personally led the army on the battle field, but let other more capable officers take command, such as von Ewald in 1806 and 1809, Prince Christian August in 1808, and Prince Frederik of Hessen in 1813.

Danish tactics have been described by many as outdated linear tactics until modern French tactics were used from 1808. In fact, nothing could be further from the truth! Danish tactics were from the beginning to the end based and modelled around advanced linear tactics with an emphasis on a high level of training, order, and speed of movement. This was then combined with advanced light infantry tactics and good use of supporting cavalry and artillery as well as efficient staff work. Danish tactics were dictated by the terrain found in Denmark and Norway, with few open fields and great deal of uncultivated rough ground, and, in the case of Denmark, a fair amount of cultivated land with a number of rivers and the sea in between the different islands.

This was no terrain for massed battles, large formations or grand batteries. Instead the main fighting formations were all-arms brigades of four to six battalions, with integrated artillery and cavalry support. A corps should, beside a number of line brigades, normally have an 'Advance Brigade' of light troops, light artillery and light cavalry. A cavalry brigade with horse artillery was usually incorporated in the corps. Danish infantry lines were always preceded by a deep screen of light infantry, who were also found within all of the battalions. All line infantry soldiers were trained in basic light infantry tactics which enabled them in case of necessity to do their own skirmishing. In 1808, a trial of column tactics was tested, but was found to be ineffective in general except for marching, reserve, and attack formations against concentrated points of resistance (fortifications, fortresses, towns or bridges) only. Instead, the formation and movement in line was made simpler and quicker. The main battle field attack formation was a deep screen of skirmishers, often with the grenadier companies as support, followed by each battalion. They formed up with two companies in line followed by a company in column of march at each angle (a formation known as 'Advance in line with both flanks refused'). This formation could march quickly, and form either a line or square rapidly. The second line would follow either in column and deploy into line when close to contact or within the range of enemy artillery.

The Light Artillery would be in the frontline as support (up till 1808 this was the regimental artillery, and from then on it was provided by the *Kørende* (mounted artillery). The light cavalry at first would scout ahead; later, when a battle commenced, they kept close to the main formation, normally on the flanks, to be able charge any weaknesses which appeared in the enemy formations. The foot artillery would be placed in central positions and from there break up enemy reserves and attack formations. Also, it would suppress enemy artillery. The heavy cavalry would be held in reserve, again to exploit any weak points where they could obtain a breakthrough or cover a withdrawal if necessary. All this was possible due to the high level of training and command.

3

The Generals and the High Command, including the Guides

Prince Frederik of Hessen 1771–1845

Prince Frederik of Hessen was a capable military officer, respected by all as a soldier, but he was not much of a politician. He displayed great courage in the field when faced with the enemy. He became loved by the Danish troops, whom he always made a habit of visiting them when they were in their bivouacs. He was promoted to lieutenant general in 1789. He was formal commander of the Kongens Regiment from 1795 to 1800, and from 1800 to 1818 formal commander of the Holstein Regiment. Besides this he was from 1800–1808 governor in Rendsborg and Inspector-General for the infantry in the duchies of Schleswig and Holstein. The Prince Regent had during the manoeuvres of the army along the borders in 1805–1807, noticed his ability's. He was following promoted to full general of the infantry in late 1808 (The highest post of the Danish army). In 1809 he was appointed to lead a Danish army from Zealand to the Swedish province of Scania, during the Danish-Swedish War. The planned attack was called off by the Danish government. In July 1809 the Prince was sent to take over as governor in Norway when Prince Christian August left for Sweden. Prince Frederik of Hesse had a special place as the King's most trusted general was the most senior officer in the army after the King, who had given himself the rank of field marshal. From 1807 to 1814 Frederik of Hessen effectively commanded all of the major campaigns.

When he was Governor of Norway he was soon unpopular in those circles working for more political independence in Norway from Denmark, and he never was as popular as his predecessor Christian August nor his Successor Prince Christian Frederik. He left in 1813. While he was in Norway he was the formal commander of the Akershus Jæger Regiment, and wore their grey single-breasted uniform with general's epaulettes and green distinctives with a pair of grey fall-fronted trousers, at least while he was in Norway. After leaving Norway, the Prince led the Danish Auxiliary Corps in Holstein, 1813–1814. This was during the War of the Sixth Coalition, in which Denmark-Norway fought on the French side. The main task of his corps was to assist the forces of Marshal Davout in defending Hamburg. When France lost the Battle of Leipzig, Frederik's corps was forced to retreat. In December 1813 he led his troops from Rostock to Rendsborg, thus saving his army from annihilation, and during the retreat he led his troops to victory at the Battle of Sehested on 10 December 1813.

After the hard campaigning he was clearly tired and his first letters to the King during the truce in December 1814 were very pessimistic, probably more pessimistic than he meant them to be, which clearly influenced the King's handling of the situation, as he trusted his advice. This led to some hard (and unjust) words to the King, when the conditions of the Treaty of Kiel were known, and this led to some cooling of the relations between the two for some time. However, after some much-needed rest, he took command of the Danish occupation force in France in 1815 to 1818. After returning home, he was once again made commanding general in Schleswig and Holstein, and governor of Rendsborg. From 1836 to 1842 he served as Governor-General over Schleswig and Holstein, succeeding his late father Carl, and was also promoted to the rank of field marshal in 1836.

As formal commander of the Holstein Regiment he wore the regimental uniform of the regiment with general's distinctions, in particular during the 1813–1814 campaign. As he was a member of the Order of the Elephant he wore the Star on the breast of his coat and on parade he wore the blue sash of the order as well, and from 1813 he also wore the cross of the Order of the Dannebrog. The Prince was ably seconded by some excellent staff officers in the field. In particular the Bardenfleth brothers, his chiefs of staff Jens Carl and Frederik Løvenørn (Løveørn translates into 'Lion eagle') who all displayed great bravery and talent during the German campaign.

The General of Cavalry, Major General von Kardorff (1756–1820)

Von Kardorff was well-liked by the King and was until 1803, the commander of the Livgarde til Hest, but he

THE DANISH ARMY OF THE NAPOLEONIC WARS VOLUME 1

Danish Generals and Senior Officers

Prince Christian Frederik in General's uniform of the Prins Christian Regiment, c.1808

Prince Frederik of Hesse in General's uniform with General's epaulettes, c.1813

Order of the Dannebrog

Epaulettes post 1808

General

Lieutenant General

Major General

Not to scale

General c.1807

General c.1810

General c.1813

Staff Officer c.1809

Staff Officer c.1811

22

THE GENERALS AND THE HIGH COMMAND, INCLUDING THE GUIDES

> **Plate 1. Generals and Senior Officers**
>
> Top row, left to right: Generals Prince Christian Frederik & Prince Frederik of Hessen in the uniform of their regiments.
> Details of the Dannebrog.
> Details of Generals' epaulettes. Note that the metals could be reversed if the general was either without a regiment or if his regiment had yellow metal buttons. After 1802 they were worn on both shoulders.
> Two variations of the Bicorn. Top a Staff Officer's Bicorn c.1808, below an early General's Bicorn c.1802.
> Bottom row, left to right: A General c.1807, drawing based on a contemporary print of General Peymann showing him wearing his regimental uniform.
> A General of Cavalry c.1810, loosely based on a portrait of Major General von Kardorff (1756–1820)
> General c.1811 (without a regiment). Clearly showing style of uniform and form of embroidery 1808–14. Based on the portrait of von Binzer. Note: If he had a regiment he would have had a white plume in full dress.
> A Staff Officer c.1809. Drawing based on a contemporary portrait of the Chief of Staff, General von Bülow.
> Details of staff lace for collars and cuffs.
> First ADC, based on a contemporary portrait of Colonel von Krogh c.1812.

left the service to marry and live a life of a landowner in Mecklenburg, so he was put 'à`la Suite'. Then, after the attack in 1807, he returned as a volunteer' with his son and was made major general in 1808, 'without a regiment'. In 1809 he was made formal commander of the Liv Regiment Ryttere, changing to formal commander of the Liv Regiment Lette Dragoner in 1810, the two finest cavalry regiments of the army. Unfortunately, the only contemporary painting shows him wearing the uniform of a 'general without regiment' In 1808. His large finger ring and a golden watch chain make him stand out. In particular his very elaborate hair style and cavalry moustache makes him out to be well favoured as few would have dared to wear a moustache in the presence of the King other than he. He soon was first made a commander of a brigade, then a division, and in 1814 the commander of the corps sent to France as a lieutenant general. Frederik VI liked him as a friend and often praised him and called him 'Our best general of Cavalry', and favoured him on several occasions, even writing personally to Prince Frederik of Hessen who was campaigning in Mecklenburg 1813, 'To take special care of all estates and land belonging to von Kardorff, as he is dear to us, and we want to show it'.

The Generals

The three principal general ranks were major general, lieutenant general and general.

Only the generals who did not command a specific regiment, or did not have any close affiliations to one, wore the specified general's uniform as was worn as well as by generals 'a la suite' (those who were not on active service). Or, to be clear, Denmark had no 'field uniform' for generals as such: the field uniform of a general was his 'regimental uniform worn with general epaulettes'. The 'general's uniform' is normally only used for generals not in active service (on pension or retired), and as such only a parade uniform. From 1806 it had blue facings, gold buttons, gold epaulettes, and embroidery and plume were in the colour of the branch of service (the difference between generals and staff officers was button colour). The bow lace on the collar and cuffs of the generals from 1811 was probably based on a stylised pen feather – the weapon most used by a staff officer! – and probably also shows von Bülow's great sense of humor as he was associated with the design.

The cloth used to make the uniforms of the senior officers was a top quality woollen worsted cloth which was shaved to make the surface smoother and also brought out the colour, the red was of a scarlet hue. The colours of the plumes for different branches of service were:

- Infantry, Artillery, and Engineers – White plumes.
- Guards – White plumes with a blue top.
- Light Infantry and Jægers – Green plumes.
- Heavy Cavalry – White plumes, but with the brass 'rhombic' plate of regiment on hat or shako, but obviously not on a bicorn.
- Light Dragoons – White plume with red top (normally they would wear a regimental helmet/Shako).
- Hussars – White plume (Hussar's mirliton).

Generals who commanded a regiment wore their regimental uniform, including the regimental colour for buttons and lace, but with general's epaulettes and any personal decorations. The plume was in the colour of their service. Until 1808 the generals wore a black felt or leather round hat with gold and red cords and tassels and a silver star plaque with a gilded centre bearing the crowned royal arms with a black cockade and a white plume on the side and a gold lace band around the base. From 1808 they adopted the officers' model shako M1808. When they wore a shako it would have had a black leather chinstrap with a black metal button, although most contemporary illustrations show them as silver/white metal. It also had gold and crimson red cords and a mixed gold and red tassel and a white plume. It had a black cockade held in place with a silver loop and bicorn hats, both with same type of fittings and feathers in branch of service colour. Most generals also possessed black bicorn hats as well. Until 1812 the bicorn was only edged with white ostrich feathers along the top. From 1812 this was to be black ostrich feathers when in field service and ordinary service. White feathers were to be reserved for parades and full dress.

Generals not in active service (on pension/retired), normally only had white feathers. However, they could, if recalled for active duty, also use black feathers on their bicorn.

Generals recalled for service (on pension/retired) who were made fortress or local commanders, and others (in war time), were allowed to also use the general's uniform, for 'as long as they were needed'.

They wore a long-tailed double-breasted crimson red cloth coat with a blue collar usually with embroidered collar and cuffs, with the same style of embroidery as used by all of the staff, in gold for the superior officers and silver for the others. The coat was generally worn buttoned over on service, with gold embroidered buttonhole lace and gold-laced edges to the lapels. The coat had blue rounded cuffs with gold trimming and two gold-laced buttonholes, or pointed blue cuffs with gold laced edges: the staff started using pointed cuffs well before the 1812 reforms. The turnbacks and lining were originally straw yellow, but later they were changed to white. The coat had false horizontal pockets which were simulated by gold or silver lace. The buttons and full fringed epaulets were either gold with three silver stars embroidered upon them very early in the period, or silver with gold stars depending on the button colour of the regiment.

In full dress, the generals wore a white waistcoat, white or buff fall-fronted breeches, and black Hungarian boots with a silver or gold lace edging and a tassel. In service dress they wore dark blue breeches with silver Hungarian knots. The form of the knots could vary, but generally it was of the stylised arrow head form with more or less embroidery around it. If the general was a member of the Order of the Elephant, he was entitled to wear a blue sash either under or over the coat and the order itself on the breast of the coat. Most generals are shown with a Danish Cross (Dannebrog), the Order of the Dannebrog, on the left side of their chest.

Their uniform was completed with the red and yellow striped silk sash worn around the waist, over the coat and knotted on the left hip. They carried either a sabre or a sword with a gilded single bar hilt, this was carried in a black leather scabbard with gilded fittings and it had a red and gold sword knot. They all wore small buff leather riding gloves, not gauntlets. Their harness was made of black leather, mostly in the Hungarian style including a hanging throat plume made of leather fringes. From 1808 the shabraque appears to have been of a fairly standard model, made from crimson red cloth with a double silver lace border and silver lace diamond motif in the angles; the older models with gold embroideries no longer appear to have been used.

Contemporary paintings show only the King using a blue shabraque with the same silver lacing, this could be his regimental shabraque as he normally wore the uniform of his regiment: originally this was the Kronprinsens Regiment which later became the Kongens Regiment and blue was the facing colour.

Aides de camp to generals, staff officers, and the general staff wore from 1806 blue facings, silver buttons, silver epaulettes and silver embroidery and a red plume. From 1801 they wore a bicorn (this was allowed for full dress for the whole period). From 1804 also wore hats. After 1808 a special staff model shako was worn by all in both the general staff and in the Guides.

Notes on Shabraques

Until 1808, the role of a general staff was in practice carried out by 'The staff of Crown Prince Frederik' and all his ADCs used red shabraque of the 1802 model. From 1808 when Frederik became the king, he then used a new model blue shabraque so that everybody could find him, but the highest-ranking officer on his staff was a major. These officers then used the new model red shabraque.

The 1802 models shown from the Brockendorff Collection show uniforms and harness as prescribed by the 1804 regulations.

The generals originally had special model saddle cloth and they did not use the new red shabraques approved in 1802 for use with the new 'Hungarian saddles' to be allowed to be used from next term (1803). This term would have a length of six years and so they could have been used until 1808–09.

This special red full-dress saddle cloth was of a style similar to the new 'Hungarian' shabraques (called a *Valdrap* in Danish), but with an 'English style' saddle over the shabraque. This saddle also had pistol holsters mounted at front and they were covered with 'old style' pistol covers.

If the general was wearing the uniform of his regiment', he would have the regimental model shabraques. So in a general's personal staff – as distinct from the general staff

– the general could be identified from a distance by his red shabraque and one of his ADCs by their blue model 1802 shabraques. The blue M1802 shabraques were only for those officers serving as ADCs to a general. Such officers rank up to colonel, but only a few would have had such a high rank, most would have been lieutenants or captains. In 1808 all the generals and staff officers all received new saddle cloths, so they were not used after then.

Regarding cavalry shabraques, the combination of figures at the rear of their shabraques clearly indicated the type of cavalry, while front figures indicated if they belonged to an officer (bows) or a trooper (chevrons). Again, details are scarce. Probably generals formally leading a cavalry regiment would use a version of their parent regiment's shabraques, but again not much different from an ordinary cavalry model, except for the quality of the cloth and lace.

After 1812 all lace was supposed to be woollen and not metallic, but whether the generals actually respected this order or not is not recorded.

Staff Officers

Before 1805 most senior staff officers wore a black felt hat which by 1808 had been replaced by a black leather officer's shako with leather bands on the top and bottom edges sometimes laced silver, it had a plume indicating his branch of service over a black cockade on the front with a silver embroidered loop and red and gold cords and tassels. The shako would have had a black leather chinstrap with a black metal button, although most contemporary illustrations show them as made of silver/white metal.

The Adjutant General's staff (*Generaladjudantstaben*) bore a red pompom-style plume and they were nicknamed the *røte fjer*, the red feathers. From 1806, they had blue facings, silver buttons, silver epaulettes and silver embroidery.

The Quartermaster Staff (*Generalkvartermesterstaben*) were probably the most numerous part of the general staff, who basically wore the same uniform as the officers of the Guides – the principal differences were the shako plates, chin scales and the collar and cuff embroidery – who were also an integral part of the Quartermaster Staff from their creation. It was for this reason they shared the same basic uniform from 1808 and this became even more evident in 1810 and 1812. The staff uniform regulations changed every two years.

The Quartermaster Staff had two types of officers: the Quartermaster officers and the 'Adjoints'/Extras, the latter were young officers learning their trade from the senior officers until they were ready to be posted to different staff commands. They did not wear the full uniform of the quartermaster staff – only the red pompom style plume, occasionally with a yellow top which indicated that they were affiliated to the Guides; in fact the officer wearing this plume were more than likely an officer of the Guides. Their officers' model shakos had gold and red flounders and long cords. In full or court dress they could still wear bicorns. From 1806 they had silver buttons, silver epaulettes, and silver embroidery on their regimental uniforms. Officers of the Quartermaster Staff wore as per descriptions of the uniform regulations of 1803 and 1808, the same uniform as staff officers, but with black facings.

In 1808 and 1810, there is clearly a question regarding which type of lace bars they wore on their collar and cuffs. Staff, Quartermaster Staff, and Guide Corpset, we are told, had 'two silver lace bows, on each side of the collar and on each cuff'. We know that at least the model of bow/lace bar for the Guides was different from that of the rest of the general staff.

In 1808 the Quartermaster Staff was permitted to wear blue facings the same as the Guides (as they were also considered as part of the general staff) in 1810, but with different lace.

The staff officers had a crimson, or more often a red, cloth coat with long tails. It had a dark blue collar with two silver loops on each side, usually worn with the lapels buttoned over, either to the left or right, apparently the reason given for this was to use the coat equally and hopefully last longer. The blue became much darker after 1811–1812; the blue was now so dark it was nearly black. The coat was piped straw yellow and embellished with silver embroidery. The round cuffs were dark blue, piped straw yellow or white with three silver buttons and silver laced buttonholes. The turnbacks were straw yellow and the coat had false horizontal pockets simulated in blue piping. The coat had silver buttons and full fringed epaulettes. The style of the embroidery on the collars and cuffs designated their rank and office. The coats of higher-ranking officers could have embroidery on the coat as well, in metallic lace up to 1812, after that date the piping and embroideries were in yellow or white wool and thread.

In full dress they wore a straw yellow vest, straw yellow fall-fronted breeches and black Hungarian boots with silver lace and tassel. In service dress they generally wore dark blue breeches with silver or more likely white Hungarian knots. Around their waist and over the coat they had a sash of yellow and red silk, later of wool, with tassels worn over their coat and knotted on left hip. They carried a sabre with silvered single bar hilt carried in a black leather scabbard with silvered fittings and it had a red and gold sword knot. They all wore small buff leather riding gloves, not gauntlets. Their horses had black leather harness and they had a crimson red shabraque which had a double silver or white lace border with silver embroideries of a model more or less the same as that used by the generals.

A staff officer who was detached from a regiment would wear the uniform of his regiment including buttons and colour of epaulettes. The plume was in his branch of service, in this case red or red tipped yellow. When serving with a general and not detached from general staff, the same would apply. They would from 1808 wear the normal officers' model shako with fittings of their original regiment.

In general, the field headquarters were clearly visible as they were marked with their own flags or, rather, fanions. They were used both in Denmark and Norway. A Norwegian model is preserved in Norway. It is blue, the surviving example is quite pale with a small Dannebrog in the top hoist, and the cross is not square but a thin Maltese style cross. In the centre the full crowned Danish arms on shield with supporters standing on the ground, the arms and supporters surrounded by a U-shaped white scroll with 'HOVED QUARTEERET' in gold lettering. Its size was roughly 60 centimetres square.

General von Huth

To better understand both the staff system and the role of the Feldjægercorpset, later called the Guides, who were very closely integrated in to the general staff, we have to look at the career and longstanding influence and visionary input in the forming of a modern army made by the General von Huth.

Firstly, as the teacher of Prince Carl of Hessen, and later of the Prince Regent, he opened the way for a whole new way of forming an army. He was recognised as both a visionary and an inspiring teacher. His ideas were also sound and well founded. His simple but logical idea was that a modern army should be led by very well-educated officers, leading well-trained soldiers, equipped with the best and most modern arms and equipment, nothing extraordinary there unless one realises the full implications: everyone should be fully educated. He first reformed the artillery and engineer school, making it both the premier school of its kind in Denmark and among the best in Europe. He also reformed the cadet academy, but as this was just as much a basic school, he created a system of further education in 'schools' where the best of the officers would learn more. One of the earliest and the best known was the formation of Slesvigske Jæger Corps which acted as a training ground (under von Ewald) of young and clever officers in the use of light infantry tactics, before being posted to different commands, promoting those same tactics. Later the Norske Jæger Corps and Sjællandske Jæger Corps performed the same mission of further education.

The Quartermaster Staff under von Binzer not only performed the same role in training staff officers, but also focused on gifted NCOs, to train them for better use. The Feltjægercorpset recruited mainly young clever and gifted volunteers or NCOs, training them, with a possibility of promotion to staff sergeants or even officers. A good example is a young 16-year-old volunteer in the Herregårds Skytterne named Fritz Hammer, the son of a innkeeper, who distinguished himself during the siege of Copenhagen, even wounding, a British general. In 1808 with the forming of Guide Corpset he was one of the Guides at the age of only 17 years. He went on to serve in 1807–14, 1848–51 and again in 1864 in different formations of the army.

A great deal of training was given to both of these formations, but this went even further, as when they were re-posted they then were able to act as instructors in their new units and therefore train the new unit. To create more officers for the army and offer officers already serving further education, a new system was created. For this a number of military institutes were formed to educate future officers, who had not been educated as cadets. These institutes were the Holstenske Militære Institut and Danske Militær Institute. Both serving officers from the Quartermaster Staff and the Feltjægercorpset and Guide Corpset were used as training personnel, as also several officers who had previously served on the Quartermaster Staff and now served as teachers.

The Feldjægercorpset, later the Guide Corpset

The Feltjægercorpset was raised in 1790 to fulfil the duties of a staff corps. This meant that they were to assist as guides, messengers, carry out missions of cartography and land measurement and mapping, or serve detached as aides de camp to the generals. Apart from this they had another more important mission as at the base they were an active service training corps for officers and NCOs. Many notable soldiers passed through their ranks.

When they were initially conceived, they were intended to have seven Officers, 10 NCOs, two trumpeters and 60 jægers, but when they were finally raised their strength had been somewhat reduced. This is the organisation of 1791, as revised in 1794 with the reduced strength.

1 *Generalkvatermesteren* (Commander)
1 *Kaptajn* (Captain)
2 *Premiere Løjtnanter* (First Lieutenants)
3 *Second Løjtnanter* (Second Lieutenants)
1 *Sergent* (Sergeant)
1 *Foureer* (Staff sergeant)
4 *Overjægerer* (Mounted Corporal)
2 *Waldhornister* (Mounted Trumpeter)
20 *Ridende Jægere* (Mounted Jægers)

The following for dismounted service only:

4 *Overjægerer* (Foot Corporals)
12 *Fod jægere* (Foot Jægers)

This remained their organisation until 1808 with a couple of minor changes.

The Feltjægercorpset Uniform

Their uniform when they were first raised consisted of an M1789 round black felt hat; on left side it had a white plume with light green top. The hat resembled a low top hat. In 1803 they were issued with a new type of hat, the M1803 with a red feather with yellow top. The yellow and red plume specified that they were part of the general quartermaster's staff; it also had silver cords and tassels.

They had a dark green cloth coatee with upturned front corners showing the straw yellow lining and black collar, lapels (closed to the waist), black round cuffs with a black flap and a black shoulder strap piped straw yellow. The coat had white metal or pewter buttons, seven on each side of the lapels. Under the collar they wore a black neck stock. Their legwear consisted of a pair of buff leather fall-fronted straw yellow breeches, sometimes the buff leather breeches were replaced with yellow *Kirsei* breeches M1802 (cloth type named after the English town of Kersey in Suffolk). These had white inside lining of the front flap and crotch (none wore underpants in those times); they had nine tin buttons around the flap, but they had no openings or buttons at lower legs, as they should fit tight, and boots always be worn over them.

Over their breeches they wore a new-style black high cuffed boots, but they changed for green fall-fronted riding trousers for service dress, probably with hessian boots. On campaign they wore a pair of green fall-fronted overalls which had black leather reinforcing on the inside legs, cut in dog's tooth style, and around the bottom of the legs. They buttoned down the outside leg with white metal buttons and the edge was piped in buff/straw yellow. They had a grey overcoat lined buff yellow.

They had a black leather belt with an open square buckle and they carried a M1792 light cavalry (hussar) sabre and they had two pistols and the M1791 Jægerkarabin which had been specially produced for them. Their horse furniture consisted of black leather harness and a dark green shabraque with black wolf's teeth piped white trim. This was the uniform they wore until they became guides in 1808.

The Officers

Not much information has survived, but we can safely make the following assumptions. They would have worn the same basic uniform as the men, but with the following differences: their coat would have had long tails, green turned back black and piped straw/buff yellow. Their rank would have been shown by their epaulettes and waist sash. Their legwear was initially as the men, buff breeches and riding boots, but like the men this was changed for a pair of green trousers with elaborate Hungarian lacing on the thighs in a style close to that of the hussars.

The Trumpeters

They wore the same uniform as the men, but with the addition of small black swallows' nests laced straw yellow. As they were NCOs they had a small simple NCO's epaulette on the right over the swallow's nest.

The Guides

In 1808 the Feltjægercorpset was renamed the Guides Corps (Guidecorpset) with a similar strength of three officers, six NCOs, two Trumpeters and 20 Guides. All the Guides ranked as NCOs. The unit was commanded by *Generalkvartermester-løjtnant Oberstløjtnant* Wolfgang von Haffner.

The Guides Uniform

From 1808, when they became Guides, the uniform was changed as well. They were issued with a black felt and leather shako with a silver-plated brass lozenge shaped shako plate, apparently stamped with an oval shield bearing the lesser arms of Denmark under a crown (a shako plate has been recently identified, now preserved in the collection of a Norwegian museum). It had silver or white metal scale chin straps and buttons, this was the only unit to officially have metal chin scales on a shako and this was a special privilege accorded by the King. It had a crimson red plume with a yellow top over with a black cockade with a silver loop and button and it had red and gold cords and tassels. The form of the Danish shako was probably closer to the early Russian or Prussian types in being more parallel or less tapered than the French style. There is some doubt as to whether or not the plates were actually stamped, as the few exiting illustrations by Senn show it as blank, but it may be the artist never actually saw a real one close up. The author's personal belief is that they were stamped. For fatigue dress they had a grey forage cap with blue brim and knot.

The coatee was changed for a single-breasted guards red cloth coat with long tails closed by a single row of silver buttons and a line of straw yellow piping; it had a very dark blue collar piped straw yellow bearing two silver buttonhole laces (in the form of bars) and dark blue round cuffs piped straw yellow with two silver buttonhole laces and buttons. The lining and turnbacks were white and the coat had false horizontal pockets simulated by straw yellow piping and silver buttons. Under the collar they wore a black neck stock. The Guides coat had a silver NCO's epaulette on the right shoulder, as all the guides ranked as NCOs. Some time around 1812 they changed the form of their cuffs to the pointed model piped straw yellow and a button, usually left unbuttoned. When they changed their cuff style the epaulette was abolished and they adopted the new distinctions, now displayed on their cuffs. See Plate 2.

In full dress they wore a pair of buff yellow tight fall-fronted *kirsei* breeches with four tin buttons. For service

THE DANISH ARMY OF THE NAPOLEONIC WARS VOLUME 1

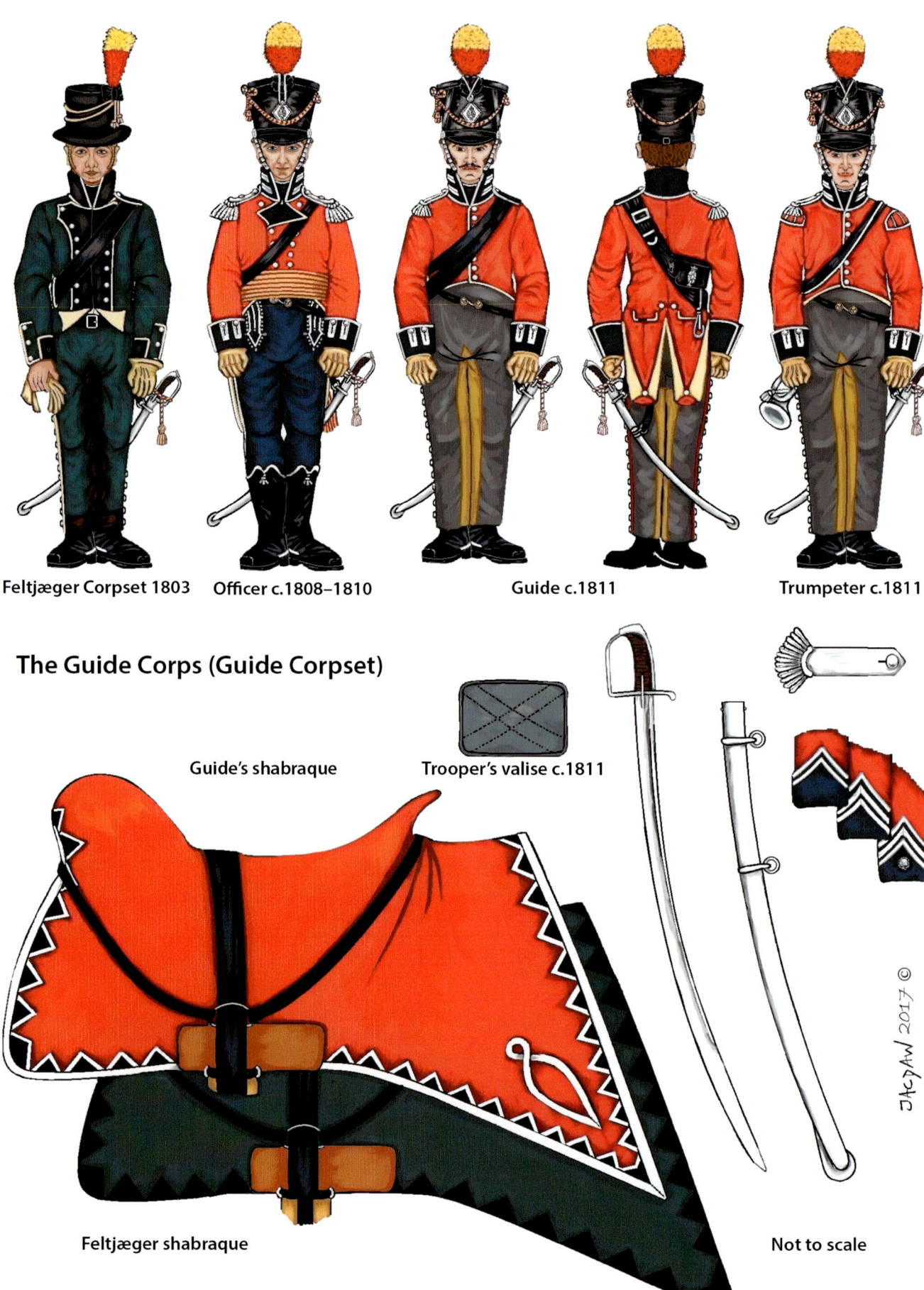

Feltjæger Corpset 1803   Officer c.1808–1810   Guide c.1811   Trumpeter c.1811

The Guide Corps (Guide Corpset)

Guide's shabraque   Trooper's valise c.1811

Feltjæger shabraque   Not to scale

THE GENERALS AND THE HIGH COMMAND, INCLUDING THE GUIDES

> **Plate 2. The Guide Corpset**
>
> Left to right: Feltjæger Corpset, c.1803–1807, Guides Officer c.1808–1810, Guide c.1811 front and back, Guide Trumpeter c.1811; note swallow's nest in coat colour.
> Guides sabre, single bar steel hilted M1808 Hussar sabre which was carried in a steel scabbard
> Ranks: the NCO's epaulette, pre 1812, a Guide had one the left shoulder and the corporal had one on each shoulder. Post 1812, the style was similar to that as used by the Livgarden til Fod. All members of the Guide Corpset ranked one rang higher than the same rank in the rest of the army; this was indicated by chevrons from 1812. As the lowest rank in the Guide Corpset was reckoned as a corporal they had two chevrons (one chevron was a vice-corporal); corporals ranked as sergeants (so they had three chevrons); sergeants ranked as staff sergeants (hence the extra button). The new regulations for the use of cuff distinctions specified that NCOs had all their distinctions on the cuff, while all officers had their distinctions on the lower sleeve, above the cuff.

dress they wore a pair of fall-fronted dark grey cavalry overalls with leather reinforcements. The outside seam had a red welt and it had a row of white metal buttons down the seam. Their foot wear was a pair black Hungarian style boots with silver lace and tassel. They were worn over the breeches and under the overalls. For foul weather dress they had a grey cape with blue collar.

Arms and Equipment
Around their waist they had a black leather belt with a rectangular silver buckle from which they suspended their sabre. Over their shoulder they had a wide black leather carbine belt and over their right shoulder they had a black leather shoulder belt and cartridge pouch with a silver badge of the crowned royal arms. As the Feldjægercorpset they were armed with the Hussar sabre M1792. Similar to the M1776, it was based on the Prussian model. It was carried until 1808.

When they became the Guides they were issued with a single bar steel hilted M1808 Hussar sabre carried in a steel scabbard. As shown in the painting by Senn, it had a silver and red sword knot and straps. The M1808 sabre was in fact the 1776 model hilt, but in a steel scabbard and with a new blade. The Guides' model M1805 *pallask*, which had a silvered single bar hilt and black leather scabbard with silvered fittings, was not issued until after 1815, probably much, much later, even if it is called the model M1805. They also carried a pair of pistols, the model is not known for sure, but it was probably the Hussar pistol M1777 and later the M1806.

The corps was officially issued with 24 M1791 carbines in 1801 for the 24 troopers; the NCOs only carried pistols. The Jægerkarabin for ridende jæger M1791 is in many ways not a true cavalry weapon. Of the original 100 rifles which were made, probably only 24 were made into the cavalry version with a slide bar. The rest were for use by infantry only. When the Feltjægercorpset was first planned in 1790–91, it was intended that it should have had a much larger contingent than in fact they finally had. The plan made in 1791 was for 60 mounted Jægers and some NCOs, all armed with rifles, and some reserves. So 100 rifles were ordered to be delivered from 1791 and made as a 'special' shortened version of the infantry rifle M1791 also in production at the same time, but in a rather special calibre (15.7mm). However, before the organisation of the corps was finalised in 1794, the corps was reduced in numbers and organisation was changed, so finally they only had 20 mounted jægers and four mounted *overjaegere* requiring the cavalry version of the rifle, with the slider. The remainder now comprised 12 foot jægers and four foot *overjaegere*, with the same rifle, but in the infantry version. So in fact only 40 rifles were ever received by the Feltjægercorpset and of those only 24 were in the cavalry version.

When the Guide Corpset was organised in 1808, all the weapons was transferred to them, and again the 24 cavalry rifles and the 16 foot rifles were put into their regimental store for their use until 1816, when they were returned to the arsenal for good. What happened to the rest of the other 60 infantry rifles is rather obscure. The problem was that the different and unique calibre made it difficult if not impossible to be used by others. One theory is that they may have been used by the Skarpskytter/Jægere in the Kongelige Livgarde til Fods, as they in 1804 received '54 carbines with Hunting knife bayonet', and that this was in fact this rifle with a new bayonet attachment and that they may have used them until 1805, when they instead received 39 'ordinary rifles' and 36 *Skarpskytte geværer*. Most probably, thoigh, they stayed in arsenal and were never used at all.

From 1808 they had black leather harness and a crimson red cloth shabraque with black wolf's teeth piped silver with a wide silver outer lace and a grey rectangular portmanteau lined black in 1809, later this appears to have been replaced with a red piped portmanteau.

The officers' cartridge pouch had a metal badge of the Kings crowned monogram in white metal or possibly silver. The other ranks had an oval badge bearing the crowned greater arms of Denmark with an elephant below them, it was cast in pewter.

NCOs' Distinctions
All members of Guide Corpset ranked one rank higher than the same rank in the rest of the army

Up till 1812 the corporals had a silver epaulette on each shoulder. The sergeants had two larger silver epaulettes and a silver sword knot, which they kept until 1816. When the new uniform regulations were issued in 1812, the Guide Corpset was to use pointed cuffs like the rest of the army. The cuffs were to be medium blue, piped straw yellow with one button, the guides had two white chevrons above the cuffs (as the guides were considered NCOs), the corporal (*kaporal*) had three chevrons and the sergeant (*vagtmester*) had three chevrons and a button/rosette. See Plate 2.

Officers' Distinctions
As the officers' uniforms were privately made there were probably some small variations in cut and cloth colour, but the basic uniform was the same as the staff officers: a red double-breasted coat with two rows of silver buttons. The coat had a dark blue collar piped straw yellow bearing two silver buttonhole laces and dark blue round cuffs piped straw yellow with two silver buttonhole laces and buttons. On each shoulder they had a large silver epaulette and fringe. Around their waist and over the coat they wore a red and yellow striped silk sash worn knotted on the left hip. From 1810, when they were in service dress, they used the same grey overalls as the men, but in full dress from 1808 they wore a pair of dark blue fall-fronted riding breeches with a white welt down the outside leg and rather elaborately embroidered arrow shaped silver lacing piped red on the thigh which continued around the seat of the breeches. These were worn with hussar boots which a silver lace border and tassels. The officers had a shoulder bandoleer with a black leather cartridge pouch with the King's cypher in gilded or silvered brass.

Their shabraques probably resembled those of the officers Livregiment Lette Dragoner. They also had a dog tooth version similar to the men for field use, but with silver lace. Armament was a Hussar officer's sabre, frequently a private purchase and a pair of pistols, model unknown. Their shakos were probably privately made.

Trumpeters' Distinctions
They are unknown, but when they became Guides the swallows' nests were red, the same as the coat with silver lace, but no ball tassels.

Colours and Standards
This corps never carried nor were they ever issued with a standard or even a marker pennon as they never served as a unit but were dispersed around the different field commands.

4

The Livgarden til Fods

The Livarden til Fods was first raised on 30 June 1658 by King Frederik III. It was always intended as a body guard, for guard duty and protection of the royal person and the palaces, only occasionally serving as a front-line fighting unit. They had fought in the Scånian War, in Flanders, and in the Great Northern War and they again took the field in 1762. With the exception of the attack on Copenhagen in 1807, where they participated in the defence, they did not see any active service in any of the campaigns in which the Danish army was engaged during the Napoleonic Wars. They were garrisoned in Copenhagen as they still are to this day. With the Livgarden til Hest they formed the royal bodyguard.

Following court intrigues, the Livgarden til Fods was briefly disbanded on 21 December 1771. They were restored on 20 January 1772 with five companies under the previous title. They were reduced to four companies in 1782. On 28 April 1772, the Dr Friedrich Struensee was decapitated, dismembered and put on the wheel, for having, among other things, dissolved the Guard in December 1771.

The Livgarden til Fods was now essentially a bodyguard unit and consisted of only one battalion of four companies. The uniform introduced in 1805 essentially remained unchanged until 1815.

The Livgarden til Fods had a regimental command. Besides the colonel, who was Carl Ludwig von Baudissin (1806–1814) and a lieutenant colonel, the staff was composed of: a quartermaster (*kvartermester*), an Auditor, a surgeon (*feltskærer*), together with a small regimental staff including two company surgeons (*kompagnikirurger*), a head nurse (*sygehussergent*), a drum major (*bataljonstambour*) and 16 musicians, a gunsmith (*bøssesmed*) and a provost (*profos*).

Each of the four companies consisted of three officers – a captain, a lieutenant and an ensign – nine NCOs, three drummers, a fifer, and 100 guardsmen. Until 1807 each company had in addition to the grenadiers, a sergeant and twelve guards who were selected to serve as sharpshooters (*skarpskytter*). After 1807 they formed their own company, wearing a uniform bearing light infantry distinctions. They were armed with rifles.

The Guard Grenadiers Uniform

The Royal Foot guards have a long tradition of keep their style of uniform much longer than the rest of the army. As they had to serve at court and had uniforms made of better cloth, meant that they had much shorter terms of issue for uniforms than the rest of the army. The jacket and trousers were issued for terms of two years (the issues for the rest of the army had six years of full service), so this would mean that between 1803–14 that the Guard received around five new clothing issues of each item (in 1804, '06, '08, '10 and '12). So the Guard apparently followed the main issue changes, but this also meant that changes of smaller details would be applied more frequently.

Up to 1805 they had worn a rather particular black leather grenadier hat based on the Potemkin model; it had a silvered embossed brass metal plate bearing the royal monogram on the front. It had a caterpillar-style woollen crest going over the top from ear to ear, in 1801 it was black, but most contemporary illustrations show it as white like the infantry of the line. It had a blue bag piped silver white and a white tassel hanging down the back. The plume was white with a blue tip. Apparently, the officers did not wear this hat, but wore a bicorn which was laced silver.

From 1805 the guard grenadiers were issued with their first bearskin cap of black/dark brown fur. It was only slightly different in form to the line model, taller with a light blue bag, which was slightly smaller than the bag found on the line infantry version and was placed higher up, with white laced borders and tassel, blue and white cords and tassels which hung down the front of the bearskin, but the cords and tassels on the side were not so long except on one side where two cords and tassels hung down to the chest. The bearskin had a white brushed wool plume with a light blue tip. The plumes on the earlier bearskins were thinner and more upright, probably made of chopped feathers, but the later models were fuller and these were probably made of brushed wool. It appears that the plumes throughout the period were dressed upright for parades, but they tended to lean them over for ordinary service and in the field, the theory being that this preserved them somewhat, this practice applied to the line grenadiers as well. Concerning the fur itself, in 1811 the King decreed

THE DANISH ARMY OF THE NAPOLEONIC WARS VOLUME 1

Livgarden til Fods I

> **Plate 3. Livgarden til Fods I**
>
> Top, from left to right. Guardsman c.1806 wearing early model bearskin. Rear view of a guardsman c.1806, showing his queue. Guard Sharpshooter c.1806 after Eckersberg (the only contemporary image – the tip could possibly have been green, but no hard evidence). An officer in full dress c.1806 with a bearskin. Bottom, from left to right. Guardsman 1808, Guard corporal wearing uniform in the version shown in contemporary illustrations. Guard Drummer c.1806, shown with lacing on the sleeve. The coat with reversed colours was worn until c.1808. Officer in service dress c.1806–1807.

that 'a load of "American bearskin" [!] is to be bought in Altona, where it is now available', and this fur is to be used for the new model bearskins to be issued for the Guard from 1812. It was made clear that this consignment was only to be used for the Guards, not for the line grenadiers. Above the black leather peak there was a stamped silvered bronze plate with the gilded Danish cabinet or lesser arms with supporters within a wreath of palm style leaves. The plate was in the style similar to the helmet plate of the Livgarde til Hest with the royal arms on a silvered brass oval plate. The bearskin had pewter or silvered brass chin scales and bosses on a leather backing.

A project in 1806–1808 to redesign the bearskin and plate in a more rounded style, and a new red feather was put forward and although a planning illustration of c.1806–07 exists, they were never made for the following reason.

From 1808, the King wished a new bearskin to replace the 1803 model with the new model which was taller and fuller in more of a sugar loaf form, generally referred to as the M1809. Also, it was wished to change the guard's uniform along same lines as that of the rest of the army in 1808. However, unaware of this, the guard had already had made a new 1803 style uniforms by private contractors. The King, although displeased, was forced to accept them, and as a consequence the Guards wore (with some smaller modifications) uniforms of the M1803 style far longer than the rest of the army. In 1812 a new bearskin was finally accepted of same design as the one use by some of the line regiments (the M1809) which was more cylindrical with a flatter top, but it still had a blue bag and the two hanging cords, now a little longer, and tassels were now looped over a button.

From 1812/1813, the bearskin cap was replaced by the shako of the line infantry, but with the plate of the bearskin for ordinary dress, from then on the bearskin being reserved for formal parades and official court duties.

The plate referred to as the 'Guards' sun' (called by many as the 'Guard's star') until recently thought to date to 1806, in fact appears to date too much later, around 1815–1817. If one looks closely at Senn's 1806–07 drawing of a guardsman, the original appears to show same type of shield with crowned arms in the centre with the supporters. What at first glance may seem to resemble the rays of the 'sun' are no doubt tufts of the fur obscuring the shield form of the plate. This brings us to the helmet M1810 of the Livgarden til Hest, which has similar shield very close in size of same model. These have the older simpler Arms of Denmark pre 1815, but this was normal, as seen on preserved cross belt and ammunition box shields, that the troopers had the 'lesser crowned Danish arms' bearing simply the lions of Denmark, the lion and axe of Norway and the crowns of Sweden with the wild men supporters and officers had the full arms. This was probably the same practice in the Foot guards, as they were closely related. The type of shield on the officers' bearskins is no doubt the one made 1806 and carried until 1812 onwards and probably also made for Livgarden til Hest helmet M1810. The 'Sun' or 'Star' probably first appeared on the new 1815 shako as it is also seen on the plates by Hyllested dated 1822–1829, a star on the shako, and a different shield on bearskin.

The sharpshooters wore bicorns with a white lace edge in ordinary service dress; it had a black cockade held with a long thin white loop and a white plume with a light blue tip. We know from an official description dated to 1809 of their *Halvmåneblæser* that the bicorn had by now been replaced with an infantry shako with green feather and cords, they had black belts with *Hirchfaengers* as their side arm, and their trousers were grey in field dress. However, in full parade dress and for official duties the sharpshooters also wore a bearskin like the rest of the regiment.

The coats of the Livgarden til Fods were cut differently from the coats of the other Danish line infantry regiments in the style of the 18th century. From 1803 they wore a red coatee worn open at the waist revealing the white waistcoat, the coat tails were lined and turned back in white. The red used by the Guards was of a different hue to the red used by the rest of the army The coat had eight pewter buttons and square white brandenburg lacing on the chest. The coat had horizontal pockets with two buttons each. The white waistcoat had small pewter buttons. The collar was plain blue, piped white, but by c.1806 it now had in addition to the piping one white buttonhole lace on each side. The open or 'French' blue cuffs were edged with a flat white lace with three pewter buttons, although at least one watercolour shows only one button closing the cuff, and this was later changed for two white laced buttonholes and pewter buttons by 1806. The shoulder straps were white piped light blue and secured with a pewter button.

Their legwear consisted of white breeches, which were of the older knee length style with both black and white 18th-century style gaiters with brass buttons. These were eventually replaced with white gaiter trousers. Usually they are shown with pewter buttons, although some contemporary illustrations show them as brass, a colourist's error. Initially they had black shoes with brass buckles; these were later replaced with black laced shoes.

A uniform of same basic cut was designed and made by the Guards themselves and was only authorised reluctantly by the new King in 1808–09, rather than stand the expense of remaking new uniforms. This was also a red coatee and it now had slightly shorter tails and was cut square at the front and closed at the waist and it was also lined white. The coat now only had seven buttons and the white brandenburgs were now larger and now finished in a point. The coat had horizontal pockets with two buttons. The collar was blue, piped white with one white buttonhole lace each side. The blue cuffs and shoulder straps were edged with white lace with two white laced buttonholes and pewter buttons.

One thing the King changed as planned was the use of the new white fall-fronted gaiter trousers of the same cut as the ones worn by the line infantry until 1809. Usually they are shown with pewter buttons, although some contemporary illustrations show them as brass, a colourist's error. From around 1810 they also had a pair of fall-fronted grey trousers, possibly as ordinary fatigue dress. A uniform with a different cut was authorised in 1807, but as some new uniforms had just been made, this new coat was not made until 1809/1810.

In 1812 they were to have the new pointed-style cuffs and, being close to the King, the new orders were probably more diligently applied than in the other corps of the army. The new pointed cuffs were blue piped white with a pewter button and a vertical square lace. The existing uniforms were simply modified; they were not replaced with new uniforms.

The men wore buff yellow leather gloves until 1811, after which they wore white gloves, probably made of cloth, but the officers continued to wear buff leather gloves.

Regarding lace and buttons, although the basic uniforms were similar for 1808–14, the haberdashery allowances for producing uniforms for the Guards did not vary. They were made for the tailors producing the uniforms, and as such these are the closest material details which exist of the actual materials used. They were written in 1807, 1809 and 1811, and they were for the new uniforms to be distributed in 1808, 1810 and 1812. What is interesting is that they are all identical, regarding the uniform coat.

The same allowances of buttons and lace lining/cords for all three dates stated that the following was to be used for one uniform:

- Two 'laced shoulder-straps'
- 20 'laced buttonholes'; there were seven on each side of the coat at the front, two on each cuff and one on each side of the collar.
- 19 'large' buttons; seven on the front of the coat, two on each cuff, one on each shoulder strap, two on each pocket and two on the turn backs.
- Four 'small' buttons; it is not specified were they were placed, but probably at top and bottom at the two lace vents on the back of the coat.

Although blue trousers were part of the official field uniform from 1808, they were kept in store for 'actual field service', but apparently they were never issued at all and they remained in store until they finally began to be worn around 1822.

In the 'Cloth Allowances', there are no notes about the new pointed cuffs of 1812 until 1816, but they would have been put on anyhow, as the uniforms first were distributed in 1813 rather than in 1812 as originally intended.

Arms and Equipment

Their cartridge box, larger than the model carried by the line infantry, had an oval white metal plate with the kings crowned monogram stamped on it and from 1807, a small white metal grenade in each corner, it was carried on a whitened leather shoulder belt. They carried their short sabre (the so called *grenadersabel*, but in fact this was the M1753 Infantry Sabre) which had a brass guard and a black leather scabbard with brass fittings and a white leather strap with a tassel of mixed white and company colour. The 1st company had pale yellow, the 2nd company had red, the 3rd had blue and the 4th company had white. The sabre and the bayonet were carried on a whitened leather shoulder belt slung over their left shoulder. This shoulder belt had an oval plate of silvered white metal bearing the crowned pre-1814 cabinet or lesser arms in gilt; it had a border of points. In October 1804 the guard received 400 Musket M1797 with a brown or white leather sling.

Instead of ordinary muskets the sharpshooters, were issued the special *Skarpskyttegevær*. In 1806 they received 36 rifles and 36 new *Skarpskyttegeværer* (until then they had had 'carbines' which may have been the foot version of rifled carbine M1791, used by the Feltjægercorpset), and they were issued with black leather waist belts for a *Hirchfaenger*, 36 with bayonet attachment and 36 (light model) without. The latter was for those using the *Skarpskyttegeværer* as this had an inbuilt bayonet. They also had a black leather shoulder belt with black leather cartridge box. In 1806 their number apparently rose from

54 to 74 officers, NCOs, sharpshooters and hornists. This is the first time the mixed armament of a light unit is clearly documented and this can be seen as an experiment first permitted for the rest of army in 1811 or a widespread practice used before this, but only officially sanctioned in 1811. Note that in 1811 not all of the sharpshooters received *Hirschfängers*; half of them received sabres.

NCOs

The NCOs wore the same uniform as the men, but with these differences: the sergeants had on their right shoulder an epaulette, quite thin, like the Guides and hussars, made of silver cord and it had a small silver fringe and crescent. Their bearskin and bicorn cords and tassels were silver. This was in fact the old 1774 system which was the basis of their rank distinction. The Guard (and possibly the Hussars) retained the use of extra silver lace on collar and cuffs as part of their NCO destinctions. The corporals had one on each shoulder.

After 1812 and the application of the pointed cuffs, the NCOs rank was now defined with lace chevrons on the cuffs, one for a vice corporal, two for corporal and three for a sergeant, they were on both sleeves, see the Guides illustration in Plate 2. The sergeant major had three chevrons and a button or rosette at the tip of the last point. Their side arms had a silver strap, knot and tassel. They probably still had some lace on their collars as well. On their shoulders they had button coloured shoulder straps with a band of facing coloured piping around it, just inside the border, not on the edge. The Guard NCOs were officially armed with spontoons/halberds until 1805, after which they were replaced with the sharpshooters' muskets.

Officers' Dress

The officers wore a bicorn with a silver scalloped lace edge; it had a black cockade with a long and broad silver loop and a light blue over white plume. It had gold or silver tassels at each end. There were some variations of the hat lace, probably signs of rank. From 1805 the officers began to wear the bearskin cap with red and gold cords and tassels, although they kept their bicorns for full dress. Both had a white plume tipped in light blue. The plate on the officer's bearskin was more finely made and bore the 'Royal' or full coat of arms, it was also gilded and silvered. The officers' bearskin caps were finer than those of the men; the hairs of the fur were longer, cut from the rump, and this tradition is still the case today.

The officers originally only had one coat, worn in undress and full dress, it was a single-breasted crimson red coat worn open on the stomach and it had long tails. The coat had an elaborate silver lace in the form of a knot on each side of the coat aligned on the buttons and silver piping down the front of the coat. The collar was light blue laced silver and there was a similar knot in silver on the collar. The cuffs were laced silver with two silver buttons and buttonhole laces. The pockets had two thin double silver laces with two buttons. Their rank was shown by their epaulettes with the similar attributes as the line infantry officers, but also on their cuffs.

By 1808 the officers received a fairly plain undress coat, it had a row of eight buttons, later reduced to seven silver buttons, placed down the front of the coat and the leading edges were laced/piped silver. The coat was lined white, white turnbacks and a light blue collar piped and laced silver; later they added one silver buttonhole lace on each side. The light blue cuffs were edged with silver lace and had a wavy silver lace and knot. The pockets were silver laced with two buttons.

In 1812/1813 the coat colour was changed, it was now scarlet, at least for the daily service uniform, and it now had pointed cuffs and they now used a rank system similar to the Livgarden til Hest. Their cuffs were now embroidered with a silver knot on the full dress coat and on the undress coat.

The officers wore a pair of fall-fronted long white breeches with black hessian boots with a silver lace border and tassel for summer wear and a pair of fall-fronted dark blue hussar-style breeches with silver lace Hungarian knots and stripes. There appears to be some variation of this embroidery, probably to do with rank, for winter wear. They also wore the hessian boots with this dress as well. They also possessed an overcoat for use in foul weather; it was made of red cloth.

Around their waist they wore the traditional yellow/gold and red sash; the different grades appear to have had more or less elaborate knots. From 1812 they ceased to wear the sash as in the rest of the army and they lost their epaulettes as well.

Officially they carried the officer's M1796 sabre with silvered single bar hilt and black leather grip, with a gold and red sabre strap and knot and the sabre was carried in a black leather scabbard with silvered fittings suspended from a black leather belt and straps, the gilt buckle plate stamped with King's arms.

Drummers and Fifers

As there are no contemporary pictures of drummers of the Livgarden til Fod between 1762 and 1837 we can only speculate as to their real appearance. What we do know is that between 1792 and 1806 they had uniforms in 'Reversed colours as ordered' as noted in their regimental account books.

In the new uniform regulations of 1806 (the same time that the new bearskin hats were adopted), they were from next issue of uniforms, to change to a uniform like the ordinary Guardsmen 'with swallow's nest and lace of drummers as before'. After the regimental accounts concerning the deliveries of cloth to the musicians, it

THE DANISH ARMY OF THE NAPOLEONIC WARS VOLUME 1

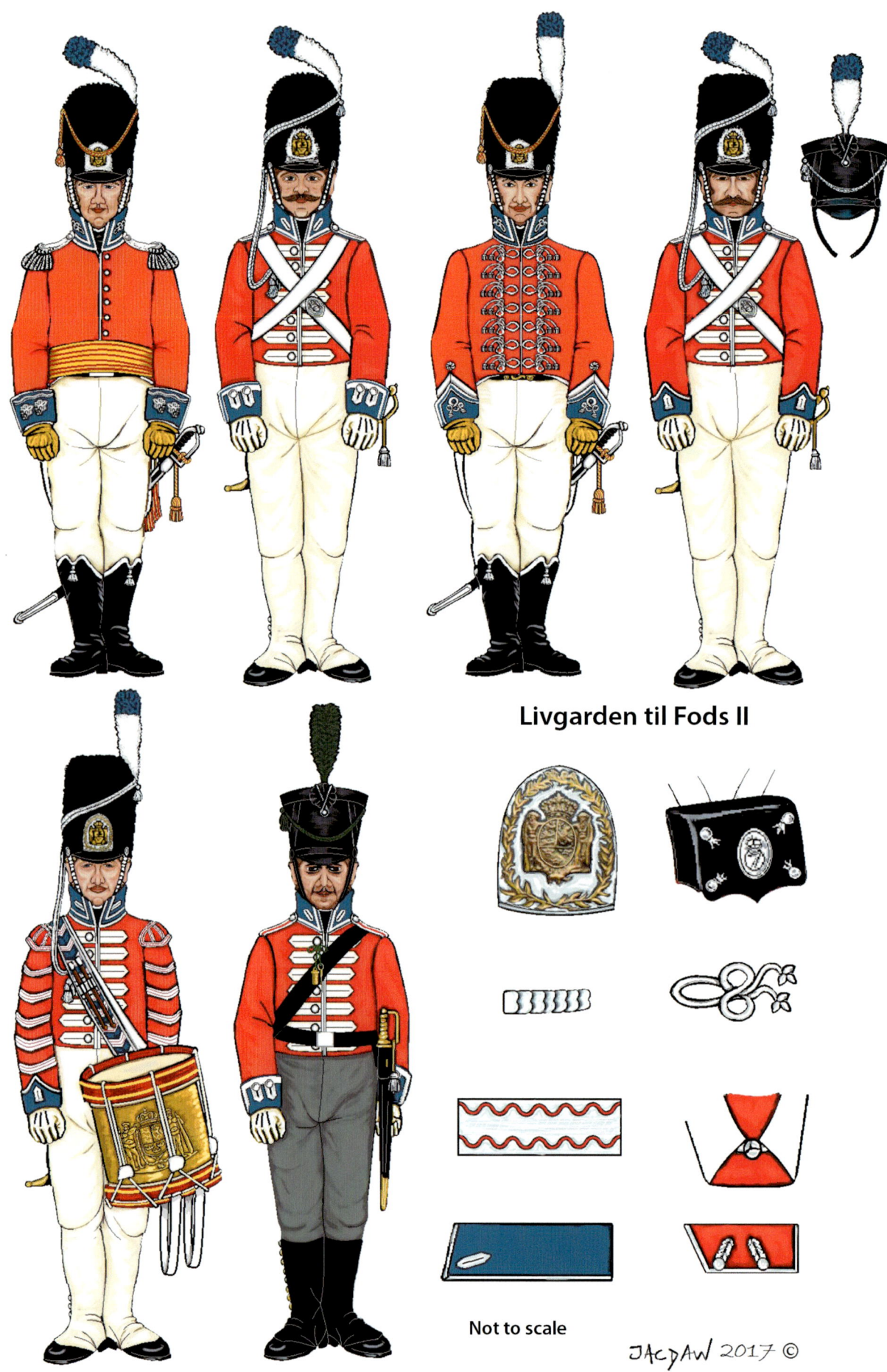

Livgarden til Fods II

> **Plate 4. Livgarden til Fods II**
>
> Top, from left to right. Officer in bearskin & service coat. Guardsman c.1811 with second pattern bearskin. Officer in full dress c.1812. Guardsman with new 1812 model coat cuffs. For ordinary duties they wore a shako from 1808/1810, the bearskin being reserved for full dress parades.
> Bottom, from left to right. Guard Drummer in the red coat worn from c.1808 with the c.1812 cuffs, sharpshooter in service dress c.1811, in full dress he would have worn a bearskin, possibly with a green plume and cords, although this is not specified.
> Details:
> Plate for bearskin, early guardsmen's version with the lesser arms of Denmark; the officers' version had the greater arms of Denmark on it; generally it was not that visible, partly obscured by the fur.
> Cartridge pouch c.1808
> Form of chinstrap scales.
> Officer's collar lace.
> Drummer's lace, white with red undulating red stripes, sometimes shown as more angular.
> Coat tail showing theturn back.
> Soldier's collar.
> Pocket flap.

suggests that they may have continued to wear out the Reversed-colour uniforms until 1808 at the very latest. This is confirmed by an order regarding the recruitment of four new drummers, when it is made clear in the accounts that in the future they will all receive the same cloth as an ordinary Guardsman. So, from 1806–08, the drummers now wore the same uniform as the guardsmen with the addition of red laced silver or white laced swallows' nests which were probably the same as they were in the 18th century. The laced sleeves of the 1770s may have continued to be worn following the text cited above when the lace was white with two undulating red stripes. The cords, knots and tassels on their bearskins were silver, not blue and white.

The drum case was made of yellow copper and stamped with the crowned royal arms; the hoops were originally painted in blue with two white stripes around them, later, around 1812, they changed to red with two yellow bands (Oldenberg livery colours) and they had white cords and white leather tension pullers and carrying straps.

The drum itself went through a number of changes. At the start of the period they still carried the stamped brass drums of the previous century which were quite large. The examples in the Guards Museum are 2–4 inches taller than the other example in the Tøjhusmuseet; this is obvious when looking at the space between the top and the bottom of the royal arms. This seems to indicate that the one in the Guards museum has probably been less altered than the one from the Tøjhusmuseet. From around 1800, when they started making smaller drums, this was simply done by cutting off a strip from the top and the bottom of the brass case both to lighten it and also make it shorter when used by the 'infant' drummer boys, who had become common around then. Some of those found today have even been cut so short that both the crown and the elephant are missing!

So the example at the Tøjhusmuseet is probably one of the 13 new drums so converted to the smaller model, but those in the Guards museum are not converted and so obviously older.

When the Guards received the new drums around 1838, these were to replace an older model of drum – the drums received in 1804, or more likely these drums were the ones which had been chopped down for boy drummers which gave them a squashed appearance. They were kept by the Guard as *Galla trommer* (formal parade drums). They were only to be used on special occasions and formal parades together with the old uniforms.

The drum was carried on a leather shoulder belt which was covered in blue cloth and it had silver laced edges and decorated with chevrons of livery lace and they had a pair of loops for the drum sticks. Drummers carried a short sabre (the so called *grenadersabel*) which had a brass guard and a black leather scabbard with brass fittings and a brown leather sword strap with a white/silver and blue tassel; it was carried on a whitened leather shoulder belt, slung over their right shoulder under the drum belt.

The two *Halvmåneblæsere* (horn blowers) of the light company had the same distinctions as the drummers, their shako with green feather and cords. They had black belts and wore grey trousers in service field dress.

The musicians of the Guards Band (*Tambourer*, *Hobister* and *Janicharer*) wore the drummer's uniform as did the Drum Major and Drum Corporal who probably had a lot of additional lace as befitted their rank with the addition of silver laced swallows' nests on each shoulder and silver epaulettes as well. It is more than probable that the musicians also had coats of reversed colours as well, changing to red at the same time as the drummers.

THE DANISH ARMY OF THE NAPOLEONIC WARS VOLUME 1

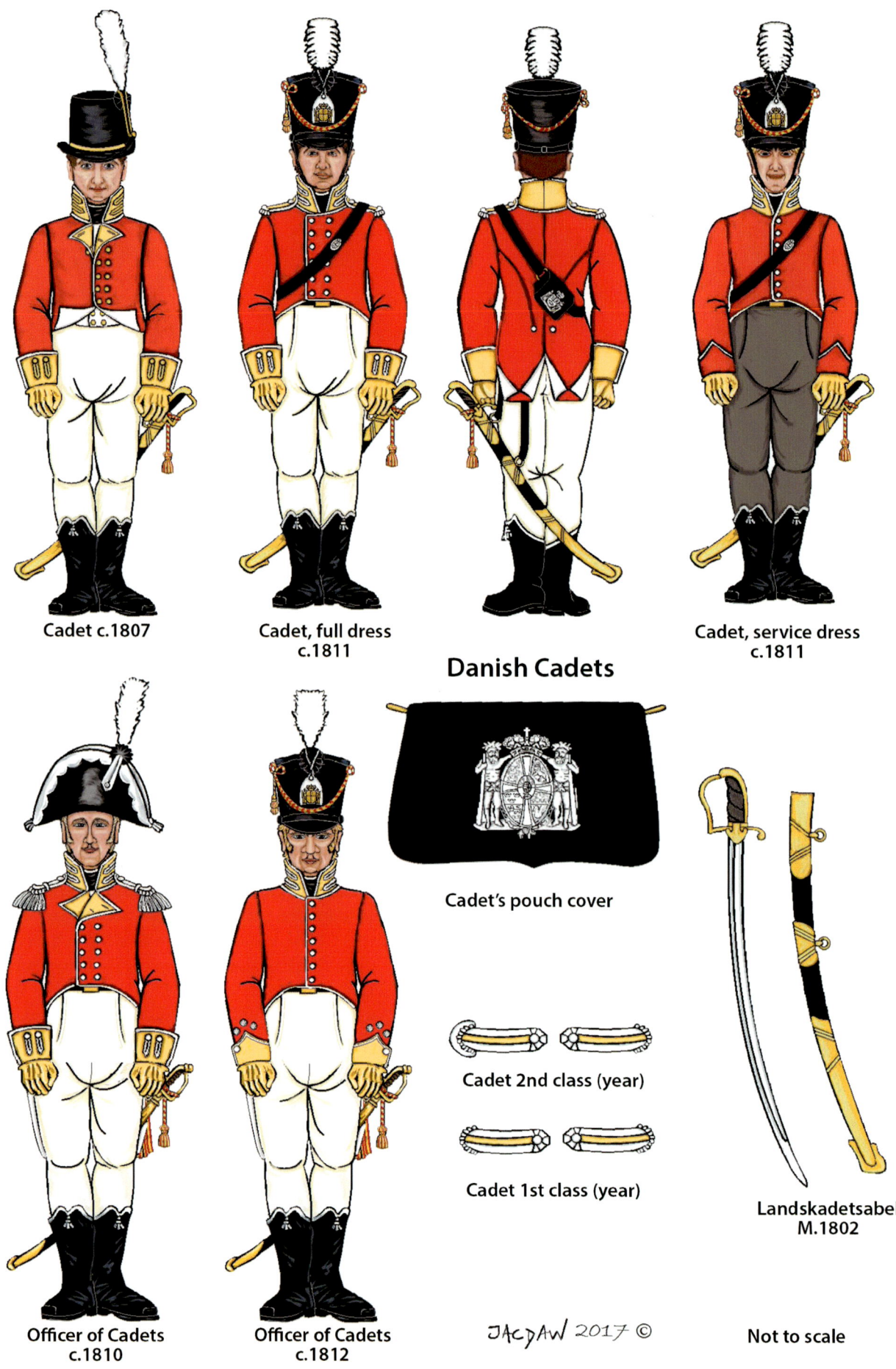

Danish Cadets

- Cadet c.1807
- Cadet, full dress c.1811
- Cadet, service dress c.1811
- Officer of Cadets c.1810
- Officer of Cadets c.1812
- Cadet's pouch cover
- Cadet 2nd class (year)
- Cadet 1st class (year)
- Landskadetsabel M.1802
- Not to scale

THE LIVGARDEN TIL FODS

> **Plate 5. The Danish Cadets**
>
> Top, from left to right, Cadet in service dress c.1807, cadet in full dress c.1811, a rear view of cadet showing the tails and cartridge pouch, cadet in daily service/school dress c.1811. Bottom, officer c.1810, showing a reconstruction of the probable officer's uniform c.1812. Inset. Pouch showing badge; official service M1802 Sabre, although the preceding model amongst others was probably used as well; shoulder straps.

Hairstyles

A particularity of the Guards is they continued to wear their hair dressed in a long thin queue, Prussian style, with a small bow of black ribbon at the level of the neck. This continued to at least 1807 and at least for parades their hair was powdered as well. Apparently they had a thin steel rod which they inserted into the centre of their queue to keep it straight.

The officers are also shown wearing this queue as well, again at least up to 1807. They all appear to have all disappeared by 1808 at the latest as testified by contemporary illustrations. The men and the NCOs were allowed moustaches, but the officers and probably the musicians were clean shaven.

The Danish Cadet Corps

The Danish Cadet college was the most prestigious school in Denmark after the university and anyone of any means or noblesse did their very best to make sure their sons went to this place if they wished to embrace a military career. A notable fact is that while the majority sought a career in the army, it was not mandatory as others became civilian engineers, civil administrators or even politicians. The cadets could enter from the age of eight years old and stay until they were 19 years old, when they graduated. When they joined their regiment they still had to go through a regimental training program and they could only go on active service at the age of 22. They were expected to buy their own uniform.

It is important to stress that this was a school unit and they were never intended to fight as a unit in Denmark, even in case of emergency. Only once, in 1807, were some of the Danish classes called out before graduating. Even here, only a few cadets from the oldest classes were distributed amongst the units defending Copenhagen, but regimental uniforms were quickly produced and issued. The rest of the pupils were used for secondary services such as fire watch, and some internal guard duties.

There were two main types of cadet training. The Land Kadet Akademiet which trained the cadets as officers in either the infantry or the cavalry and the Artilleri Kadet Institutet which trained the cadets to either become artillery officers or engineers.

The headwear of the cadets of the Land Kadet Akademiet was originally a black bicorn which had a black cockade with a gold loop and a white plume. From around 1802 this was replaced with a black hat with a gold hat band around the base, a black cockade with a gold loop attached to the brim with a gilt button on the side and a thinnish white plume. This was replaced c.1810/1811 with a shako which had a reversed silver shield-shaped front plate with the royal arms in brass in the centre; it had a black cockade with a silver loop, a white plume with red and silver cords and tassels.

From 1802 for formal or parade dress the cadets wore a red double-breasted tailed coat which had straw yellow collar and cuffs piped white on the leading edges and around the cuffs. They had two brass or gilded buttons and two laced buttonholes on the collar and cuffs. The double-breasted red coat had six pairs of gold buttons and gold buttonhole lace. The coat had short tails with white turn backs. The waistcoat was white with brass buttons; the shirt was white and worn with a black neck stock. This coat was worn with white breeches and black officer's boots.

In 1810 they received two new uniforms: a formal dress uniform, probably in the Guards red, and a service uniform. The colour of the buttons and buttonhole lace was changed; they now had two silver buttons on their cuffs with white laced button holes, two white buttonhole laces on each side of the collar and two rows of silver buttons down the coat front and two on the back of the coat on the full dress uniform all piped white. On their shoulders they had fringeless epaulettes to denote rank; these were yellow with silver laced edges and crescents. The coat had short tails with white turnbacks and was lined white. They wore a pair of fall-fronted white breeches with short black hessian boots. The service dress was much simpler and the cloth was probably ordinary red cloth, this coat had a yellow collar with two silver buttons on the collar and white laced button holes the cuffs were simulated with white piping stitched in a V and were closed with a button. In this dress the cadets wore grey cloth breeches.

Until c.1811 only the senior cadets were allowed long tails on their coat, as they were by then classed as officers. Note that there was no lace on the collar and cuffs on the senior cadets' uniforms.

Although the original Page Corps had been abolished in 1791, there were still pages at court. When senior cadets had finished their training, the 12 best suited were transferred and served at court. This was an old tradition that a young officer who was in his final year, that he should do duty as a page in the royal household so that he could meet personally his King, the royal family, and all the senior commanders to get to know them, both formally and informally. When their period of service as pages was completed, they were duly transferred as officers to various regiments.

Those who served as pages continued to wear hats long after the change to shakos had been made by the rest of the college. The cadets who served as pages wore a similar uniform, but with long tails on the coat, white silk stockings and shoes. They wore gold epaulettes on both shoulders as a sign of their rank as senior cadets. Also, page service gave the page a new uniform of fine cloth, which most young officers, when first sent to a regiment, could use as a basis for their new regimental uniform. Many officers were poor, so this was a way to help them along in their career.

For service dress the cadets wore a single-breasted short-tailed red coat with pointed cuffs defined by white piping and it had white piping on the edges of the coat. The coat had a straw yellow collar edged white with two white laced button holes on each side. The coat had a single row of silver buttons and no epaulettes. The coat had short tails with white turnbacks and was lined white. They wore a pair of fall-fronted grey breeches for service dress with short black boots; they are also recorded as having trousers made of blue and white ticking, although this may have been a little later, just after the end of the Napoleonic Wars.

The cadets of the Artilleri Kadet Institutet, and probably the engineer cadets as well, wore similar uniforms with a red double-breasted coat, but which had dark or medium blue cuffs and collar and the coat had brass or gilt buttons. The pre-1801 uniforms show a single gilt-fringed epaulette on the left shoulder. They had two gold laced buttonholes on each side of the collar, without a button and on the cuffs with buttons. The coat was lined blue and had blue turnbacks. They had blue waistcoats and breeches. They had a black waist belt with a square brass buckle bearing crossed cannons. Sometimes they served directly in the batteries as part of their education and were permitted to wear the same uniform as *stykjunkere*, but without any distinctions as such.

From 1812 the lace was no longer metallic, but it was changed to white, or yellow in the case of the artillery cadets, cloth tape.

The Danish cadets they were supposed to have been armed with cadet officers' sabres, but contemporary sources mentions that due to a shortage of these sabres, they were given stored cavalry *pallasks* and hussar sabres (the troopers' model) from the arsenals, which sometimes would have seemed ridiculously large compared to their small size of the cadets, particularly the youngest cadets, although this remark is probably much more pertinent to Norwegian cadets than to the Danes. The official model shows a scabbard with a stud to go in an infantry sword bandolier, but all of the contemporary illustrations show a black leather cavalry frog with a rectangular brass buckle, as used by infantry officers around 1810. They carried a small black cavalry-style leather cartridge pouch with an embossed silver or pewter badge with the crowned royal arms with supporters on the flap, slung over their shoulder on a black leather shoulder belt with a small brass badge placed at chest level.

The Officer-Instructors of the Cadet Corps wore a bicorn which was replaced with a shako sometime around 1811. They wore the same tailed coat as the cadets, but they had silver-fringed epaulettes on their coats. It is not clear how their uniforms were modified after 1812. They were not permitted to wear a waist sash as this was reserved, only to be worn by officers on active service.

The Cadets possessed an infantry colour for use when on parade.

When the cadets served in the regiments they conserved their cadet service uniform until either the regiment was able to provide them with regimental dress or they could afford buy one themselves.

In 1811 a simple grey uniform of standard cut was made; this was issued to volunteer cadets. It was approved for use because of the growing numbers of extra volunteer officer cadets, who were not from typical officer families, but from the bourgeois and merchant classes, to meet the growing demand for young officers as the war advanced. These cadets received a shorter, more compressed form of education. They wore a shako without cords, plume, or shako plate, but with the black cockade. They carried a small black cavalry-style leather cartridge pouch, slung over their shoulder on a black leather shoulder belt, but with a small brass badge placed at chest level.

This was not the only military college in Denmark. There was another college in Holstein, their uniform was similar, but was said to have green facings. The uniform the commander of the Holstein military academy, von Mollowitz, was a unique model made especially for him. Von Mollowitz had served in the Feltægercorpset and then in the Guide Corpset and Quartermaster Staff and it was because of this that he was allowed to wear a modified version of his previous uniform. However, he was not allowed the waist sash and his embroidery had to be of 'ordinary cloth not true lace'. He wore the uniform of the Guides, but with green collar, cuffs and lining. His shako did not have a plate and his plume was to be white.

5

The Line Infantry Organisation, Basic Tactics and Uniforms

Composition of the Line Infantry Regiments

Until 1803, the line infantry regiments were composed of a headquarters staff (*Mellemstab*) and two infantry battalions

The regimental staff consisted of the colonel (*Oberst*), usually a general officer assisted by four senior officers: two majors, a quartermaster (*Kvartermester*) and a surgeon major, the other officers, (the *understab*) were; a senior juridical officer (*Auditor*), a surgeon (*Feltskaerer*), and an assistant surgeon (*Underkirurg*), who in turn was assisted by five company surgeons (*Kompanikirurger*), a master medical orderly (*Sygehussergent*), a regimental police sergeant, overlapping somewhat with the *Profos*; it was they who carried out the actual physical punishments (*Regimentsgevaldiger*); a provost (*Profos*); and a gunsmith (*Bøssesmed*): there was also a drum major who may have been included within this number.

Up to 1803 the two infantry battalions were composed of a Grenadier company (*grenaderkompagni*) and four musketeer companies (*musketerkompagni*). Each company was composed of three NCOs, (sergeants) nine under officers (corporals), three drummers, a fifer, two carpenters/sappers, and 12 sharpshooters and 136 musketeers or grenadiers. Each company was commanded by a captain, a first lieutenant, two second lieutenants and a sergeant-major.

From 1803 the sharpshooter contingent was disbanded and the grenadier company of the 2nd battalion was converted into a light company (*jægerkompagni*). Thus the 1st battalion retained one company of grenadiers and four of musketeers, whilst the 2nd now had four of musketeers and one of jægers. Each company was now composed of thee NCOs, nine under officers, three drummers (or three hornists in the light companies), a fifer, two carpenters/sappers and 157 musketeers, grenadiers or jægers. Officers and NCOs remained as before. A company had two platoons of four sections and two companies formed a division. This gave a battalion a theoretical strength of 900 officers and men.

In 1808 when the *Landeværn* was disbanded, all the men fit for active duty were used to form two reserve battalions, the 3rd and 4th battalions, for each of the line infantry regiments. These reserve battalions, called *Forstaerkningsbatalioner*, were composed of four musketeer companies and a light company. Their jæger companies were armed with the jæger musket M1794/1808 and, where available, a sabre M1756 as their side arm. Their shakos had the standard yellow and red shako cords; only the 2nd battalion jægers had green cords.

The junior officer rank of *Fændrik* (Ensign) was abolished in 1809. The colours were now carried by senior NCOs.

The jæger company, sometimes assisted by either the grenadier company or a line company detached for light duty, would always form at the front and on the flanks protecting the different formation changes. When line was ready to fire, they would form up on the flanks, ready to move forward to harass the enemy. If battalion formed a square, the jægers would protect this, and then form up on the angles of the square, together with the grenadiers.

A battalion normally had a colour party of two ensigns, later NCOs, as colour bearers and a colour guard of six NCOs. They were used for directing the manoeuvres, and were an important asset in formation and alignment the different formations. In the following diagrams they are shown by a small square with a colours symbol. The battalion's eight to 10 sappers would normally form a section of their own, following the orders of the battalion commander, and they were normally placed on the right of the battalion, together with the two guns of the regimental artillery, which they were to aid as well until 1808. The NCOs would normally form the end of sections, while the 'first class NCOs' and officers would be alternatively in front of or just behind the formed formations, depending on any given situation. The drummers and the fifer would normally stand behind or follow their parent company, but in some situations like parades they could be formed into a massed band led by the drum corporal. The regimental band was led by the drum major who normally followed the regimental commander, and was normally positioned

THE DANISH ARMY OF THE NAPOLEONIC WARS VOLUME 1

Danish Line Musketeers

1805   1808   1812

Corporal 1805   Sergeant 1811   Sergeant 1812   Campaign Dress

> **Plate 6. Danish Line Infantry Musketeers**
>
> Top, left to right, Musketeer c.1805, Danske Livregiment til Fods (Danish Life Regiment of Foot) in winter dress. Musketeer c.1808 Norske Livregiment til Fods (Norwegian Life Regiment of Foot) in summer dress. Note this regiment continued to carry a sword by special permission. Musketeer c.1809 Kronens Infanteriregiment in winter dress showing a rear view of a musketeer of the regiment's 3rd & 4th battalions. As there were not enough waist belts available, their bayonet scabbard was attached to their cartridge box. Note the two buttons on the rear of the coatee above the vents. Musketeer c.1812 Kongens Infanteriregiment wearing the new grey trousers. Musketeer c.1812 Dronningens Livregiment til Fods (Queen's Life Regiment of Foot) in winter dress, rear view showing knapsack, bread bag and canteen. Bottom, from left to right. Corporal of musketeers c.1805 Danske Livregiment til Fods, in winter dress. Sergeant of musketeers c.1811 Københavns Infanteriregiment in summer dress. Sergeant of Musketeers c.1812 Prince Christian-Frederiks Regiment in summer dress. Musketeer in campaign dress c.1814 in full marching order. Musketeer Holstenske Infanteriregiment wearing campaign dress c.1814 in full marching order. Musketeer Oldenborgske Infanteriregiment wearing winter campaign dress c.1814 in full marching order.

between the two battalions, they was also supposed to aid the regimental surgeons and doctors in combat.

Until 1808, all movement was done at a slow or fast walk. After 1808 running was allowed while changing formation and charging.

In 1811, all of these regiments had 20 companies each, divided into four battalions of five companies, four centre companies and one elite company, a grenadier company in the 1st battalion and a jæger company in the other three battalions. There were 830 men in each battalion excluding officers and NCOs; this was the official strengths for the following units:

Danske Livregiment til Fods
Norske Livregiment til Fods
Kronens Regiment
Kongens Regiment
Dronningens Livregiment til Fods
Prins Christian Frederiks Regiment
Fynske Infanteriregiment
1st Jyske Infanteriregiment
2nd Jyske Infanteriregiment
3rd Jyske Infanteriregiment
Oldenborgske Infanteriregiment
Slesvigske Infanteriregiment
Holstenske Infanteriregiment

The Københavns Infanteriregiment was originally raised in 1808 as the Københavns Borgerlige Infanteri; a militia unit primarily with volunteers of the surplus young men in Copenhagen, normally to serve in the regular army, a two-battalion regiment. This regiment was only to serve in and close to Copenhagen, and service was only to last until end of hostilities. It became the Københavns Infanteriregiment of two battalions totalling one grenadier, one jæger and eight musketeer companies amounting to 1,200 men.

The Marine Regiment was the last bastion of the old enlisted foreigners (18th-century style professional soldiers) who were considered as untrustworthy and were eventually disbanded and the best of them were transferred and incorporated into the new Københavns Infanteriregiment. Thus in October 1810 the Københavns Infanteriregiment was reformed and mixed with the disbanded Marine Regimentet. New Organisation: 1st battalion, the Marine Bataljonen, had five ordinary musketeer companies or 'sea companies', the 2nd Københavnske Garnisons Bataljon had one grenadier and four musketeer companies and the 3rd Københavnske Garnisons Bataljon, had one jæger and four musketeer companies; total strength was around 1,800 men.

The grenadier companies of the line regiments were sometimes regrouped into grenadier divisions of two companies. These were not ad hoc units, but were organised and based on the regimental distinctions: for example, the Holstein and Oldenborg regiments, which both had black facings, were grouped into one brigade, within a combined grenadier battalion. At least this was the official view; however in practice this was sometimes not respected.

All the line infantry regiments were grouped by pairs in infantry brigades where both units wore the same facings colours, one with white piping and the other without. The Holstein and Oldenborg regiments were known as the Black Brigade.

Basic Tactics

As the terrain in Denmark and Schleswig-Holstein was mainly cultivated, broken or of a closed nature without room for large formations, the brigade was the main fighting formation. This was an all arms 'battle group', normally

Danish Line Grenadiers and the Company Jægers

THE LINE INFANTRY ORGANISATION, BASIC TACTICS AND UNIFORMS

> **Plate 7. Danish Line Infantry Grenadiers and Jægers**
>
> Top row, from left to right, Grenadier c.1806, Dronningens Livregiment til Fods, winter dress. Grenadier c.1810 of the Norske Livregiment til Fods in summer dress. Grenadier c.1812, Prince Christian-Frederiks Regiment in campaign dress. Grenadier c.1812, rear view, Kongens Infanteriregiment, campaign dress. Grenadier c.1813 wearing an overcoat, Kronens Infanteriregiment.
> Bottom row, from left to right. Grenadier of the 3rd Jyske Infanteriregiment wearing a shako and campaign dress. 2nd Battalion Jæger company c.1806, Kronens Infanteriregiment, winter dress; note the Jæger company of the 1st battalion was armed with rifles. Jæger company NCO 3r /4th battalion 1st Jyske Infanteriregiment, campaign dress c.1808. Jæger of the 3rd/4th battalion c.1810 Slesvigske Infanteriregiment, campaign dress. A Jæger c.1812, 2nd battalions 2nd Jyske Infanteriregiment, campaign dress.
> Note: the jæger companies of the 3rd/4th battalions were armed with muskets, not rifles. We know from regimental documents regarding the formation of the regimental jægers of the Kongens Regiment's 3rd and 4th battalions that they had no sidearm/sabre at all, only one black cross belt with an attached bayonet frog. Those formations formed on Zeeland from the former Landeværn were still suffering from the equipment losses sustained by the Landeværn (and army) on Zeeland in 1807. Also, it was necessary to equip the Norwegian army and the new navy, so this meant that extra uniforms and sidearms of any kind, were generally rather scarce on Zeeland. Units formed in Holstein, Jutland, and Funen generally had access to better and more equipment from the start, so they were generally much better equipped. A few regiments, like the Dronningens Livregiment, confirmed from a contemporary picture of 3rd battalion, had even been able to supply the musketeers in the 3rd and 4th battalions with a sidearm (Sabre M1756) by 1810.

composed of four infantry battalions, a light battalion and a cavalry regiment. Until 1808 there were eight regimental 3-pdr guns which was a part of the brigade as well. After 1808 a full 10-gun 3-pdr mobile battery became part of the brigade. The mobile battery was akin to an Austrian cavalry battery, with all the gunners mounted on the guns and wagons.

This was obviously not a weak force. Strong in both defence and attack, and the large amount of light infantry and close rank firepower, combined with long training, were the major assets of the infantry. The cavalry was well mounted and armed and aggressive in tactics. At first glance perhaps artillery was the weakest part of the formation, since although they were quite manoeuvrable and numerous, the calibres were a little light. The gunners were also well trained and would, if necessary, fight until overrun, even though they now only had sabres to defend themselves with. However, as the army was only quite small it was probably best suited for the defence of Denmark, not for war on a European battlefield.

Although the Danish army had been involved in a great deal of combat, it had not fought any major campaigns before 1812–1814. They had been besieged in Copenhagen by the British, the assault on Stralsund and the winter wars with the Swedes, but that was the Norwegian troops who fought there. Its only true campaign was that of Germany with the Danish Auxiliary Corps in 1813. Thus, the officers as well as the troop lacked experience in the Napoleonic Wars and were shocked by the horrors of war during the 1813 campaign. What they lacked in experience they made up for with bravery, good training and good sense.

The Danish army had, like many other European armies at the time, based their training, drill and tactics on the drill and doctrines of the Prussian army, which had functioned brilliantly in earlier wars. This all changed in 1787 when Prince Carl of Hessen, the formal commander of the army, influenced by his old teacher General von Huth and with the blessing of the Prince Regent, decided to make a clean break with the old complicated doctrines and drills. Instead a simpler, quicker drill was introduced, as the Prince recognised the need for quick formation changes and the necessity to be able to fight and manoeuvre in skirmish formations, but still retaining some Prussian influences.

The two basic combat formations used by the Danish infantry battalions 1803–14 were the line and the square. Generally, the Danish infantry fought in line, just like the British, but in three ranks as Danish units were always closer to full strength at 800.

Both jægers and grenadiers could skirmish (the grenadiers could also be held back as a reserve or used to lead an attack). However, as nearly all the soldiers had two years of basic training together with some wartime service, so the musketeers had also received basic skirmish training. Any company could form a skirmish line for the battalion by deploying its third rank after the Prussian norm. By doing so the battalion did not shorten the line by deploying a complete company.

In battle the battalion would form a line, three ranks deep, either in an unbroken line, or occasionally in echelon by company. Each soldier in the battalion was expected to aim and fire three shots per minute. The battalion would fire volleys by platoons from a compact linear formation to obtain maximum effect. This volley was usually fired by to the two first ranks in such a way that a platoon would fire their muskets while the next platoon was reloading. This made it possible for the battalion to keep up a constant rolling volley fire. The square formation was used for protection against cavalry attacks. It involved the battalion forming a rectangle, which made it easier to repulse mounted attacks.

While the line battalion was forming line, their light company would spread out in skirmish lines to the battalion's front. The light troops would protect the battalion when it was formed and continue to provide harassing fire upon enemy battalions trying to attack their parent battalion. The skirmishers would also try to protect their parent battalion by engaging the enemy skirmishers trying to harass it. It is to be noted that the light troops (*skarpskytter* and *jæger*) could also form a circle in defence against cavalry. This was a formal tactic, not an improvisation. Until 1803 each Danish company had 12 sharpshooters, which would link up with the sharpshooters from the other companies to form the skirmish lines. After 1803, as noted above, the sharpshooters were removed from the line companies and formed into a complete elite company of their own.

The second line/reserve normally stood in column with a company front, but if in line of fire they could also change to 'line with refused flanks' or to line as the situation dictated. The Danish infantry (not the Norwegian) was equipped with mainly M1794 muskets (50,000 made), which had a cylindrical ramrod that did not need to be turned when used, and a self-priming pan. Further, it had a screen at the pan to protect the eyes of the soldier standing to the left, so that everyone could aim better when firing in line.

When attacking, the battalion would march towards the enemy in a linear formation; the elite grenadier company would usually lead the 1st battalion into battle. The battalion would open fire when it came within 200 metres of the enemy. The fire would be either a battalion volley or a platoon volley (starting from the right, even numbered battalions fired first then the odd numbers would fire). After each volley the battalion would advance before reloading. When the battalion came within 20–30 meters of the enemy they would charge using bayonets. All through the combat, the light companies would continue to skirmish with the enemy, maintaining a steady fire on the enemy battalion. One of the musketeer companies could be detached as extra skirmishers in support of the sharpshooters.

On the march the infantry had three standard marching speeds. First was 90 steps a minute (before 1808 it was 76 steps a minute), the second was 120 steps per minute and the third pace was running. During formation changes the first marching speed was used to avoid disorder and confusion. To maintain order during formation changes non-commissioned officers would take up position on the terrain marking where the battalion and companies should be placed. The battalion standards and company fanions were then used to guide the troops into their positions as quickly as possible. On the march, the elite company (the grenadiers) of the first battalion was placed at the head of the column.

The Diagrams

The following is a extract of the different diagrams found in the 1787 rule book for the Danish infantry, with different additions 1803/10. Skirmishers are not shown here as they had their own set of rules, but they would normally always be placed at the front and on the flanks patrolling/skirmishing in front to protect their parent formation.

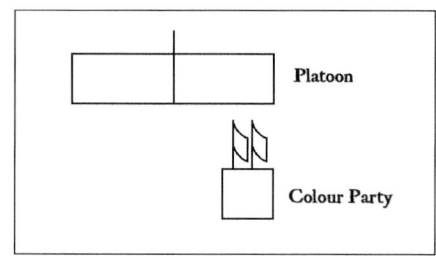

Column of March

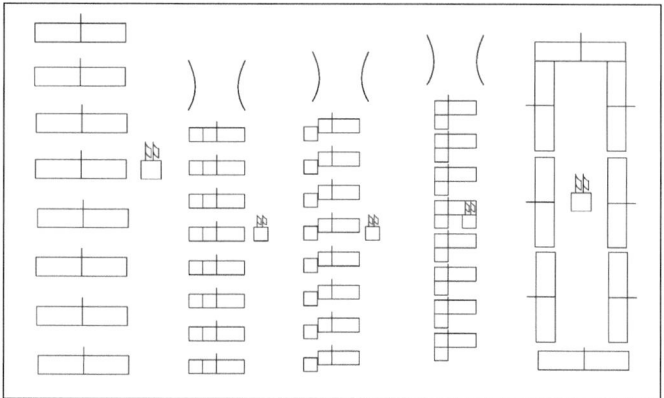

1. The basic column of march in the field with a platoon front. Note the placing of the colour platoon.
2. Column of march making ready to pass a narrowing road, bridge or other kind of narrow defile by refusing the left-hand section. If very narrow both flank sections could be refused behind the two in front, and this could also be used for 'road march'.
3. Forming the narrow march column to the left.

4. The column fully re-formed, and ready to march through the narrowed passage. After passing the obstacle the formation resumed its original formation.
5. From same the column of march a hollow marching square could be formed against a sudden cavalry attack.

Battalion Columns

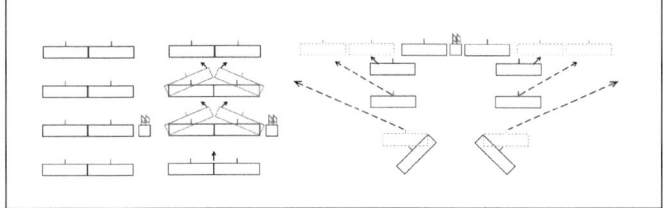

1. The normal 'column by companies' or a 'column of attack' was normally only used in Denmark for the movement of the second line/reserve on the field of battle. The first line would always deploy in line as intensive field manoeuvres had shown that although a 'column of attack', was easier to control, and to manoeuvre, it took more time to deploy and lacked firepower as well as offering an easy target for enemy artillery fire and close fire. Note the placing of the colour party.
2. The 'column by companies' or a 'column of attack' always had room between companies to turn and deploy.
3. The 'column by companies' or a 'column of attack' deploying into line. This was a difficult manoeuvre to execute directly in the face of the enemy.

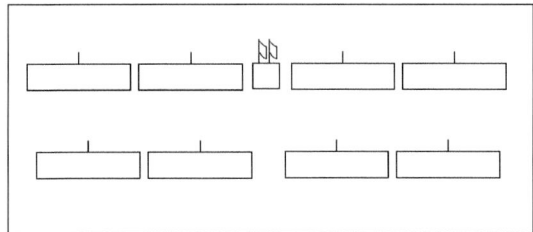

4. In 1810, a new 'Column by division' or 'Division Column of attack' was taken into use and now there were pictures in the rules. This was a two company (a 'division') facing followed by another. It was again only used for movement of the second line/reserve, and was thought to be less exposed to artillery fire and easier to deploy.

The Line and Square

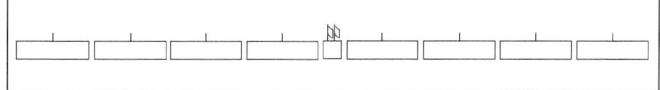

The line was the formation found to have the most firepower and the formation least exposed to artillery fire. It demanded a lot of training on the part of the soldiers and could be slow to move because of the need for constant realignment. It was also vulnerable against a sudden attack by cavalry or on the flank.

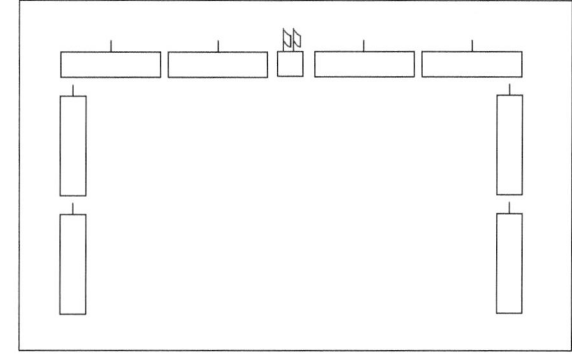

The need for more speed and the need for constant realignment of the line when moving, lead to the adoption of a compromise the *Line med højre og venstre om*; a line formation with both flanks refused. This formation could march as quick and as easy as a column of division or a column of companies and it was less exposed to artillery fire, was easy to reform into either the line or the square. This was the formation:

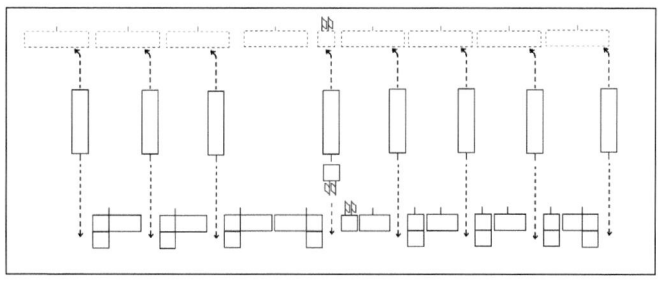

An important change formation was the 'passing of the lines', both backwards and forwards, so the lines could replace each other when needed.

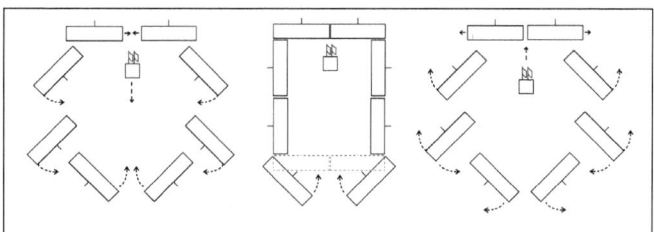

1. Forming a square from the line (or any other formation) was a formation change and it was a drill which was practised regulary. This was to be carried out with the utmost speed, but also the utmost calm.

2. Square nearly formed. Note how the rear ranks are the last to close. At same time the regimental jægers and grenadiers would do theit utmost to harras and disperse the enemys initial attack, until the square was formed, they would then regroup on the angles.
3. The drill for reforming the line was regulary practised as well.

The Uniforms

Firstly, one must remember that changes of uniform, and as a result change of appearance and style, was regulated and normally closely observed in Denmark.

There were two main issues of uniform clothing and they would not necessarily happen the same year.

- New trousers and footwear: every two years
- New uniform coat and headwear: every six years (cavalry helmets were not normally changed, but simply repaired and modernised).

The issue of uniform coats and trousers did not necessarily occur at same time. As these changes of clothing did not occur at the same time in each regiment, it obviously produced a difference of appearance between regiments. Normally a year, sometimes two years or more, would be allowed for the old items to wear out. The officers would normally change their clothing before that, if it did not make them appear too different to their men. In between these main issues, other changes of details or new equipment could occur (like the one in 1812 which changed the rank insignia).

These were the main changes which occurred within our time-frame.

- In 1803 the Infantry, artillery and cavalry were to receive a new style of uniform coat and hats. Bearskins were to be issued to the grenadiers (M1803 uniform); this was more or less completed by 1806.
- In 1808 the infantry, artillery and cavalry, including the reserve formations, were to receive a new style of uniform coat cut shorter in front, buttons evenly spaced in pairs, wider lapels and different lower lapels, this change was more or less completed by 1810.

Since the uniform reform of 1789, followed up by those of 1795 and 1802, the importance of more practical uniforms, was dealt with in several new ways, turning the uniform into a true field uniform, no longer just a Parade dress as had been the case up till then. The uniform reform of 1808 in many ways was based on modern thinking regarding, of how to make a uniform work better.

Around the turn of the century the idea of gaining a better control of one's body by performing gymnastics, became popular in parts of Europe, and the Prince Regent, himself a man of movement and action, had taken up this discipline himself. This he also saw to it that this practice was taken up by the army. The new army of recruits, nearly all of young men from a rural background, meant that nearly all were already 'formed' by the hard-working life of the peasant class so it was much easier to turn them into good active and effective soldiers. If the new regulations and new ways to fight, with speed and light infantry tactics were to work, the soldiers needed to be able to move better themselves. They were taught to use their bodies in better ways by drill and gymnastics. So, in the uniform reform of 1808, a number of improvements were made to the uniform to aid ease of movement of the body were carried out. To have a free movement of the under-body, the trousers now had a very high waist line (between navel and breast, instead of just under navel as before) and uniform coats sat higher on the body, both to avoid hindering the movement of the lower torso and limbs.

The use of the waist belts was reduced, now most infantry men had just one crossbelt over one shoulder, combining bayonet-frog and ammunition pouch into one load, and the bread bag and water bottle over the other shoulder. Those who still carried sabres had two buttons to support the waist belt at back of coat above the vents. The back pack now had two straps so to better place it on back, so better to ease the loads of a soldier. Another point taken care of was protecting the neck and his head; this was done by a looser neck cloth, but higher stiff collar. On his head he now wore a new well-designed tall shako with leather reinforcements on the sides and around the top to protect against cuts and blows with a good visor protecting the eyes and sitting firm on the head. This was perfectly in line with Frederik VI's own motto: 'Always seek to combine the practical with the useful'.

Theoretically the shako was to have been issued to all from 1808. The light infantry, who should have had their uniform changed at same time, had their change postponed until 1810 but they did receive the shakos. However, many reserve formations continued to wear hats as well as a number also had ersatz shakos of modified hats (the hats were apparently blocked up to reduce the taper, the rim was cut off except at the front to form a small visor, and the plume was moved to the front).

A change of trousers was made in 1809–10, when new grey service and white summer trousers were introduced to be worn with short black gaiters.

The changes in 1812 were based on both practical and economic reasons and a number of details were changed. Uniforms as such were not issued, but starting with the officers and NCOs, new cuffs where to be made for existing uniforms displaying the new signs of rank. As the soldiers' uniforms had to last for two or more years according to planning (1808 + 6 years = 1814), the regiments where given the choice to wear out the M1808 uniforms until then or, if possible, add the new cuffs to old uniforms (in Norway only slight changes were made – basically they modified the cuffs to the new pointed style – until after 1814). However, if regiments had to make any new uniforms, they were to have the new cuffs from the start.

The next major change saw the attempted introduction of grey uniforms in 1814 in same style as light troops, to be issued to units due for an issue of new uniforms (Officers had already been allowed to buy these grey uniforms privately in 1813 and eventually to wear them). However, due to economical restrictions, this change never really took effect, and instead a new uniform issue was ordered in 1816 (completed in the 1820s and thus outside the scope of this work). These new uniforms would not have been seen on the battlefields of this war.

The basic regulations, as they were laid down in 1803, remained the standard rule until 1814. When the soldiers were mustered, each soldier was issued with following items from stores: one pair of summer trousers and one pair of campaign trousers, one 'daily uniform coat' (service dress, from used stock, rarely new) and one 'campaign uniform coat' (normally kept in stock, in their depot, only to be issued when they actually went on campaign); A hat (from 1808, a shako), belts, backpack, kit and 'under garments'; basically the shirt, stockings, and a neck stock.

Other kit was issued on a yearly basis. For a musketeer of a line regiment this would be: once a year, two pairs of shoes, two linen shirts, one neck stock (black), one pair of stockings (no more), and one pair of fall-fronted white trousers made of sailcloth; once every two years: a pair of full fronted blue cloth trousers. After six years he received a new hat (from 1808, theoretically a shako), a vest and enough cloth and buttons to repair both of his uniforms. The rest of his kit he had to provide himself.

The Musketeers

From 1803 they had a tall black round felt hat with a narrow brim, slightly turned up at the sides, very similar to the hat used in the Swedish army of the period, with a band of lace corresponding to the button colour (yellow or white lace) around the base. The officers and NCOs had gold or silver lace, but of poorer quality for the NCOs. On left hand side of the hat there was a white plume over a black cockade with a button-coloured loop reaching down to the brim and a button. Denmark had been the only country in using hats as headgear from 1789–1808 followed by Sweden. This was found to be light, and practical, and giving good shade for the soldier's eyes.

From 1808 this hat was replaced progressively with a black felt shako reinforced with waxed black leather bands around the top and bottom; the lower one had a buckle for adjustment. It had a height of 22 to 24cms and the top had a diameter of 26 to 27cms. It had a waxed black leather top and reinforcing side Vs and a black leather peak and chinstrap with a buckle and a black leather button. On the front there was a fairly tall white chopped feather plume over black cockade held in place with button coloured loop. It had a single mixed yellow and red woollen cord and tassel, this was part of the shako and as such and even if the plume was not worn, the cords were still worn. The line infantry model did not have a plate. A popular misconception is that the M1808 Danish shako was a Danish copy of the French model, because Denmark had joined the French as allies in 1807. The decision to introduce shakos into the Danish army was made in 1805–06 during the preparation of a major reform of uniforms for the year 1808. The design was mainly influenced by the early Russian model with some Prussian and German details, who were also working on several designs of their own at same time. During the rule of Frederik VI, Denmark was always at the forefront of military science and so uniform trends were up to date as well. So Denmark never just copied anything, and they nearly always managed to add a Danish 'twist', formed for specific Danish needs and praxis. The M1808 shako was not a just copy of any other European model of shako, but was different in several important details. Firstly it was higher than any other shako model. It had also a leather top on the ordinary shakos, and a metal one on the officer's model, to give some (rudimentary) protection against cuts and blows, but far better than that of the old hats. Also, this top partly protected the shako as a whole against the elements. The Danish shakoes also had the visors turned down, so that it gave a good protection against the sunlight; Something several other European models was either missing or only received much later. They all had a height of c.23–25cms and a diameter of 26–27cms around the top.

Between 1811 and 1813 the size of the plume diminished and it now appears to be a cheaper woollen plume shaped in a carrot, oval or ball. Most of these later plumes appear to have been made of brushed white or dyed wool. There were a number of ersatz shakos made by reshaping the brims from the M1803 hats, blocking the crown out and moving the cockade and plume to the front, more generally used in the militia and some artillery units post 1808. From September 1813, it was decided to remove the plumes from the shako, but this was apparently not carried out with much diligence as a resolution regarding replacing the grenadiers' bearskins with shakoes clearly states: 'naturally plumes on this are to be carried as has been done until now'. In 1814 the plumes were not to be carried in the field, but they were probably kept for parades.

The musketeers also had a stocking-style fatigue bonnet, very similar to the French model of the period; it was red for grenadiers, grey for the centre companies, generally with a facing coloured turn-up. It had white piping

Danish Hats and Legwear 1789–1815

THE LINE INFANTRY ORGANISATION, BASIC TACTICS AND UNIFORMS

> **Plate 8. Danish Hats and Legwear**
> 1. M1789–1803 hat, three quarters view
> 2. M1789–1803 hat, face view. This hat continued to be worn by some militia units until 1807 at least.
> 3. M1803–1808 hat, three quarters view
> 4. M1803–1808 hat, face view
> 5. Fatigue bonnet or cap, three quarters view
> 6. M1808 ersatz shako, converted from M1803 hat and lacquered
> 7. M1808 other ranks' shako, left side
> 8. M1808 other ranks' shako, face view
> 9. M1808 other ranks' shako, rear view
> 10. M1808 officers' shako, right side
> 11. Gaiter trousers
> 12. M1808 gaiter
> 13. M1810 'Hessian'-style jæger's gaiter with tassel
> 14. M1810 'Hessian' gaiter variant without tassel
> 15. Officer's hessian-style boot

only if there was white piping on the facings. The tassel was in the button colour; when not in use it was probably rolled and strapped under the cartridge box French style, it has not been possible to confirm this assumption.

The infantry wore a short tunic of red cloth (*Kjole*) with upturned front corners (*Oppbret*) showing the white lining used by all of the line infantry regiments. This is not part of the actual lining, but pieces of lining cloth stitched on as false turnbacks: this was a continuation of the style of the previous jackets, which were meant to appear like cut down coats with no tails. The M1803 coatee was cut longer with larger turnbacks, the lapels were quite narrow and the tops were more rounded. The buttons were placed at regular intervals. The M1808 coatee was shorter; the lapels were much larger with the tops scalloped and pointed and the turnbacks wider and more pointed. The coatee had seven buttons with one at the top and the others placed in three pairs, the coatee had two buttons in the small of the back with piped pleats. All the buttons were the same size and fairly large. The collar and lapels were in the facing colour. The cuffs were in the facing colour and had a red cuff flap (rectangular with three buttons), piped when the facing colour was piped. The flap is generally depicted as scalloped to a greater or lesser degree. The piping was applied around the base of the collar and at the throat, but not along on the top edge, this rule applied to all arms.

In 1812, a new set of regulations was issued, it was stipulated that only grey cloth should be used for manufacture of uniforms in the future. By this time Denmark was near to bankruptcy due to the wars and the blockade. The new grey uniform was not issued to the troops, although a few officers had the coat made up.

Finally in 1812 following a new approbation, the coat was modified by the regimental tailors and it now had pointed cuffs, as only a limited amount of new uniforms were made before the end of the war. The white turnbacks were smaller as well, although some examples are still quite wide, but the coat continued to be made of red cloth. Although some grey uniforms had started to be issued, it appears that this was more of a stopgap measure due to shortages. This new uniform does not appear to have been that widely used, at least in the field as most contemporary illustrations made after 1812 still continue to show the previous model of cuffs as well as the officers still wearing their sashes and epaulettes.

The shoulder straps were also in the facing colour, generally piped in white. The buttons were made of either pewter or brass depending on the regimental colours.

Under the collar they all had a black neck stock and they wore linen shirts, these were generally of the smock style and made of unbleached linen, so could be greyish white or a light beige colour, and had one button at the neck and one on each cuff.

Before 1800, musketeers had worn fall-fronted white knee breeches with high M1789 black gaiters, which were still being worn during the 1801 attack on Copenhagen; these were replaced with fall-fronted medium blue woollen gaiter trousers for winter wear and fall-fronted white gaiter trousers for summer dress. These trousers had a very high waist, rose over the stomach to the level 'of the heart', according to the texts, and a fall-front flap with three buttons, usually hidden by the coatee; by 1810 the flap was now much larger. There were five buttons on the bottom of each of the legs, which, when closed, formed the gaiter part of the trousers.

Officially in 1808, they still had gaiter trousers and black leather shoes, which were already being worn during the 1807 attack on Copenhagen and in Stralsund in 1809

THE DANISH ARMY OF THE NAPOLEONIC WARS VOLUME 1

Danish Infantry Equipment

THE LINE INFANTRY ORGANISATION, BASIC TACTICS AND UNIFORMS

> **Plate 9. Danish Infantry Equipment**
>
> 1. Cartridge box showing the box from the front, open with drilled wooden block for 15 'ready to use' cartridges and rear showing the strap arrangement. Some illustrations suggest the straps were crossed over.
> 2. Belts, top the musketeer's standard model and below for grenadiers, København Regiment, and some NCOs.
> 3. M1789 jæger's 'shooting bag' the combined cartridge and kit pouch made of badger skin, three quarters view, in its original form before conversion into a knapsack like No. 4.
> 4. M1803–1808 knapsack for musketeers and grenadiers.
> 5. Tin canteen.

and during the Norwegian campaign in the late summer of 1808 through to spring 1809. These gaiter trousers are shown as fairly tight fitting in both length and width. Around 1809, they were issued with short black gaiters, apparently these gaiters were made by cutting down stocks of the old pre-1800 knee gaiters and were worn with either grey or blue woollen trousers, or white linen trousers for summer. Note that the white gaiter trousers were never cut down in Denmark, but they were worn as originally made up till 1809 at least as shown in the watercolours by von Prangen.

In 1810 they changed for fall-fronted grey breeches or overalls/long trousers worn with low M1808 black gaiters, which were worn during the German campaign of 1812–14 and in the Norwegian campaign of 1814. However, this was a gradual change that took many years and depended on the supply situation, so many variations would have been found in use at the same time. Suhr shows some musketeers in white trousers in 1814, but it is unclear how many wore these trousers, probably more than is generally thought. At least by 1810 they were suspended with off white cloth braces. As late as 1813, the 3rd Jyske Infantry Regiment is known to have used the old white gaiter trousers during the winter campaign in Holstein, as did some Norwegian regiments in 1814. This may not be as strange as it sounds; the quality of these older trousers would probably have been a lot better than most of the new grey ones.

For winter and foul weather the men were issued with grey double-breasted overcoats, which were worn in action during the winter campaigns. When it was not worn, it was rolled and strapped on to their calfskin backpack. These coats were issued in the autumn and returned to stores in the spring. Some of these coats may have had their regimental facings added to the collar and cuffs like the jæger battalions. During the 1814 campaign it was remarked upon the fact that the grey greatcoated units had suffered fewer casualties than those wearing the red coatee.

The musketeers equipped with a white leather shoulder belt with a black leather cartridge box; some of the pouches had a brass badge on the flap, either a crowned cypher or a flaming grenade. The interior had a wooden insert which was divided into a large and small space. In the large space a packet of 15 cartridges was placed on the bottom and then a wooden block drilled with 15 holes for another 15 cartridges was placed on top. The small space contained a phial of oil, tools, cleaning rag, a tompion and wooden practice 'flints'. Spare flints were carried in the front pocket, see Plate 9.

They carried their bayonet on a white leather waist belt which had a simple open square brass buckle. However, for the 3rd and 4th battalions there were not enough waist belts to go around so in 1809 as a stopgap measure the bayonet scabbard was attached to the back of the cartridge box. A large number of this model were also shipped to Norway where they became a standard issue from 1810 to 1814 as shown in the illustrations of Mørner and Ljunggren.

During the 1813/14 campaign, illustrations show troops of the Auxiliary Corps with cross belts, so it appears that they either acquired white leather shoulder belts for their hangers at least, probably recuperated in the field, or they were issued with old belts of the previous century which had been conserved in the arsenals, they were never worn in Norway and probably not in Denmark either.

At the start of the period the Danish infantry used a rather obsolete 'rounded' backpack of calfskin with just one white strap until 1807–1808. This backpack had probably been influenced by the Prussian/Austrian or British model which had the furry side out. This pack was tiring for the men as all the weight pulled to one side. This was replaced from 1808 with a square French-style backpack again made of calfskin which had the furry side out and it was carried on whitened tan or buff leather shoulder straps and the flap was closed with three leather straps and brass buckles. The contemporary traditional breeds of cattle of Denmark were principally the Jutland, which could have a light grey, dark grey or black piebald coat or the Holstein breed, now known as the Danish red which had a reddish-brown coat. These variations of colour would show on the backpacks, possibly denoting the regions of the regiments or where the backpacks were made. Following the psychology of the Danish army, these new packs were probably made from the old models. They had straps provided on the

THE DANISH ARMY OF THE NAPOLEONIC WARS VOLUME 1

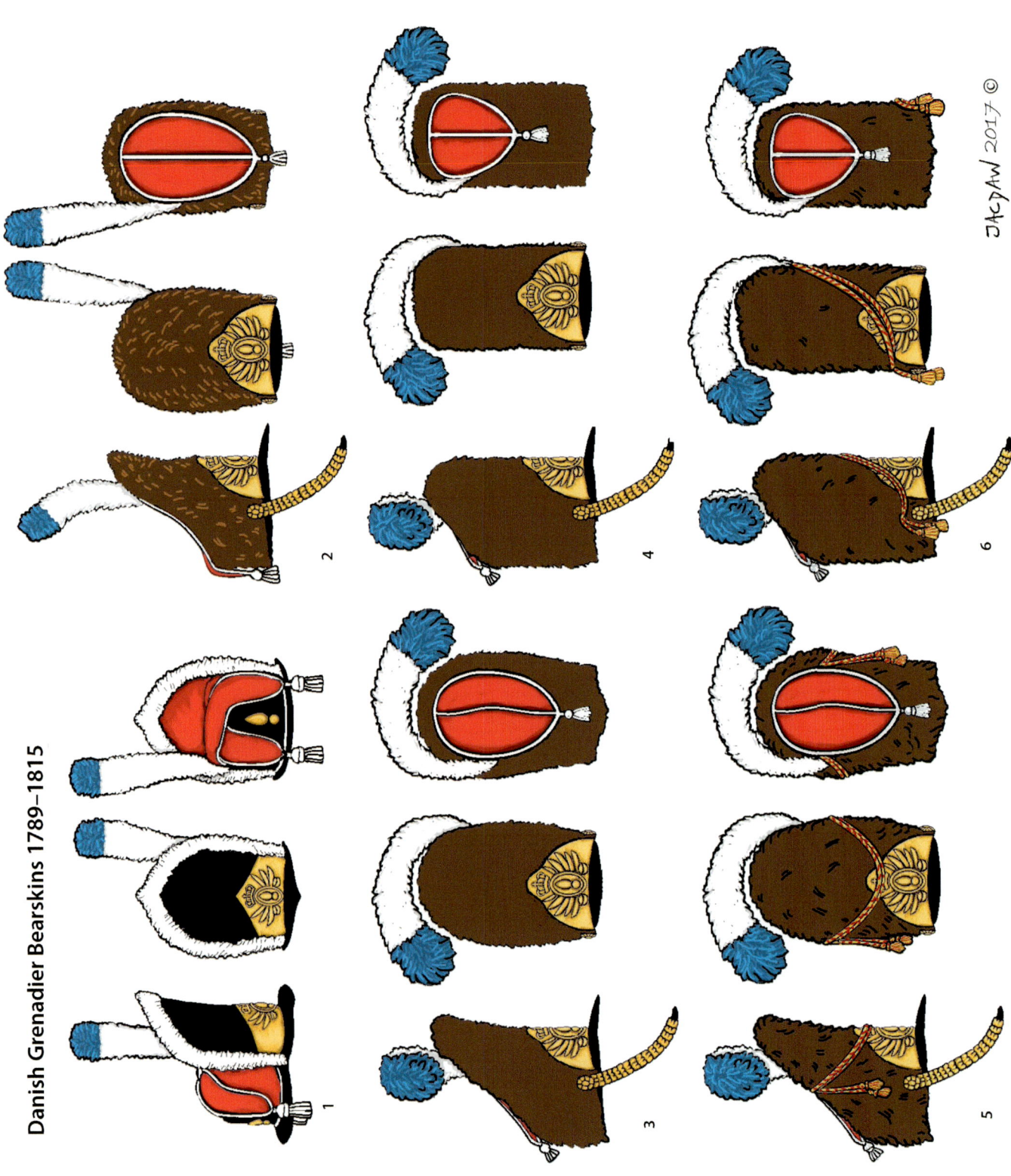

Danish Grenadier Bearskins 1789–1815

THE LINE INFANTRY ORGANISATION, BASIC TACTICS AND UNIFORMS

> **Plate 10. Danish Bearskins**
>
> 1. M1789 other ranks' grenadier hat, side view, face view and rear view. Plate shown is the later M1803 model, probably for the Jydske Regiment, earlier models were simpler with just a grenade on it and those made in Norway had some foliage stamped on them as well.
> 2. M1803 other ranks' bearskin, side view, front and rear view.
> 3. M1808 other ranks' bearskin, side view, front and rear view.
> 4. M1812 other ranks' bearskin, side view, front and rear view. Probably only issued to the Livgarde til Fods and the 1st or 3rd Jyske regiments pre 1817.
> 5. M1803 officer's bearskin, side view, front and rear view.
> 6. M1812 officer's bearskin, side view, front and rear view. Probably only issued to the Livgarde til Fods and the 1st or 3rd Jydske Regiments pre 1817.
> Note. The colour of the bearskins would obviously vary; no doubt darker fur would be preferred, especially for the officers. The colour of the fur was noted as fading and becoming lighter in colour over time.

top to attach the greatcoat. The jæger company had black leather straps. The grenadiers used the same model as the musketeers. During the 1812–1814 period, some troops simply carried a rolled blanket over their shoulders on a leather strap.

Other equipment consisted of a tin or copper canteen they were made of tin thin metal plate welded together with an alloy of tin and lead. This was easy to work with but had the sad side effect that some soldiers suffered with lead poisoning with time, today it is thought to have led to some of the sickness and death of soldiers in 1813–14. The top was slightly larger and narrower at the top and could be used as a small cup; very practical when receiving the daily ration of schnapps. It was carried on a brown or white leather bandolier. In the Norwegian regiments it was only issued to one man in two, but it has not proven possible to ascertain whether this rule applied to the Danish troops as well. They had a natural linen bread bag. This bread bag had a white leather strap for the centre companies and the grenadiers and black leather straps for the jægers.

The Grenadiers' Uniform

Grenadiers wore the same uniform as the centre companies but with the following distinctions. In 1802 they had a Potemkin-style grenadier hat. It had a large varnished leather top trimmed with a white fur crest from ear to ear. It had a large brass plate stamped with grenade. It had double facing-coloured bags (red for black-faced regiments) each with button coloured lace and tassel. The plume was white with light blue tip.

This hat was replaced in 1803 with a dark brown or black fur bearskin cap bearing a new brass plate, stamped with a crown over a grenade with some regimental variations; it had a black leather peak and brass rosace and chin scales. Following research into these early bearskins it appears that in fact the first bearskins were made from the previous hat by eliminating the crest and putting a bear skin sleeve over the hat and then stitching one of the bags and the plume back on. This is yet another example of the Danish method of recycling older elements to make 'new' items.

The bearskin had a reputation of fading to light brown after a while. This bearskin, known as the model 1803, had a steep profile when seen from the side and the plume was more or less vertical showing its origin. The bag is frequently shown with a central line of piping but this is not correct; if one looks at contemporary non-official art it is not shown. This detail was not added until much later, post 1812.

In the period 1805–07, the reform of standard uniforms was planned and designed, following the latest trends and experience, to modernise the uniforms as war was becoming more likely. These reforms also concerned the bearskins it was decided that they were to be improved. In the Approbation 22 January 1808, it was stated: 'That the now used bearskins, shall be altered according to the shipped sealed proof models, And from now on the inside part, the top and visor, will be made of leather, instead of the previously used felt'. The old M1789 hats had been made of felt and, being some 15 to 17 years old by now, they were probably quite worn out.

However, in February 1809 the King decided 'As [the first] 2 grenadier companies have received Bearskins of a new and larger design [M1808], I cannot allow them [in the future], as they are more expensive than the previous model [M1803]'. This may not be so strange, as the M1803 had re-used the old M1789 hats, this way it had reduced costs. The new bearskin, were also to have a new 'inner hat' as well as more fur and trimming, and so would as a consequence, be more expensive. This new 1809–1810 model was more rounded and voluminous, with more of a sugar loaf form with a smaller bag, but in March 1809, after having reconsidered, the King concluded 'If this new type of bearskin could be made smaller, in same design [M1808] and at the cost of the previous model of bearskin [M1803] they would be allowed. If not [possible], then the design of the 1803 bearskins should then be used also for making the new ones'. These new bearskins were generally disliked by the men, being both heavier and uncomfortable; this eventually led to the use of shakos on campaign.

The first to receive bearskins in spring/summer 1809, were the Kongens Regiment and then Prins Christian's Regiment, in that order. Then after March 1809, logically they should then have been followed by, Holstenske Regiment, Danske Liv Regiment, Norske Liv Regiment.

Of these regiments the two first had received the M1808. There is only one picture of the Kongens Regiment in a bearskin (Voigt 1815–17) so logically this must show the M1808 bearskin. There is also one attributed to Holstenske Regiment (Mørner 1814), but the details show that this must be wrong, and that this is in fact the 1st or 3rd Jydske as both were to receive bearskins c.1811–12 as the last regiments, together with the guard. However, what is interesting as they show a completely different type of bearskin! This model, judging from contemporary drawings had a more rounded plate and the plume now fell over the top. The other nine regiments instead appear to have received a M1803/09 refurbished with new fur, a little higher and with a longer plume.

From 1806, all the regiments now had a red cloth bag with white lace and tassels. From November 1813 the men were ordered to no longer to wear their plumes while they were on campaign. From November 1814 it was decided to start replacing the grenadiers bearskins with a shako, but they would continue to use the same plate as the bearskin, at least for campaign dress; they were to have white cords, to distinguish them from musketeers. The shako also had a blue over white plume.

The grenadiers carried a white shoulder belt with a brass match-case. The black cartridge box had a brass grenade badge. Besides the bayonet, they carried an M1753 infantry sabre which was 76cms long with a blade of 60cms, with a brass single bar hilt and guard, or a M1756 musketeer hanger, usually shown with a red sword knot and strap and carried in a black or dark brown leather scabbard with brass fittings and slung from a white leather waist belt.

The M1753 infantry sabre was the workhorse of the army, first as an infantry sabre, later as grenadier, artillery, light infantry, and royal life guard sabres. It is frequently misnamed as the M1753 grenadier's sabre, but this is a modern term. This sabre was occasionally carried by the line companies NCOs, musicians, and possibly some enlisted units of the infantry battalions. The only specific mention is for the grenadier companies of some or all of the regiments garrisoned in Copenhagen around 1808, who were allowed to use white leather sword straps with red tassels, as long as they were paid for by the regiment or by the men themselves.

The standard musket for the musketeer and grenadier companies of the line battalions was the M1774 smoothbore musket. Several modified versions of the M1774 existed (the M1785, M1789, M1791, M1794, and M1807) as all existing muskets were modified and pressed into service. Each new modification showed improvements with a tendency of each new model becoming lighter and the M1807 being a little shorter. The modified M1774 versions were the most widely used musket. A trained soldier could theoretically fire up to three aimed shots per minute with the M1774 musket. The musket's calibre was 18mm, the overall length was 144cms, the barrel being 105cms, and it weighed in at 4,086 grams. The butt and stock were generally made of beech wood and they were originally painted black in the early part of the period. In Norway birch wood appears to have been used to repair stocks.

The Regimental Sharpshooters' Uniform

The sharpshooters or company jægers were dressed in the same uniform as the centre companies, but with the following distinctions: the shako was the same as those in the musketeer companies but with a brushed woollen white plume with light green top.

From 1808 the light companies of the 2nd, 3rd and 4th battalions of the line wore the same uniform as the centre companies, but they now had an all-green plume and a green cord on their shako. The light companies had black leather belting. Most of them appeared to have a pick and brush on a knot of green ribbon for their musket hung from a tunic button on their left breast for rapid access.

The 2nd battalion jægers were armed with a special light infantry musket, the light infantry rifle M1807. At least that was the theory, but as only some 2,000 of them were made, obviously not all of the men were equipped with them. The 3rd and 4th battalion jægers were armed with standard infantry muskets. This rifle was a highly precise weapon with a very slow rate of fire. Loading, aiming and firing a shot could take several minutes. It was effective up to 200 paces; maximum range was 500 paces. The rifle's calibre was 16mm, the overall length was 113cms, the barrel being 73cms long and it weighed in at 4,005 grams. Obviously they did not have a bayonet sheath on their waist belt as such, but carried *hirschfängers* on their waist belts.

The *hirschfänger* was a short sword which was modified into a sword bayonet. In 1801 the Danish high command decided to mount a heavy steel bracket with a spring on the two *hirschfänger* models, so that it could fit be used as a bayonet on the jæger rifles. This was fitted to the rifle by means of a bracket and sprung lever which slotted on the side of the barrel. It was 76cms long, the blade being 63cms with a brass handle and guard and was carried in a black or dark brown leather sheath with brass fittings. This was not a very good invention as the *hirschfänger* was already a heavy weapon on its own and adding this steel bracket did not make it any lighter. In addition, it made the *hirschfänger* stand out to the side another 55mm on the left side of the rifle, thus the balance was terrible; not only for shooting, but also when fighting with the bayonet. It is sometimes shown with a green wool sword knot and strap.

On their black leather waist belt there was a powder horn slung by a simple leather strap on their right side and a bullet bag also on a simple brown leather strap slung on the left by the *hirschfänger*; they were called the *krutthorn* and *kulepung*. Over their shoulder they carried a black leather bandoleer for their cartridge box, containing their cartridges, spare flints and tools for their rifle.

Their officers carried a M1789 officer's sabre. Musicians carried a coil-shaped horn (*Waldhorn*) wrapped with green cord and tassel and they would have had swallows' nests in regimental facing colour, laced with the button colour.

NCOs' Distinctions

When new NCO destinctions were introduced in 1789 for the infantry and artillery, they were to be easily visible. Their shako had a thicker double cord than the troops; this goes for the light infantry, cavalry and artillery as well. As shoulder belts were used by both officers and NCOs, as well as the infantry and artillery, their distinctions were stitched directly onto the uniform, on the shoulder opposed to their shoulder belt, as they were not intended to retain a strap. Now that they had distinctions on both shoulders it was neccessary that the shoulder strap held the shoulder belt of their sword. The officers received special 'Dragons' and distinctions at the same time. This was before NCOs and officers used waistbelts to carry their swords. The NCOs distinctions were probably placed on top of the shoulder strap as they were made of lace. Shoulder belts were only used by some officers and the Livgarde til Fod. In 1790 the soldiers were re-issued with the old waist belts and the officers were also issued with a new type of waist belt as well.

Previously the NCO distinctions had apparently been sown directly on to the uniforms, but probably in 1798 when breadbags and backpack were issued, to be carried over their right shoulder, they had to have a proper shoulder strap, stitched on one end and retained with a button on the other end so a belt could be retained. Therefore, when in 1805 when NCOs halbards and espontons were abolished and they were rearmed with sharpshooters' muskets (which were lighter than ordinary infantry muskets), they had to have them as well for the shoulder strap of the cartridge box. By 1808 when the new backpacks and waterbottles were issued, only the drum majors and senior NCOs still had theirs sewn on. According to regulations (as found on existing uniforms and contemporary illustrations) one had to have a special NCO distinction on one shoulder (normally the right shoulder), or to put it simply this is the mark of an NCO. Without it, you were not an NCO, whatever the form of the NCO's distinction (which differed from service to service). This had nothing to do with a particular rank; that was shown on the other shoulder in the form of a plain shoulder strap for a *Gefreiter* (vice corporal; not a professional but rather a 'common' soldier who, during his ordinary service, was promoted temporarily to the rank of NCO), and a corporal in the cavalry. The cavalry normally had no need for vice corporals, so it was only when they were actually going to war that some troopers were promoted to this rank as a wartime combat rank for the duration.

The NCOs wore the regimental uniform. The sergeants of the line infantry had double cords and tassels on their shakos. They were all green for the jægers, and red and yellow for the line. The sergeants' shakos were the same size as the privates' model, but better made and the button for the chinstrap was metallic, generally of pewter.

From 1801 the sergeants wore epaulettes with button-coloured metallic lace and fringes on one shoulder with facing-coloured straps, and the other side had a facing-coloured shoulder strap trimmed with button-coloured metallic lace. The corporals had ordinary facing-coloured shoulder straps trimmed with button-coloured metallic lace on both shoulders. The lance or vice corporals had an epaulette on their right shoulder and a simple shoulder strap on their left. Contrary to the contemporary illustrations, these epaulettes were in reality a lot thinner and the fringes was not very full, in fact a little scraggy, little more than tufts, and there appears to be some regimental variations to the lacing, not all had a figure-of-eight style.

At some point, to difference vice-corporals more clearly from the 'real' NCOs, the corporals were allowed two NCO epaulettes to clearly show him apart from 'a mere vice corporal'. All the NCOs carried sticks as a mark of rank. In addition to these distinctions, grenadier NCOs also had a small brass grenade badge on their epaulette. The jæger company NCO had, apart from the other distinctions, a whistle on a chain looped across his chest and hung from the buttons with a green or blue ribbon on the other end of his picker. Possibly, the only difference in the uniform itself was, theoretically, a better quality of facing cloth on sergeants' jackets, along with the metallic lace and the sword knot and strap, a sword knot corresponding to their rank was gradually introduced.

As already stated, the fusilier NCOs were still officially armed with a M1769 sergeant's halberd (*lilje*) and a sabre up until about 1805, when the halberd was officially replaced with the M1789 sharpshooter musket and they were issued cartridge boxes along with the fusils and a grenadier sabre at the same time. It is more than likely that the halberds had already been replaced and the approbation simply put the seal on an established practice.

Carrying a 'swagger stick' was part of an NCO's attributes and a symbol of his rank, but it was officially abolished prior to the period under study here. Up to the end of the 18th century these sticks were the visible symbol of a NCO's rank. He was allowed a beat the disobedient soldier with this stick to enforce discipline and respect. In Britain it is still remembered by the expression 'corporal punishment'. However, towards the end of the late 1700s, probably around 1789, this stick fell out of use as an official part of the attributes of an NCO. The amount of punishment allowed was now restricted and regulations were made for its use. NCOs were now only allowed to 'correct with lashes', as part of the training of soldiers, but not to hand out any kind of other type punishment which could be perceived as 'dishonouring' the recruit. A 'correction with lashes' was so common generally in society that this was not seen as dishonourable but simply normal behaviour.

To ensure that a soldier's honour was respected it was forbidden to use one's hand or whip as part of this 'corrections'; only 'a short stick', or the flat of a sabre if an NCO was himself was being 'corrected'. Other older punishments like 'sitting on the wooden hose' and flogging were also abolished as 'dishonouring'. Prison was now more common as a punishment, but for severer crimes like stealing or mutiny the punishment of the '*Spidsrod*' or running the gauntlet was still in use for 'crimes dishonouring the army and his fellow soldier'. In this case the soldier was punished by his own unit for not living up to the moral codex of being a soldier. However, whilst the NCO's stick was no longer part of their attributes when 'under arms' after 1789, it was accepted and used (probably rather freely), by nearly all NCOs during training. Also there are examples that some NCOs carried them 'concealed', often inside the barrel of the musket, 'to have them to hand if needed'. Even during 1848–50 and 1864, this was still remarked upon. The officers also liked to have a 'walking stick' and there are several examples that 'corrections' were also handed out with this.

So, to resumé: before 1789, NCO distinctions appeared on the right shoulder only and were stitched on. In 1789 new NCO distinctions were issued to be shown on both shoulders, so now they were stitched at one end and retained with a button by the collar allowing the passage of a shoulder belt. This applied to officers as well.

From 1812, when their cuffs were changed for the pointed style, NCOs received button-coloured shoulder straps (white or yellow cloth) with facing-coloured stitched trim all around, on both shoulders, plus rank chevrons in yellow or white woollen lace according to the button colour, on both arms inside placed on the cuffs: The vice corporal had one chevron; the corporal had two chevrons: both had a yellow sword strap with two red stripes with a mixed red and yellow tassel. The *Vagtmester* and *Kommandersergeant* had three chevrons. They had identical sword straps, but with one silver thread worked in next to the red stripes, and silver thread mixed into the tassel. The sergeant-major had three chevrons and a button or rosette at the tip of the cuff point.

Just to confuse things a little more, the Danish also had an award system of special or honorary distinctions. The NCOs were allowed to wear them on parade only, but not in the field. This system was of '*Præmie epauletter*' (prize distinctions) was created in 1809 and they were awarded to those NCOs who had studied at the special NCOs' school and had graduated with the best results of their class/year. These special distinctions were considered the private property of the NCO, and they were still permitted to wear them after the orders of August of 1812, where all other epaulettes made of silver and gold metal had been abolished. They were all metal, of the button colour, including metal fringes and measured 15 x 7.2cm. They were to be worn over the top of the normal shoulder strap, fixed by two rivets, and the 'regimental colour' could be seen then through the gap at the middle. The name and details of bearer were written on the back of the epaulettes.

- 1st Prize: A silver epaulet with metal fringes on right shoulder (this epaulette was much fuller than the service one) and a full silver strap on the left.
- 2nd Prize: Full silver strap on both shoulders.
- 3rd Prize: A silver epaulet with metal fringes on right shoulder and a normal 'regimental' strap on the left. At the same time this does appear to mirror the standard system.

The Officers' Uniforms

The officers originally wore a black felt cocked hat with the company coloured plume over a black cockade with silver or gold loop and a red and gold tassel. From 1805 at the latest, these bicorns were replaced with round hats with gold and crimson cords. As illustrated in the Suhr sketches, the infantry officers affected cavalry-style cap lines and flounders, which they later added to their shakos and their bearskins, probably reusing the old cap lines from their earlier round hats, judging from the diameter of the cords.

This hat was replaced in 1809 with the shako which was more or less the same size as the privates' model. They were generally made of felt cloth with leather reinforced top and bottom and interestingly a metal plate on the top (as extra protection against sword cuts) and covered with silk or another fine cloth without the V strengtheners on the sides. However, as the officers had to buy them themselves, several had them made of silk cloth instead of ordinary cloth with both lacquered leather and waxed leather; some still had metal tops. They had gold and crimson cords,

THE LINE INFANTRY ORGANISATION, BASIC TACTICS AND UNIFORMS

Table I. Officers' Rank Distinctions: Epaulettes pre 1812	
Second Lieutenant (*Sekondløjtnant*)	Strap FC, lace trim B with 1 button B, Crescent and fringes B
First Lieutenant (*Premierløjtnant*)	Strap FC, lace trim B with 2 buttons B, Crescent and fringes B
Captain (*Kaptajn*)	Strap B, Crescent and fringes B
Major (*Major*)	Strap B with 1 rosette IB, Crescent and fringes B
Lieutenant-Colonel (*Oberstløjtnant*)	Strap B with 2 rosettes IB, Crescent and fringes B
Colonel (*Obrist*)	Strap B, counter stripes IB, , counter stripes IB Crescent IB and fringes B
FC= facing colour. B= button colour (in gold or silver). IB = inverted button colour (silver on gold or gold over silver)	

tressed thicker than those of the men, including tasselled flounders (or rackets) on long cords which hung down from the right of the cap to the breast and were looped over a lapel button on the left side (the third button from the top on the lapel). It had a black cockade held in place by a button-coloured loop and regimentally coloured metal button and a white plume. The shako had a black leather chin strap and a black button.

The shakos worn by the officers were occasionally a little different in form as they had a reputation of having theirs made privately; the couple of preserved shakos are privately made models. One of these models preserved in Norway is made entirely of leather. Note that the long cords of the officer's previous hat were not normally worn on the shako, except by some of the more elaborately dressed dandy officers or on formal parades. By 1813 it is not confirmed that they continued wearing their plumes when they were on campaign or on the battlefield.

The grenadier officers wore the other ranks' bearskin cap, but with red and gold cords, including tasselled flounders on long cords which hung down from the right of the cap to the breast and were looped over a lapel button on the left side the same as for the shako. It had a blue-tipped white plume.

Feathers on officers' hats/bicorns/shakos were often mentioned in regulations, as officers often used taller plumes than they were supposed to according to regulations. For bicorn hats of the guard and others, a maximum length of c.20–22 centimetres was ordered. For hats and later for the shakos, the maximum height of plumes officially allowed was to be the 'same height as the hat from top to bottom'. However, many dandy officers did not obey these regulations and used privately-made plumes of greater lengths.

The officers wore long tailed coats of crimson red cloth with same regimental coloured facings as the men. They had white turnbacks, except for the Copenhagen Infantry Regiment. The coat had two buttons in the small of the back with piped pleats. The coat had two small false horizontal pockets on the back, piped straw yellow or white, but no buttons. Some officers returning to Denmark who had served alongside French troops started to add three buttons under each pocket in an 'un-regulated fancy fashion'. The collar was as for the men, although, strictly against regulations, some officers started adding piping to the top of the collar in regiments that had piped uniforms

We have a statement from the King to the officers returning from service in France, in 1814, who wrote: 'I have noticed that several officers, against regulations have added several extra buttons underneath the pocket flaps, this is not the correct dress, but I will allow it for now, and take it into consideration, for future uniform regulations'.

Again, no metallic thread piping anywhere after 1812, except for the Marine Regiment officers, who had gold embroidered button holes and horizontal pockets until the unit was disbanded. The buttons and piping were in the regimental colour, but in non-metallic thread. Theoretically, the crimson coat was replaced with a bright red/scarlet coat after 1808, but the officers continued to use the crimson coats for parades at least, right up till 1814. We know this because some of these coats which were altered in 1812 with the addition of pointed cuffs still exist. Some officers even had coats made up with the same coloured cloth as the men's coats.

Around their waist the officers wore a sash until these were officially abolished in 1812; they were not embroidered, but woven in the Sprang technique (an ancient method of weaving fabric that gives it a natural elasticity; its appearance is similar to netting, but unlike netting, sprang is constructed entirely from warp threads), with red and yellow stripes and terminated in a tassel and fringe. They were long enough to go twice round the waist and worn knotted on the left hip.

From 1812 when they received new coats made of scarlet cloth; the epaulettes and silk sash were abolished and they were replaced with the new rank insignias in button colour, which were worn on both arms over the pointed cuffs. However, judging from contemporary illustrations, the vast majority of officers continued to wear their epaulettes and sash up to the end of the war in Denmark.

THE DANISH ARMY OF THE NAPOLEONIC WARS VOLUME 1

Danish Line Infantry Officers

THE LINE INFANTRY ORGANISATION, BASIC TACTICS AND UNIFORMS

> ## Plate 11. Danish Line Infantry Officers 1805–1814
>
> Top row, from left to right: officer of the Kronens Infanteriregiment in summer dress c.1806; officer of the Holstenske Infanteriregiment in summer dress c.1808; officer of the 2nd Jyske Infanteriregiment c.1811, rear view; officer of the Danske Livregiment til Fods c.1812; rear view of an officer of the Norske Livregiment til Fods c.1812. Bottom row, from left to right: grenadier officer Slesvigske Infanteriregiment, winter dress c.1806; grenadier officer Prince Christian-Frederiks Regiment, campaign dress, c.1808; Jæger Officer of the Oldenborgske Infanteriregiment c.1810 off service; officer of the Jæger Company of the Slesvigske Infanteriregiment wearing campaign dress c.1812; officer wearing campaign dress in 1814. He is wearing an old red M1798 overcoat; the new overcoats were to be made of grey cloth.

In 1812 it was ordered 'Because of the state of economy all officers and NCOs will from now on use the new system of rank. Only higher graded officers will, at their own expense continue to use the previous marks of rank'. The major and the higher ranks are known to have retained their old symbols of rank. These new distinctions were placed over the new pointed cuffs.

It should be noted that the officers wore their coat fully buttoned up when on service. Many contemporary illustrations and paintings show them open at the throat with either a cravat or shirt visible; this was because they were off duty getting their portrait painted, in town they would be seen like this, never on duty. This remark concerns all officers.

Table II. Officers' Rank Distinctions post 1812	
Second Lieutenant	1 rosette
First Lieutenant	2 rosettes
Captain	4 rosettes
Major	1 chevron lace and 1 rosette
Lieutenant-Colonel	1 chevron lace and 2 rosettes
Colonel	1 chevron lace and 3 rosettes

In service dress, the officers had a coat without lapels but with the same distinctions. For winter and foul weather dress the officers had a double-breasted red cloth overcoat closed by two rows of seven buttons with inverted collar, it was supposed to be made in grey cloth from 1810 but this does not appear to have actually happened.

In full dress the officers wore fall-fronted white breeches and black leather Hungarian boots. In service dress, a few had dark blue breeches with white Hungarian knots. In campaign dress a pair of fall-fronted dark blue overalls (grey from 1810) but plain grey trousers became the norm. Regulations state, and supplies prove, that the officers were to wear the same legwear as their men, in both the style and the colour – so, white in summer. All the officers would have worn light buff-coloured buckskin gloves both on service and on campaign.

The officers wore a black leather waist belt which had a gilded buckle plate and was worn under the sash and the coat, from which their sabre was suspended. Sometimes the belt was worn under the fall-front of their trousers or breeches. The buckle could either be a rectangle in brass or gilded with either a plain edge or with a tressed border. In the centre there was a stamped or cast plate of the crowned royal arms with supporters, either gilded or silvered in contrast or an S buckle with two lion's head bosses.

They were armed with the M1789 officer's sabre which was 89cms long with a blade of 76cms with a silvered single bar hilt which had a leather-bound grip. It was carried in a black leather scabbard which had two brass carrying rings with silvered fittings, red and gold sword knot and strap. Several different variants existed. The artillery and cavalry officers also carried a modified version of this sabre. When they were on mounted duty, the officers, this being the colonel, lieutenant-colonel and major, had a red or regimentally coloured shabraque (both types are noted at different times, but only the red is ever shown) with silver or white lace; all the regiments had a similar model.

In Denmark a great effort was always made by the young officers to get uniformed, 'so as not to lose the respect of their men' as the uniform equalled respect. One young officer (Ræder, a Norwegian serving in Denmark), wrote in his diary:

> By mistake I was first ordered to join the 'Kongens Regiment', but upon arrival in my nice newly tailored uniform, following closely the prescribed appearance, I was informed that it was a mistake and I should instead report to 'Fynske Regiment'. In all haste I had to have my uniform altered at my own expense as they had a different facing colour. So now I started in debt and with no money for food the first couple of days. But such is the life of an officer, better to go hungry, than to lose face and the respect his men and fellow Officers.

THE DANISH ARMY OF THE NAPOLEONIC WARS VOLUME 1

Danish Line Drummers, Hornists and Drum-Majors

THE LINE INFANTRY ORGANISATION, BASIC TACTICS AND UNIFORMS

> **Plate 12. Danish Line Infantry Drummers and Hornists 1805–1814**
>
> Top row, from left to right: drummer of the Arveprins Frederiks Regiment c.1805 in summer dress; drummer NCO of the Norske Livregiment til Fods in winter dress c.1808; drummer of the København Infanteriregiment wearing campaign dress, c.1812; rear view of a drummer of the 1st Jydske Infanteriregiment, c.1813 in campaign dress; drum major of the Holstenske Infanteriregiment in service dress c.1808.
> Bottom row, from left to right: grenadier drummer of the Danske Livregiment til Fods c.1806 in winter dress; grenadier drummer of the Dronningens Livregiment til Fods in campaign dress c.1812; hornist of the 2nd battalion of the Slesvigske Infanteriregiment carrying a Halvmåne (half-moon) horn wearing campaign dress c.1808, note the corporals distinction and tassels on the swallows' nests; hornist from the 2nd battalion of the Oldenborgske Infanteriregiment in campaign dress carrying a Waldhorn, c.1812; drum major from the Prince Christian-Frederiks Regiment wearing his service dress, c.1808.

Drummers' Uniforms

The Drummers wore the same regimental coat as the men, but with the addition of facing-coloured swallows' nests which were generally trimmed with button coloured lace. Those who held the rank of vice corporal or sergeant had an epaulette as well placed over the swallow's nest. These musicians' NCOs had a lace border around the edges of their cuffs.

Towards the end of the period they started to experiment with Prussian-style shoulder rolls: the little information that has survived indicate that they were made in the facing colour and trimmed with a thin, almost piping, button coloured lace around them. They wore shakos in the centre and light companies and bearskins in the grenadier companies.

The drum case could either be made of wood and painted with a 'C7' with the royal or provincial arms painted on them or of stamped brass sheet with the royal or provincial arms stamped on them (first introduced in 1738); generally they had red hoops under Frederik VI, possibly they had medium blue hoops during the early part of the reign of Christian VII. The Queen's Regiment had red hoops and white cords and was carried on a large white drum belt which had brass tubes for the drumsticks. The brass drums originally belonged to the 'old' formations, the regiments and units existing with the army circa 1762, and they kept them as parade drums. It is quite likely they were reduced in size as were those of the Livgarden. By this time most, if not all, of the regular troops had brass drums and the diameter was somewhat smaller than the older wooden drums. The older wooden drums appear to have been recycled out to the militia formations. Wooden drums were used later in Norway. A post-1815 regulation explains to a drummer how he should be able to make his own wooden drum.

The relatively few period illustrations usually show the drummers as very young men or boys. They all carried an infantry sabre slung from a white leather belt, again misnamed as a grenadier sabre. The drummers occasionally carried extra and different sticks in a special brass case; originally they were brass with a red leather cover, possibly recycled fife cases.

The light companies' musicians were hornists and they classed as the *spillemænd*, generally they carried waldhorns or *Halvmåne* (half-moon) horns. Both the drummers and hornists carried 'grenadier' sabres with their knots in their company colours.

The drum major was counted among the *spillemænd*. In 1807 the drum major of the Holstenske Infanteriregiment had a very elaborate uniform; he wore a black shako with a red over black over white plume, and a black cockade with a silver loop and button, white or silver cords and tassels. He had a regimental coat red faced black with wavy large pale blue lace with a space then a line of white piping; the collar was black with on the front edge a large pale blue wavy lace with a red border piped white; black drummers wings laced pale blue, a band of red piped white and hanging white ball tassels, over the wings; silver epaulets, the left one did not have fringes. Under the collar was worn a black neck stock. He had grey breeches with elaborate white Hungarian knots and a pair of hussar-style boot laced silver with a tassel. Over his shoulder he carried a large black drummer's belt which was heavily laced on both sides, a large wavy pale blue lace with a red border and white piping. It had two ornamental silver-butted black drumsticks held by silver loops which had multi coloured cords and large hanging tassels (red, white and blue). He carried a black wooden mace which had a silver head and ferrule with multicoloured cords wrapped round crossover style and ending in silver tassels, and strangely enough, he had a beard.

A couple of other illustrations of drum majors show similar details. One has a uniform with green facings, probably the Prince Christian-Frederiks Regiment, and the basic details are quite similar except that the plume is white and the drum belt is not as decorated; it was green with

THE DANISH ARMY OF THE NAPOLEONIC WARS VOLUME 1

Danish Musical Instruments

Not to scale

THE LINE INFANTRY ORGANISATION, BASIC TACTICS AND UNIFORMS

Plate 13. Musical Instruments

1. Large wooden drum with cypher of Christian VII, the main difference in drums was the size; these older wooden drums were much larger. The color of rim was blue until 1808. Now used principally by the militias.
2. Brass Drum Frederik VI, with red rim from 1808 used by most of the line regiments.
3. Klokkespil (Jingling Johnnie) of the 2nd Jydske Regiment. A number of these have survived, but some doubts have been made as to whether they were used before or after 1815. This one has mixed black and white horsehair tails, but all the other existing models have black only.
4. Waldhorn, as used by the jægers and the light infantry.
5. Halvmaane horn, as used by the jægers, the light infantry and the foot and mobile artillery.
6. Wooden fife and fife case. This is a simple wooded model, the fife cases were made of rolled brass, and some were quite elaborate.

Musician's swallows' nests. The colour usually corresponded with the facing colour and the lace with the button colour A. M1789–1808, for the infantry, continued to be used in the cavalry; B. M1808–1815, for use by all musicians; C. M1810–1822, for drummers.

white or silver lace edging, a gold badge, probably stamped with the royal arms, and double loops for the drum sticks and he wears a moustache. The other regiments undoubtedly had well-dressed drum majors as well, but unfortunately the details for the others have not survived.

The Musicians

The music was divided in two groups; the first consisted of the regimental drummers and fifers (*spillemænd*) and the musicians. The former were soldiers, but the latter group were contracted civilians and not under military law but could be expected to wear a uniform if on the parade ground. On the official regimental lists each regiment had the right to have six hautboys, but most regiments had their own band usually of more than six musicians. These bands did not necessarily all have the same composition. Regiments could have larger musical bands, but in that case the extra musicians were paid for privately by the officers and or the colonel of the regiment.

We know that the following regiments had bands, the Livgarden til Fods, Kronprinsens/Kongens Regiment and Livjægerecorpset had larger music corps than most, and they competed in popularity each Sunday in the *Kongens Have* (The Kings Gardens). The Kongens Regiment had 19 hautboys and occasionally they gave concerts in the town as well. The 2nd Jyske Regiment is recorded as having had a band. The Oldenburg Regiment also possessed a band. Most of the line regimental bands also appear to have had a *Klokkespil*, otherwise known as a '*chapeau chinois*' or 'Jingling Johnnie' at the head of the band; we know this because at least three have survived, one of which has definitively been attributed to the 2nd Jyske Regiment. There is a little doubt as to the age of these items, so although some researchers think they are possibly post 1815, but as there is no proof, doubts persist.

The light troops had bands as well, for example the Holstein Skarpskyttekorps had two French horns, two bassoons, two clarinets, a trumpeter and two fifers. It seems that three extra musicians for a band, as here, was quite common. There exists a picture of a band with Hertuginde Louise Augustas Jægere. A German engraving/picture of a funeral of some well-known poet or philosopher circa 1808, shows Danish musicians wearing the old grenadier cap.

The Regimental Sappers

In 1792 it was decided that the sappers should have entrenching tools, called *skansetøj*, to build redoubts for the regimental artillery. Half of the regimental sappers would each carry two spades, a quarter should each carry a wide pickaxe, while the last quarter should carry an axe. As spades were particularly heavy, those who carried them were to be spared the weight of bearing the saw, carried on the waist belt like a sabre, normally carried by regimental sappers. To carry these new tools special carrying straps were approved at the same time for each type of tool (for the pick axe and spades, the axe probably had the straps as used previously). The design of these straps is unknown.

The provision for sappers' uniforms is strange, since sappers no longer appeared in the army lists of 1789, but they reappeared in the army lists from 1803 where their number had been increased from the numbers allocated previously. There were now two sappers in each of the musketeer companies and in the grenadier companies, but not in the new jæger companies.

A small watercolour dated 1816/1817 gives some of the very little information we have about their uniform. Here they are shown wearing full beards, a shako with red cords and bands round the shako with a large elongated pompom-style black plume, long brown leather aprons, saws and they still carried their axes. It seems unlikely

THE DANISH ARMY OF THE NAPOLEONIC WARS VOLUME 1

Danish Line Sapper

4

Not to scale

> **Plate 14. Danish Line Sapper c.1813 of the Prince Christian-Frederiks Regiment**
>
> 1. Spade; 2. Axe; 3. Saw & sheath, it was either carried on the sword belt instead of the sabre or possibly on the side of the backpack as it was done as late as 1848–50; 4. Cartridge pouch, it may have been larger than the normal cartridge pouches, probably similar to the ones used by the Royal Life Guards, as the surviving plates are rather large. Top, earlier model, below later model.

that they would have had the red bands on their shakos or the black plume during the Napoleonic Wars: modern research suggests they wore the same shako as the rest of their company. The leather aprons could be dark brown or black. The sappers of the grenadier companies probably wore the same bearskins as the rest of the company.

Originally, they had been equipped with fascine knives carried in sheaths on their belts; but they now carried saws instead. These saws were carried in sheaths on waist belts; occasionally on shoulder belts. The sheaths metalwork would be in the regimental button colour. Their black leather cartridge case would probably bear a brass crossed axe and saw or just crossed axes under a crown. This case was probably larger than the infantry model judging from the size of existing badges and the watercolour. The badge for the musketeer companies was a crown over two crossed axes with a horizontal saw, the grenadiers would have the same, but with the addition of a flaming grenade below. They were armed with muskets, and carried bayonets.

Regimental Artillery

Originally each battalion had a regimental artillery battery with strength of two officers, five NCOs and 40 gunners manning two 3-pdr guns. The two pieces of artillery were 3-pdr 22 calibre pieces, at least from 1800; before this they used the old 3-pdr M1687/1748/57 16 calibre *Harboe* system as regimental pieces. They were manned by men from within the regiment and given the necessary training to manipulate them. They wore the regimental uniform, but were equipped as artillerymen. They were armed with either the infantry model M1753 infantry sabre or an old short sword. Their equipment and the pieces will be covered fully in Volume II.

In 1808, those batteries were regrouped in 'light batteries' (*kørende batteri*), and reinforced the Mobile Artillery with eight 3-pdr guns and four 10 pdr howitzers, which were attached directly to the infantry brigades.

Regimental Train Drivers

These were chosen among the soldiers within the regiments, who had some knowledge of horses and were familiar with handling them. Often these men suffered with some disability, so whilst they did not make them ideal combatants they continued to be of service to the regiment. They were issued extra equipment, including spurs, whips and gloves as needed, but they wore the standard regimental uniform and were probably unarmed except for a short sword of some description.

The regimental wagons were painted as follows. The two-wheeled ammunition carts and four-wheeled supply wagons for the infantry and cavalry: red wood and yellow iron fittings. The general supply carts and wagons from the general park allocated to the infantry and cavalry: dark red wood and dark red iron fittings.

The infantry and cavalry ammunition and supply wagons/carts had the name of the parent unit (e.g. '1st Jydske') painted on them. No other numbers were painted on the wagons and carts other than those of the parent unit. The lettering could apparently be in either white or black paint.

Winter Wear

Initially, early in the period, the officers had red knee length surtouts (frock coats) for winter wear, they were double breasted, and in some cases they had regimental facings and buttons, probably replacing the coat with the surtouts as daily wear in the field and for daily service. These surtouts were replaced with red double-breasted greatcoats around 1804: sometimes they had capes added onto them and sometimes they had their facing colours on the cuffs, they could be worn in foul weather or for long route marches. After 1812 these red greatcoats were abolished. Officers were still allowed to wear the red coats that they still owned, but only grey material was now given by the state for the subsidised greatcoats which were issued each year. It appears that some officers continued to wear red overcoats which they had made privately.

The men were issued with grey woollen greatcoats, probably without capes, with the cuffs and collar in regimental colours for the Danish infantry. These regimental facing colours were abolished around 1810; after that only grey coats without any distinctions were produced and issued.

Some troops were issued with cavalry overalls and a short double-buttoned jacket, like a modern sailor's jacket, normally in grey, with no distinctions, was approved in 1809, more specifically for the Norwegian army instead of greatcoats. These were used up until the 1814 campaign, some line units preferring them to their red jackets in the

THE DANISH ARMY OF THE NAPOLEONIC WARS VOLUME 1

Danish Regimental Distinctions c.1808

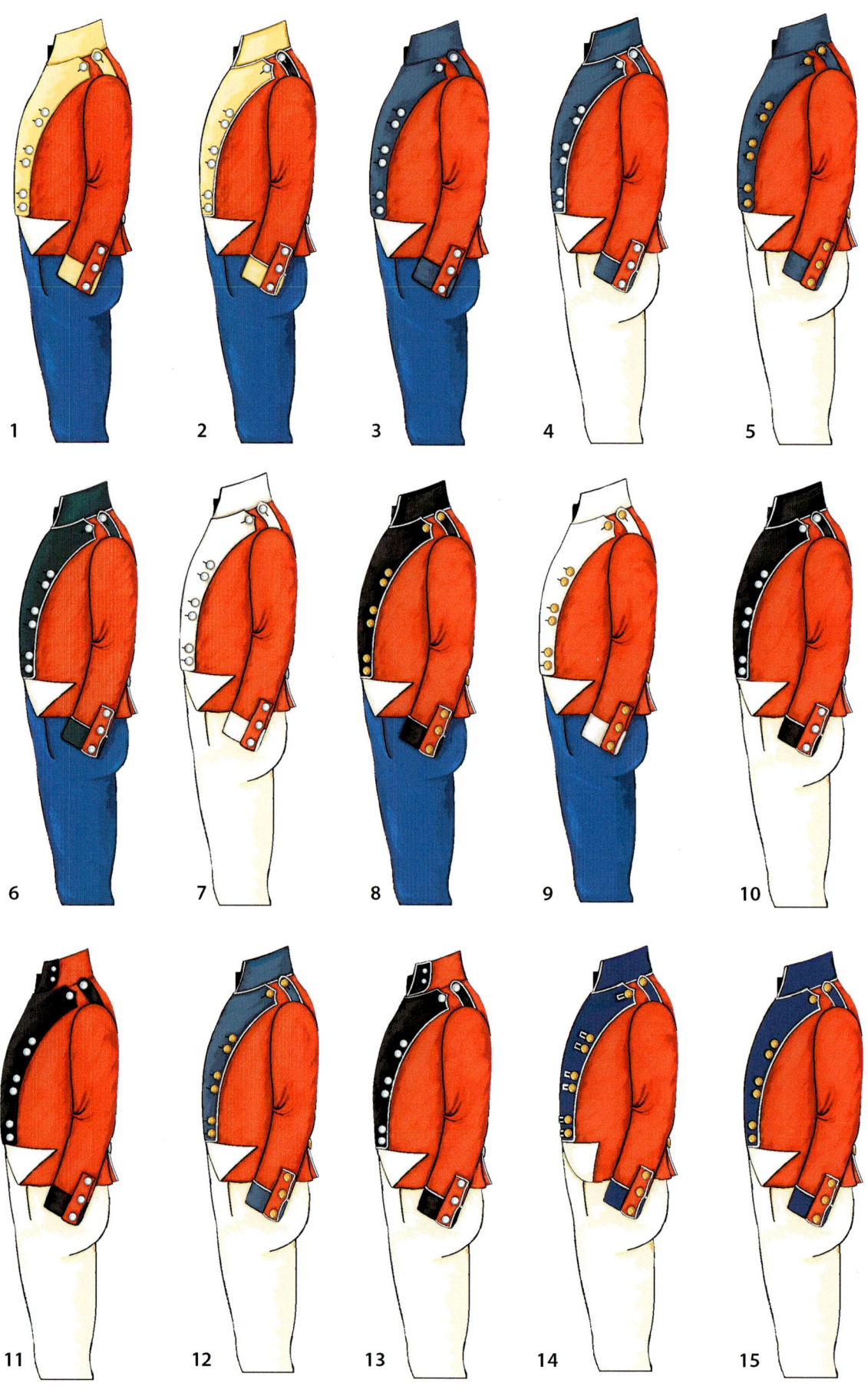

> **Plate 15. Danish Line Infantry Regimental Distinctions c.1808**
>
> 1. Danske LivRegiment til Fods (Danish Life Regiment of Foot) in winter dress.
> 2. Norske LivRegiment til Fods (Norwegian Life Regiment of Foot) in winter dress.
> 3. Kronens Infanteriregiment (Crown Regiment, until 1808 they were called the King's Regiment) in winter dress.
> 4. Kongens Infanteriregiment (King's Regiment, until 1808 they were called the Crown Prince's Regiment), in summer dress.
> 5. Dronningens LivRegiment til Fods (Queen's Life Regiment of Foot) in summer dress.
> 6. Prince Christian-Frederiks Regiment (until 1806 they were called the Arveprins Frederiks Regiment) in winter dress.
> 7. Fynske Infanteriregiment (Regiment of Funen), in summer dress.
> 8. 1st Jyske Infanteriregiment (1st Regiment of Jutland) in winter dress.
> 9. 2nd Jyske Infanteriregiment (2nd Regiment of Jutland) in winter dress.
> 10. 3rd Jyske Infanteriregiment (3rd Regiment of Jutland) in summer dress.
> 11. Oldenborgske Infanteriregiment (Oldenburg Regiment) in summer dress.
> 12. Slesvigske Infanteriregiment (Regiment of Schleswig) in summer dress.
> 13. Holstenske Infanteriregiment (Regiment of Holstein) in summer dress.
> 14. MarineRegimentet (Marine Regiment) in summer dress. The Regiment was disbanded in 1811 and the personnel were incorporated into the Copenhagen Regiment. Note the officers had large rectangular gold-laced buttonholes including two on each side of the coat collar and on the cuff flaps.
> 15. Københavns Infanteriregiment (Copenhagen Regiment), raised in 1807) in summer dress. In 1811 one battalion (the Sea Battalion) was transferred from the disbanded Marine Regiment and was reserved for sea service on board the warships.
> Note on the colours: it has been endeavoured to match the colours on the plates as close as possible to existing cloth samples in the Tøjhusmuseet, Copenhagen. The real cloth colours are much duller than the colours in most contemporary watercolours.

field, with the officers having matching garments made up to blend in with the troops.

All the different types of winter wear were supposed to have been issued in the autumn, and then collected and returned to storage again in the spring as an economy measure, both in Denmark and in Norway, so anything strapped on top of the knapsack in the summertime would be very unusual.

Facing Colours

Table III on the next page gives the regimental facing colours. This includes the collar, shoulder straps, lapels and cuffs and the piping where applicable and regimental variations. All were lined white.

Regimental Variations

Norwegian Life Regiment of Foot. They had black shoulder straps piped white. It was to placate the regiment, which had originally been the Crown Prince Regiment and they had carried that title since circa 1650. Their regimental facing colour had always been black, in remembrance of the Student Corps and the Swedish attack on Copenhagen. Now not only were they no longer a royal regiment, but they had also lost their old black distinctives, so they were rather unhappy and took this as a social disgrace. So they got back their black shoulder-straps as compensation and also received the surname of Livregiment. A rather sad story and one from which the regiment never recovered their original esprit de corps. The entire regiment, or at least the first two battalions, were also authorised to carry M1756 infantry sabres. This honour was possibly extended to the Danske Livregiment til Fods as well.

The King's (Kongens) Regiment circa 1807. A senior officer is shown still wearing a bicorn with ornate silver lace with a white plume with a light blue tip and gold tassels, fall-fronted blue breeches with ornate silver/white Hungarian knots and lace down outer leg, boots with silver tassels, this was probably full dress. The grenadier officers are shown with silvered bearskin plates and silver-plated chin scales and the men with brass bearskin plates and chin scales in 1811.

The Oldenborg Regiment. The officers of this regiment continued to wear their pre-1812 uniforms, including their epaulettes, in 1813. The officers of the musketeer companies had an oval silver plaque on their shako and silver lace around the top of the shako; the officers were also wearing blue hussar-style breeches with white Hungarian knots and piping down outer leg, boots with silver or white tassel.

THE DANISH ARMY OF THE NAPOLEONIC WARS VOLUME 1

Table III, The Infantry Regimental Distinctions				
Regimental Name	Facings & Piping	Button Colour	Shoulder Straps	Particularities
Danske Livregiment til Fods (Danish Life Regiment of Foot)	Straw Yellow	White Metal	Straw yellow	Coatee with short tails for OR
Norske Livregiment til Fods (Norwegian Life Regiment of Foot)	Straw, piped White	White Metal	Black, piped white	Coatee with short tails for OR
Kongens Infanteriregiment (King's Regiment)	Light Blue	White Metal	Light Blue	Renamed in 1808 as Krønen (Crown) Regiment
Kronprinsens Infanteriregiment (Crown Prince's Rgt)	Light blue, piped white	White Metal	Light Blue, piped white	Renamed as King's Regiment in 1808.
Dronningens Livregiment til Fod (Queen's Life regiment of Foot)	Light blue	Brass	Light Blue	
Arveprins Frederik's Regiment (Heir-Prince Frederik Regiment)	Yellow, white piping. Green facings, white piping from 1806	White Metal	Yellow piped white, green from 1806	Renamed Prince Christian-Frederik Regiment in 1806
Fynske Infanteriregiment (Funen Regiment)	White	White Metal	White	
1st Jyske Infanteriregiment (1st Jutland Regiment)	Black/white	Brass	Black, piped white	
2nd Jyske Infanteriregiment	White	Brass	White	
3rd Jyske Infanteriregiment	Black/white	White Metal	Black, piped white	
Oldenborgske Infanteriregiment (Oldenburg Regiment)	Black	White Metal	Black	Red collar with black patch with 2 buttons
Slesvigske Infanteriregiment (Schleswig Regiment)	Light blue/white	Brass	Light Blue, piped white	
Holstenske Infanteriregiment (Holstein Regiment)	Black/white	White Metal	Black, piped white	Red collar & black patch piped white with 2 buttons,
Marineregimentet (Marine Regiment)	Dark blue, white lacing on lapels & cuff flaps	Brass	Dark blue, piped white	Disbanded in 1811. Officers had gold lace
Københavns Infanteriregiment (Copenhagen Regiment)	Dark blue/pale yellow	Brass	Dark blue piped yellow	Raised in 1811, including elements of the Marine Regiment

Some of the grenadiers had been forced to replace their bearskins with shakos, as their bearskins were thoroughly worn out, but they kept the bearskins' front plates and mounted them on to their shakos.

The Marine Regiment and its successor, the Københavns Infanteriregiment (1st Battalion) essentially served on board ship, rather like the Royal Marines in Britain. They were still wearing hats until quite late and the change to shakos was also to be 'Postponed until later'; instead the older hats was first used up, and from 1810 shakoes made from old model hats, by reducing the brim, and adding a special 'Lacquer composit', a form of resin varnish, or paint to stiffen them (Shako-hat M1810). When these 'new' shakos were made, the plumes shifted from the side to the front to accentuate the difference of these ersatz shakos. Officers had gold lace and piping, including two gold lace bars on the collar. After 1807 when a large number of British deserters, in fact mostly Germans from the King's German Legion, were incorporated in to the regiment. They kept their stovepipe shakos and some of the other captured shakos were re-issued as well. The original British shako plates had the British crown and surround cut off and the round centre part stamped KGL was conserved and worn. The companies assigned to the fortress on the island of Christiansø, east of Bornholm, were dressed as such. It was noted that the 'Grenadiers will have to wait for their Bearskins until a later date, until then white feathers with blue tips are to be worn on the normal hat' to differentiate them from the other companies. It is not known if or when they eventually received their bearskins:

probably never, as as late as 1814 they were still wearing shakos with blue-tipped white grenadiers plumes on them. When the Marine Regiment was disbanded, one battalion was transfered to the new Københavns Regiment, and they formed the 1st battalion was now the 'Sea Battalion' which was reserved for sea service. The 2nd and 3rd were garrison battalions, and although it is possible that the regiment changed uniforms completely this is unlikely as the old uniforms had to be used as long as possible, and the previous stocks of reserve uniforms for the Marine Regiment was taken over by the new formation, but they had the button hole lace removed.

General Appearance

Their general appearance was not that different from the other Scandinavian countries where blond hair was fairly typical. Hair was worn rather long to start with, but by 1808 at the latest they now cut their hair short, at least in the regular army; things were probably more lax in the volunteers. Most soldiers appear to have worn sideburns and moustaches, worn indifferently by both the men and officers, except the higher ranks. Strangely enough, only a very few show grenadiers with moustaches, officers or men. The grenadiers were officially permitted moustaches from 1809.

Final Note

The uniformity of the infantry dress must be regarded as relative. Shortages, new recruits, campaign wear, old uniforms reissued from central stores, and new regulations all contrived to thwart this. One Danish Officer complained in his memoirs: 'My [Musketeer] company wore uniforms of all descriptions and colours, some of the men have even received headgear from cavalry stocks! We looked more like a band of robbers than an army … '

THE DANISH ARMY OF THE NAPOLEONIC WARS VOLUME 1

Danish rank Distinctions A. Pre-1812

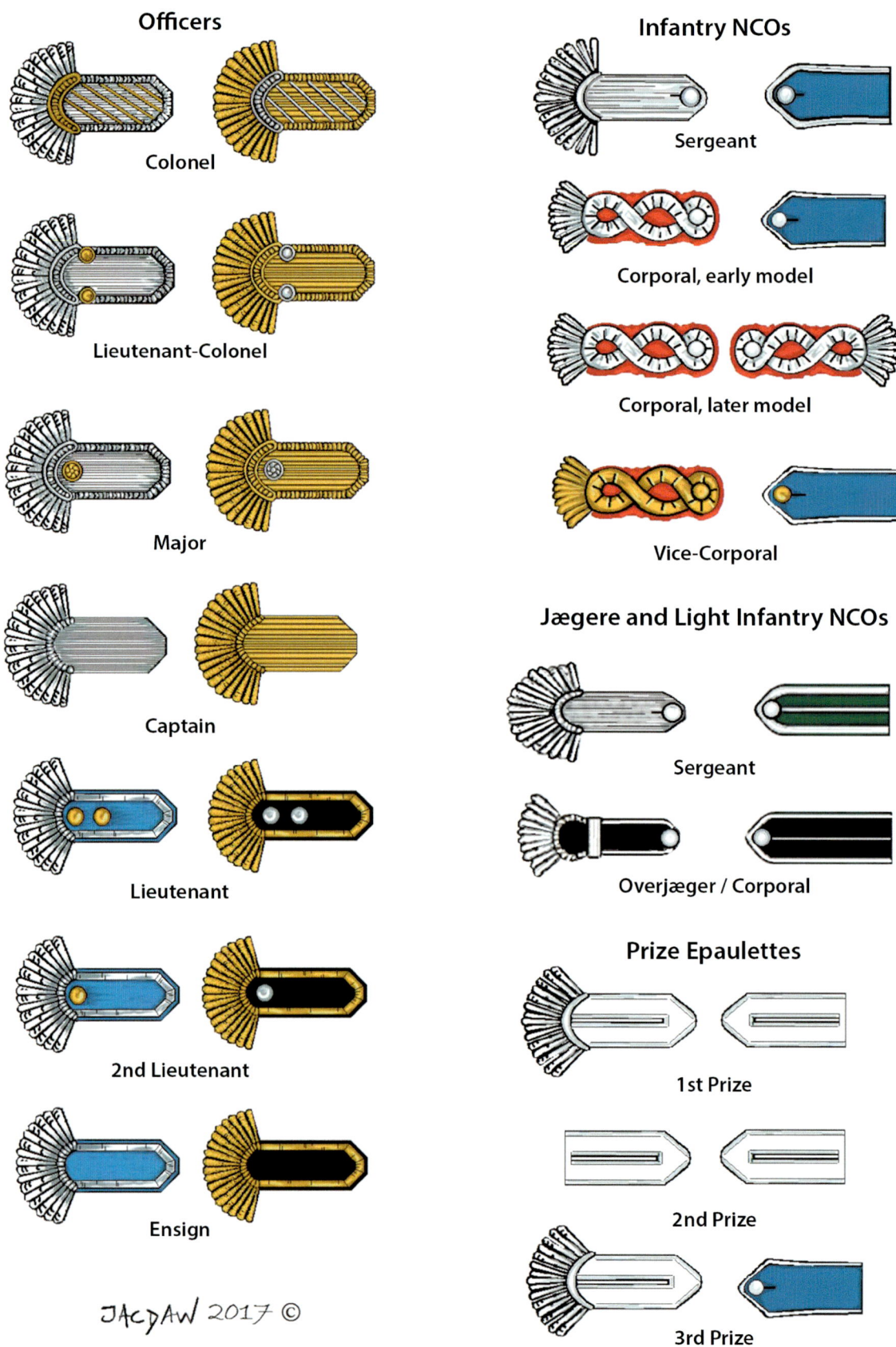

THE LINE INFANTRY ORGANISATION, BASIC TACTICS AND UNIFORMS

Plate 16. Danish Rank Distinctions: Officers and NCOs' Epaulettes 1801–1812

In the 1801 regulations, the colours of the metal usually corresponded to the button colour and for the 1st lieutenant, 2nd lieutenant, ensign and NCOs, the lace was in the button colour and the rest was in the regimental facing colour. See table I.
Notes. For a regiment which had brass buttons, the colours would be reversed for colonel, lieutenant colonel, major and captain: gold epaulette with silver buttons, rosettes etc.
The prize distinctions were never worn in the field, they were shown uniquely for special parades.

Danish Rank Distinctions B. Post-1812

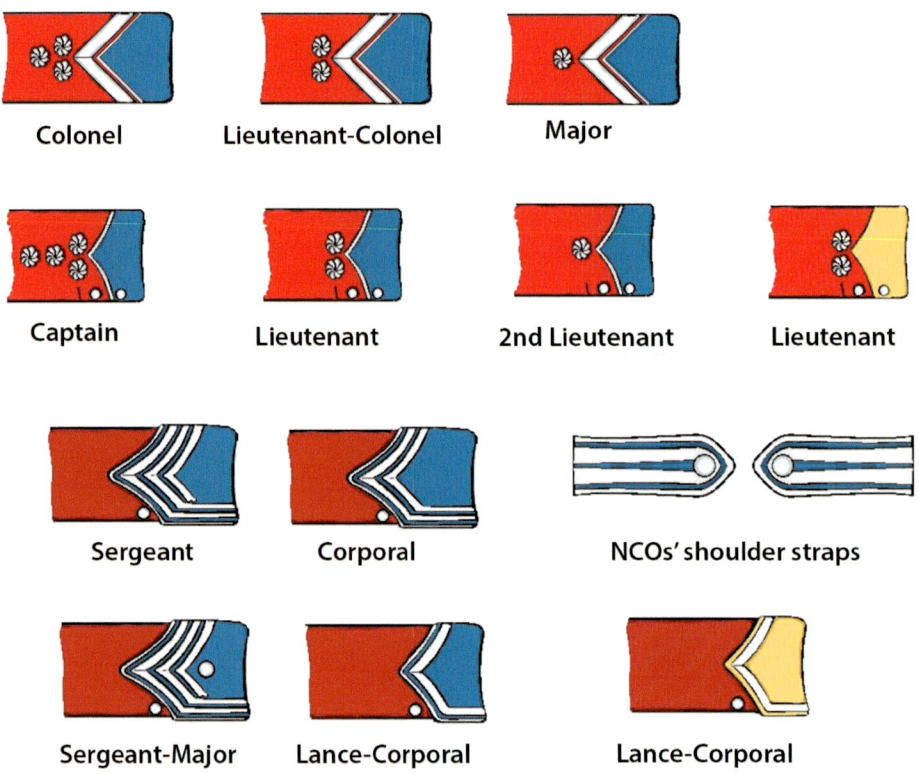

Rank Insignia Volunteers and Citizen Militia c.1801

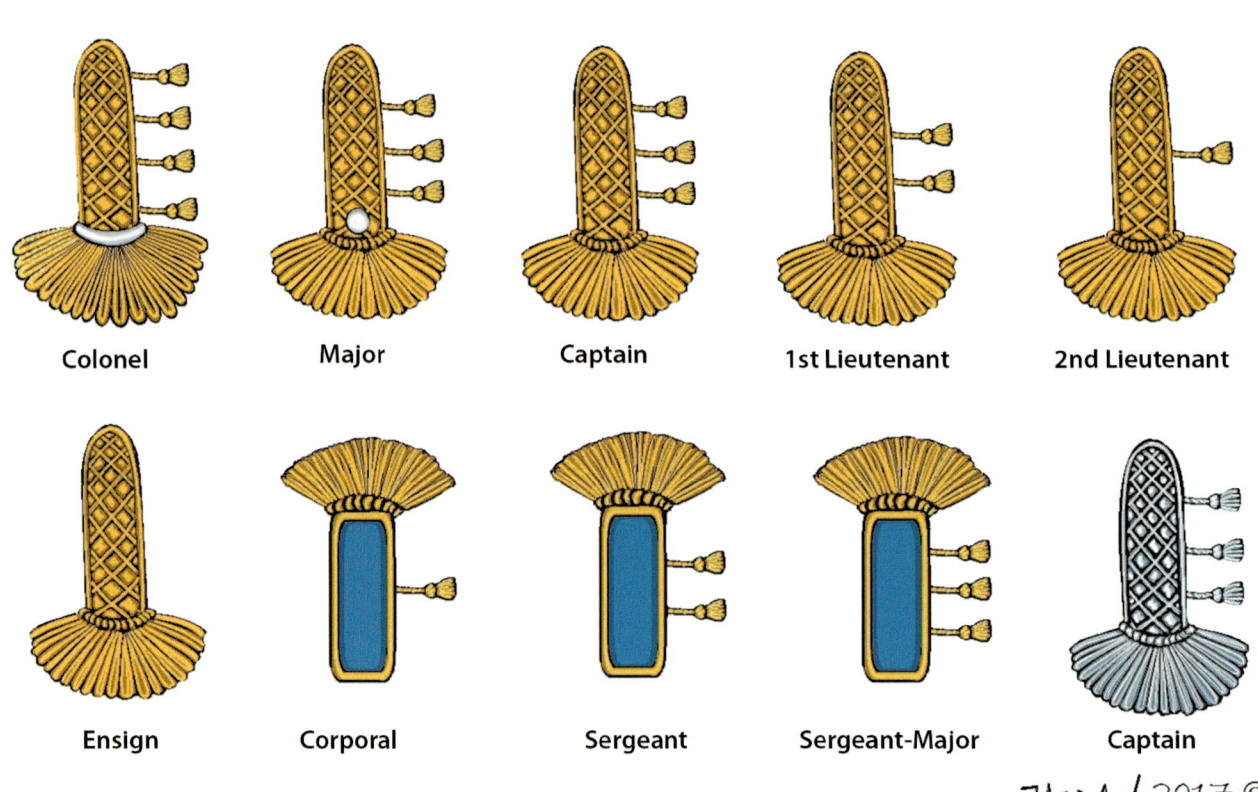

THE LINE INFANTRY ORGANISATION, BASIC TACTICS AND UNIFORMS

Plate 17. Danish Line Rank Distinctions 1812–1815

In 1812 a new system of showing the ranks was instituted. The epaulettes were abolished for all except general officers. In the new system the rank was shown on the cuffs, the lace and rosette were usually in the button colour, usually in white or yellow wool for the NCOs. The new regulations for the use of cuff distinctions specified that NCOs had all their distinctions on the cuff, while all officers had their distinctions on the lower sleeve, just above the cuff. See examples with piped and un-piped cuffs.

Danish Volunteers and Militia

In 1801 when new officers' and NCOs' distinctions were ordered for the regular army, a slightly different model was ordered for the Town Volunteer and Citizen Guards officers and NCOs. The epaulettes were no longer to be made of metal, but with knotted silver or golden cord, according to their regimental button colour. Officers were to have two epaulettes and a system of knots would define the rank.

The NCOs would only be allowed one epaulette and it was to be worn on the left shoulder only, as at first this was usual in light infantry, the line infantry wore theirs on the right shoulder (later the regular light infantry were allowed to wear theirs on the right shoulder too). The NCO's epaulette was to be in the facing colour; knot, lace and cord in the button colour as well.

Officers' Epaulettes
No knot: *Fändrik*/Ensign (rank abolished in 1809).
One knot: *Sekondløjtnant*/second lieutenant.
Two knots: *Premiereløjtnant*/first lieutenant .
Three knots: *Kaptajn*/captain. See version in silver.
Three knots and a button: *Major*/major
Four knots and metal 'half moon': *Stadshauptmand*/town commander/colonel.

NCO's epaulettes
One knot: *Korporal*/Corporal.
Two knots: *Sergent*/Sergeant.
Three knots: *Kommander sergent*/Sergeant major.

A consequence of these epaulettes being sown directly on to the coat was that until 1808 some NCOs wore their cartridge belt over their right shoulder as the belt could not pass under this epaulette. This could no longer be done when they received cross belts in 1808. It is possible that they, like regular NCOs at a later date put the NCO distinction on a separate shoulder strap.

It is possible that an epaulette without any knot was taken into use (after 1808?) for the rank of *Gefreiter*/vice corporal.

6

The Jægerkorps and the Light Infantry Battalions

It is impossible to really write separately about the uniform as of these two corps as they were so close in both their mission and their uniforms and they were eventually merged. Therefore sometimes it is not possible to be 100 percent sure which unit is meant. They are separated here simply to try and make things easier to follow.

The two Rifle battalions (Jægerkorps) were raised in 1785 by enlisting mainly Danish subjects, but they also included a number of Germans, Norwegians, and Icelanders who were, at the time (a difference of which they were conscious of) known for their marksmanship. In battle they covered the troops of the line with a screen of skirmishers, using the classical tactics of the period, although they differed in forming a long line of jægers in spaced out pairs. They were also trained to fight in open order and were frequently employed for reconnaissance work and harassing the enemy.

The first to be raised was the Holsteinske corps in 1785, but they were sent to Norway as a cadre for the Norwegian Jæger Corps. This cadre later returned to Denmark and was incorporated into the Slesvigske battalion.

Each battalion was composed of a headquarters staff of a quartermaster (*Kvartermester*), a juridical officer (*Auditor*), a surgeon (*Feltskaerer*), who in turn was assisted by two company surgeons (*KompaniKirurger*), a master medical orderly (*Hospitalsergent*), a provost (*Profos*), a gunsmith (*Bøssesmed*) and a master hornist (*Stabsvaldhornist*).

The four rifle companies were each composed of three officers, five *Overjægere* (master riflemen/sergeants), eight *Jægere* (senior privates/corporals), 120 *Underjægere* (riflemen/privates) and two hornists.

In 1808, a reserve battalion was attached to both rifle battalions. The first battalion was classed as a regular battalion; the new battalions were called the *Forstærkningsbatalioner* (reinforcement battalions).

The light battalions were to be used as elite line battalions, fighting both in line formation and in skirmish formations in front of the other Danish units. They would function as an addition to the line battalions' light companies. The light battalions could therefore function both as a regular line battalion but also as traditional skirmishers. The normal way to deploy a Danish light battalion was to form it into a line with a deep screen of skirmishers to the front. The skirmish lines would deliver precise and devastating fire upon their attackers as they advanced before they fell back behind the parent battalion which would then fire a series of heavy volleys into the disordered attackers.

The Jægerkorps were to be used differently than the light battalions. The Jægerkorps were an elite reconnaissance and patrol force. They would set up forward observation posts and shadow the enemy's movements while remaining unseen or sniping at the enemy from great distance. In combat the Jægerkorps operated in *roder*. A *rode* was a small three-man team which was designed to give each other mutual fire support in combat. The three men worked together in all combat situations; both in unit skirmish formations but also in other looser formations. The Jægerkorps were a highly mobile and very fast moving force. They were trained in silent rapid movements, in silently seeking cover and in understanding field sign language from their officers. All the things one would expect to find in modern elite formations. The Jægerkorps achieved a high rate of professionalism and respect from the other branches of the army

The Jægerecorps Uniforms

For headwear they were originally issued with the standard M1802 black round felt hat as in the line infantry but with a black leather band on the lower edge, instead of the white/yellow lace band of the line regiments. On left side it had a green plume made of dyed cut feathers over a black cockade with a button coloured loop. From 1808 the hat was replaced with a black felt shako with black leather top and lower bands and reinforcing Vs on the side, a leather peak and chinstrap. The shako had a green plume over a green cockade with a button coloured loop and it had green cords and tassel. The Jyske Jæger Corps is shown with brass diamond shaped plates on their shakos in contemporary illustrations.

They wore a short coatee in green cloth with upturned front corners showing the white lining. It had a black collar and narrow black lapels closed to the waist with seven

Table IV, Jæger Corps Distinctives

Battalion Name	Shoulder straps c.1805	Button Colour	Shoulder straps c.1810	Button Colour
Sjællandske Jægerecorps (Zealand)	Dark green piped white	White Metal	Dark green piped white	White Metal
Slesvigske Jægerecorps (Schleswig)	Dark green piped yellow	Brass	Dark Green piped yellow	Brass

evenly spaced buttons and black cuffs. The black cuffs had green cuff flaps (slightly scalloped as for line infantry with three buttons) with either white or no piping, depending on the corps. From 1808 they received new coatees which were even shorter with the buttons grouped in pairs and white piping. The coatee had green shoulder straps with white or yellow coloured piping. The buttons were pewter/white metal or brass. Under their collar they wore a black neck stock.

From 1810 the coatee was supposed to be replaced with a grey cloth jacket without lapels, it was to be closed by a single row of ten buttons with a line of green piping on either side of them, at least for Sjællandske; the collar, round cuffs and shoulder straps were in their facing colour. The change to grey uniforms was made by a Royal Resolution dated 23 Feburary 1810, and it was stated that: 'It is to be single breasted with green lining'. This was the Resolution which was used for describing the new uniform: in fact this was a reintroduction of the pre-1803 uniform, but it was now made of grey cloth. However, another change was then made: probably the King reconsidered his decision, influenced by the Jæger officers, finding this uniform 'too plain'. This resulted is a new resolution. This Royal Resolution dated 9 May 1810, was only for the officers of the Sjællandske Jæger Corps, the Sjællandske Skarpskytte Corps and Jyske Skarpskytte Corps.

This new coatee does not seem to have entered into service until around 1812 as contemporary images still continue to show the previous uniform. The upturned corners were also in the facing colour. The tunic had white metal buttons. From 1812 the coat had pointed cuffs. Zealand is shown in one print with green braid on the chest; this is somewhat doubtful. The new grey uniforms with three rows of buttons on the coatee were to be worn by the men as well, but they continued to wear their existing uniforms and they were allowed to be worn out before they received the new model.

The shade of grey was generally very dark, blackish, although there were a number of variations ranging from a medium warm grey for the trousers through to a bluish grey up to the darker grey; all these variations are shown in contemporary prints and the few surviving articles of clothing. One could even find either all the uniform in the same grey or with the breeches in a lighter grey. The uniform of the Slesvigske Jæger Corps possibly had three rows of buttons from 1810, as shown in the KM Manuscript, but this manuscript only shows the project, not what necessarily was really made. The colour of the collar and cuffs was not clearly defined when they changed uniform 1810–11. We know from the regimental records that the King in 1810, allowed extra money to pay for the change 'Into the new grey uniform'.

This change to grey was apparently permitted so as to differentiate them from the sharpshooters. Their officers also had three rows of buttons on their jacket, but with dark grey wollen tresses between them. The two Jæger corps in Denmark and Norske Jæger Corps were considered as elites, so it was normal to be able to 'single them out' from the other light troops. However, as in all the Danish army, most changes took quite some time with many earlier uniforms continuing to be worn until the end of the conflict. In Norway the Norske Jæger Corps continued to wear their green uniform until 1815.

Legwear was, to start with, fall-fronted grey gaiter trousers and black leather shoes for general service wear and white gaiter trousers for parade dress. From 1808 they were gradually replaced with a pair of fall-fronted grey breeches and black short gaiters. The previous gaiter trousers continued to be worn until they were worn out. In winter they were issued with a grey overcoat with a green collar and cuffs. Note the tone of the grey could vary somewhat.

They were equipped with a black leather bandoleer and cartridge box. The sword-bayonet (*hirschfänger*) was suspended from a black leather waist belt, which had a small belly box for cartridges and badger-skin 'shooting bag' (combined knapsack and ammunition pouch) until 1802 when it was converted with new straps into a simple backpack which was slung over one shoulder like the line infantry except it was of badger skin. Their cartridge pouch was the mounted on the shoulder strap of the shooting bag, although there is a possibility that they continued to use the belly pouch on the waist belt: as there is little contemporary iconography this remains a dark area until 1808 when the new equipment was issued. Later they were issued with an ordinary cartridge box and a powder horn on a green cord. From 1808 they used a square cow-hide knapsack like the line infantry, but the shoulder straps and buckle fastening straps were made of black leather.

Danish Jægere

Jægere Officer, Jægere, NCO, Hornist c.1806

Jægere Officer, Jægere, NCO, Hornist c.1808 / 1810

Altonaiske Jægere Grenadier

THE JÆGERKORPS AND THE LIGHT INFANTRY BATTALIONS

> **Plate 18. Danish Jægere I, 1806–1810**
>
> Top row left to right: Jæger officer; Jægere; NCO; Hornist, all of Sjællandske Jægerecorps (Zealand), the sergeant is wearing the white full dress trousers; Jæger Slesvigske Jægerecorps (Schleswig). Bottom row left to right: Jæger officer; Hornist; Jæger, all of Sjællandske Jægerecorps; Jæger Slesvigske Jægerecorps wearing the short gaiters over his trousers; Altonaiske Jægergrenadier.

They were all armed with a special light infantry musket, a modified version of the M1774, called the *Skarpskyttegevær* M1789. The reason for this was that the Light Infantry Rifle M1807 (which was used by the light companies in some the line battalions) had a slower rate of fire when compared to the three shots a minute for the M1774.

The *Skarpskyttegevær* M1789 was therefore used by both the Sharpshooters and Jægers as it had a higher rate of fire that the M1807 Rifle. A trained marksman could fire one aimed shot a minute with the M1789. This weapon's calibre was 19.1mm, the overall length was 141cms, the barrel being 102cms long, and it weighed in at 4,030 grams. A curiosity was the ramrod, which had one end sharpened and was to be stuck in reverse into its emplacement and served as a bayonet. Obviously they did not have a bayonet sheath on their waist belt but carried either hangers or *hirschfängers*.

The Jæger Grenadiers Uniform

Two companies of the Zealand battalion (Sjællandske Jægerecorps) were called grenadiers (Jægeregrenader). These grenadiers wore the same uniform as others troopers but with a grenadier cap similar to the one of line infantry with black fur and a non-metallic front plate. It had a green bag with white laces and tassels and adorned with a green plume with crimson top; from 1808, the bearskin cap no longer had a plate, the rest as before. They had a brass match case on the cartridge box bandoleer.

The Jægere-Grenadiers were in theory the elite company of light units. However, in most cases, they were special units often made up of former regulars, surplus to requiremnts after the National Army reforms of 1789–1803.

The Altonasiske Jægere Grenader Kompani was formed in 1799. Until 1813 this unit never served with its parent unit the Slesvigske Jægerecorps, but their role was guarding the Royal Bank in Altona near Hamburg! They wore the uniform of the Slesvigske Jægere Corps, but with grenadiers' distinctions including a bearskin cap without a plate. There appears to be some confusion about the colour of the bonnet: it has been described as a green bonnet piped white and a white tassel, but the contemporary or near-contemporary illustrations show a red bonnet without piping and tassel. It also had a green plume with a red tip and brass chin scales and they had a brass match case on their black leather cartridge box bandoleer. Apparently, they received their new bearskins only very sparingly, four M1809 in 1809 and five more in 1810. In 1811–12 the Altonariske Jæger Grenader Kompagni, should have received new bearskins (as the only unit outside the guard and line infantry to wear bearskins, but there was no shield on theirs), probably of M1809 style. They should have been armed as Jægere, but as contemporary illustrations testify, they were in effect armed with muskets and carried the grenadier sabre.

Sjællandske Jæger Grenader Kompani; two companies were formed in 1799, and attached to the Sjællandske Jæger Corps. They were mainly formed from former foreign regulars. In 1803 they were both transferred to the Marine Regiment and given same uniform as them.

NCOs' Uniform

The NCOs wore the regimental uniform with epaulettes in the facing colour with gold or silver embroidery and fringes. The Jæger sergeants wore their epaulette on the left shoulder and the corporals had one on each shoulder. There are also indications that the Jæger NCOs had green/white and green/white/silver sword knots before the grey 1810 uniform was issued.

As for line regiments, when cuffs became pointed, the shoulder straps were in the facing colour with white lace trim on both shoulders, but epaulettes were replaced with rank chevrons in white woollen lace on both arms on the cuffs below the regimental piping.

The 'Pricker' was worn at the left Buttonhole. The official regulations stated that these were only worn by the NCOs. The original Resolution of 24 August 1804 placed them on left side, but Senn shows his *Overjæger* with it worn at right side in 1807, so it may have changed, but we have only Senn`s drawing regarding this. What is most interesting is that this way to carry the 'Pricker', was only to be used by NCOs and 'Jægers'. As noted, *Jægere* was also the term used for senior privates/corporals. They normally had no distinctions, but this is apparently the distinction they wore. What we would term an 'ordinary jæger', the lowest rank of soldier, was called a *Underjæger* and is not mentioned in the official text. However, this is maybe not so strange as they had prickers in the top of their powder-horns.

On 18 May 1808 it was further ordered that all infantry and cavalry (musket or carbine armed), should always

THE DANISH ARMY OF THE NAPOLEONIC WARS VOLUME 1

Danish Jægere II

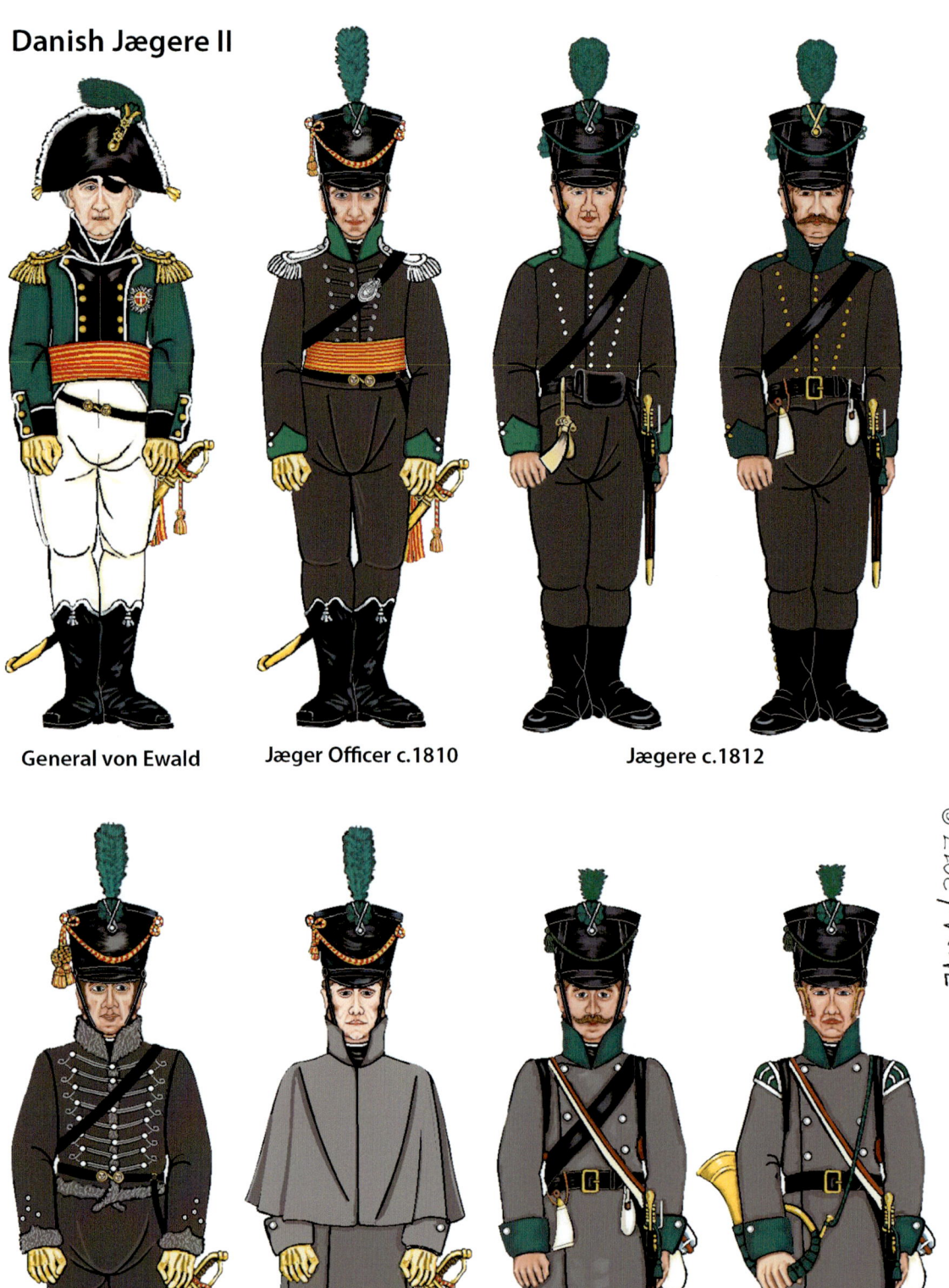

General von Ewald — Jæger Officer c.1810 — Jægere c.1812

Officer winter dress c.1813 — Jægere and Skarpskytter winter dress 1812°1813

THE JÆGERKORPS AND THE LIGHT INFANTRY BATTALIONS

> ### Plate 19. Danish Jægere II, 1810–1814
>
> Top row, left to right: General von Ewald c. 1808, the founder of the Danish Jæger and Sharpshooter corps – it is not generally known that he wore an eye patch as his portraits were in profile; officer in new uniform, after a miniature in the Brockdorff collection. Jæger, Sjællandske Jægerecorps wearing the new belly-box on the waist belt; Jæger, Slesvigske Jægerecorps c.1812.
> Bottom row, left to right: officer in pelisse c.1813; officer of Jægere or Skarpskyttrer in overcoat with cape; a Skarpskyttrer or Jægere and Hornist, both in overcoats 1812–1813.
> Note. In the contemporary illustration the cords worn between the buttons ('à la hussar') are not particularly obvious, as they are dark grey like the uniform. This is confirmed by the King because in 1814 he sent out a direct order to all Jæger and Sharpshooter corps in Denmark (Confirming that all Danish units should now have the dark grey uniform with three rows of buttons) 'that I have been made aware that some officers have allowed themselves to wear light grey and even white cords/strips between the buttons instead of the dark grey as ordered (uniform colour). This is to stop at once, and the ordered dark grey be worn from now on'.

receive a 'pricker', and this would be kept in a space in the ammunition pouch, and to be used after each fourth shot at least.

Officers' Uniforms

To begin with, the Jæger officers wore the standard black felt cocked hat with a green plume over a green cockade with silver or gold loop and red and gold tassels at each point. From 1805, the bicorns were replaced by the round hat with gold and red cords, and again replaced in 1809, as for troop, by the shakos. The hatband was also black, not button colour as frequently shown in modern reconstructions. The officers of the Altona Jægergrenadiers probably wore the other ranks' bearskin cap, but with red and gold cords and tassels on formal duties.

Theoretically the officers wore a long tailed green coat which had green turn backs, although there are some indications that some continued to wear their short green M1789 jacket. Later they had gold horn badges on their turnbacks. The rest of their uniform was as the other ranks' dress. They had gold or silver rank epaulettes depending on the button colour as for the line infantry officers.

From 1810 the tunic was supposed to have been replaced with a dark grey single-breasted jacket with short tails and buttons in the regimental colour. Some of the officers wore a grey dolman style jacket with three rows of eight buttons with a green collar and cuffs with their epaulettes on the coat until their suppression in 1812 when they were replaced with rosettes and chevrons on the cuffs.

For winter dress, some of the officers wore a dark grey hussar pelisse which had dark grey fur trim and dark grey braiding on the chest; some officers unofficially replaced the dark grey braiding with a lighter grey to make them more visible. Although the fur should have been dark grey, it is sometimes described as silver grey fox fur, but probably more often was dyed sheepskin for most, due to the economic situation. Wurgler Hansen describes the pelisse as green with grey fur, but without giving a source. They also had a large overcoat with a cape which could be worn over the dolman.

In 1809 the commanding officer of the Slesvigske Jægerecorps, General von Ewald, is recorded as wearing a bicorn with a green plume, black cockade and a gold loop and a white feather border and a gold tassel at each end. He wore a long tailed green coat with black collar cuffs and lapels piped straw yellow and cuff flaps with three buttons. The coat had a white lining and the buttons and epaulettes were gold. His breeches were green with gold lace Hungarian knots and worn with gold laced Hungarian/Hessian boots. Around his waist he wore the usual sash and wore a Dannebrog on his chest.

Officers wore a pair of fall-fronted grey cloth trousers, sometimes with button colour stripes on the outer seam. These trousers were replaced with fall-fronted grey breeches and black leather boots around the same time, 1812; sometimes these boots were laced and tasselled in the button colour.

As with the line regiments, their epaulets were suppressed in 1812 and new rank insignias in button colour were worn on both arms over the cuffs as for the line infantry officers.

They were equipped with a black leather cartridge pouch bearing the crowned royal cipher in the button colour, and a black leather bandoleer with a silver shield badge on the breast. They had a black leather waist belt with gilded buckle plate worn over the red and gold embroidered silk waist sash which was knotted on the left hip until it was suppressed in 1812. From the belt they hung their version of the infantry officers' sabre. The M1789 sabre was 89cms long with a blade of 76cms with a silvered single-bar hilt which had a leather-bound grip and was carried in either black leather or steel scabbards which had two brass carrying rings with silvered fittings, red and gold sword knot and strap. In later contemporary

Danish Light Infantry / Sharpshooter Corps

Lette Infanteribataljoner, Officer, Light Infantrymen and Hornist, c.1806

Skarpskyttecorps, Officer, Sharpshooter and Hornist c.1810 / 1811

Skarpskyttecorps c.1812 / 1813

> **Plate 20. The Light Infantry/Sharpshooters.**
>
> Top row, from left to righ: officer & light infantryman 1st Sjællandske Bataljon Let Infanteri, which became the Sjællandske Skarpskytte Corps; corporal & sergeant hornist of the 2nd Sjællandske Bataljon let Infanteri, which became the Jydske Skarpskytte Corps; light infantryman of the Slesvigske-Holstenske Bataljon Let Infanteri, which became the Holstenske Skarpskytte Corps in 1808. Bottom row, from left to right: officer Sjællandske Skarpskytte Corps c.1810; corporal hornist Holstenske Skarpskytte Corps c.1810; sharpshooter of the Jydske Skarpskytte Corps c.1810; sharpshooter of the Sjællandske Skarpskytte Corps 1813; sharpshooter of the Holstenske Skarpskytte Corps 1813.
> Source: Drawn from contemporary watercolours and engravings preserved in the Tøjhusmuseet, Copenhagen.

illustrations the scabbards are shown in yellow orange so possibly at least some of these sabres had gilded or brass scabbard fittings. It is also possible that they acquired both new and old hussar sabres due to shortages as well as personal preferences.

Note that the colonel, lieutenant-colonel and major were mounted as was the regimental staff hornist (he carried a waldhorn, likely placed round his arm, as being a horn first designed in Germany for hunting on horseback, having it round your arm, under your armpit, was the easiest way to play it when mounted). They all had green shabraques with silver/white lace border of the same design as used by cavalry officers.

Hornists' Uniform

The hornists wore their regimental dress with black swallows' nests with button coloured lace trim. As they were regarded as specialists they had an NCO's epaulette on their left shoulder over the swallows nest. They carried a brass *Halvmånes* horns which were bound with green cords by 1808–1810.

The *Waldhornister* (French horn players) comprised the staff hornist and a group of extra bandsmen (eight were allowed circa 1809). They had a swallows' nest in the regimental colour with a button coloured (metal) lace and three knots to each swallows' nest.

The *Halvmåneblæsere* (Crescent hornists) were the company signallers, two to each company. They had swallows' nests in regimental colour with button coloured (wool) lace and three knots to each swallows' nest.

In 1812 all metal lace was to be replaced by wool and the knots were apparently discontinued: 'knots not to be carried by any more except for a few specially designated units'. In October 1813 an official order was written that specified that 'from now on signals are to be kept to a minimum on the battlefield, so as not to give away your position to the enemy and lose the element of surprise'.

Notes

From 1813 at least, some of the jægere, if not all, used a ventral cartridge box to hold 10 ready-to-fire shots on their waist belt like the early model (or possibly the same which were reissued). Normally a jæger used a loose ball, with a patch and loose powder, so as he could dose the different quantities of powder for different ranges. He also had to hammer down each shot in the barrel. However, when the enemy came too close, he often was left defenceless due to the length of time needed to reload. Therefore the meaning of 10 ready shots tells us that this was a pre-packed cartridge with a ball of a slightly smaller calibre wrapped in paper with the powder. It was destined to only to be used for rapid firing at close range. The shot would not be patched, obviously undersized, and was only retained in the barrel by being rammed down with the paper. This meant that he now was able to fire as quickly as a standard line musketeer, but also with the same lack of precision.

Table V Light Infantry Sharpshooter Battalions 1805–1810

Regimental Name	Shoulder straps in 1805	Button Colour	Regimental Name	Shoulder Straps in 1810	Button Colour
1st Sjællandske Bataljon Let Infanteri	Dark green	White metal	Became Sjællandske Skarpskyttecorps	Dark green piped white	White metal
2nd Sjællandske Bataljon Let Infanteri	Black piped white	White metal	Became Jyske Skarpskyttecorps	Black piped white	White metal
Slesvigske-Holstenske Bataljon Let Infanteri	Dark green	Brass	Became Holstenske Skarpskyttecorps	Dark green	Brass

THE DANISH ARMY OF THE NAPOLEONIC WARS VOLUME 1

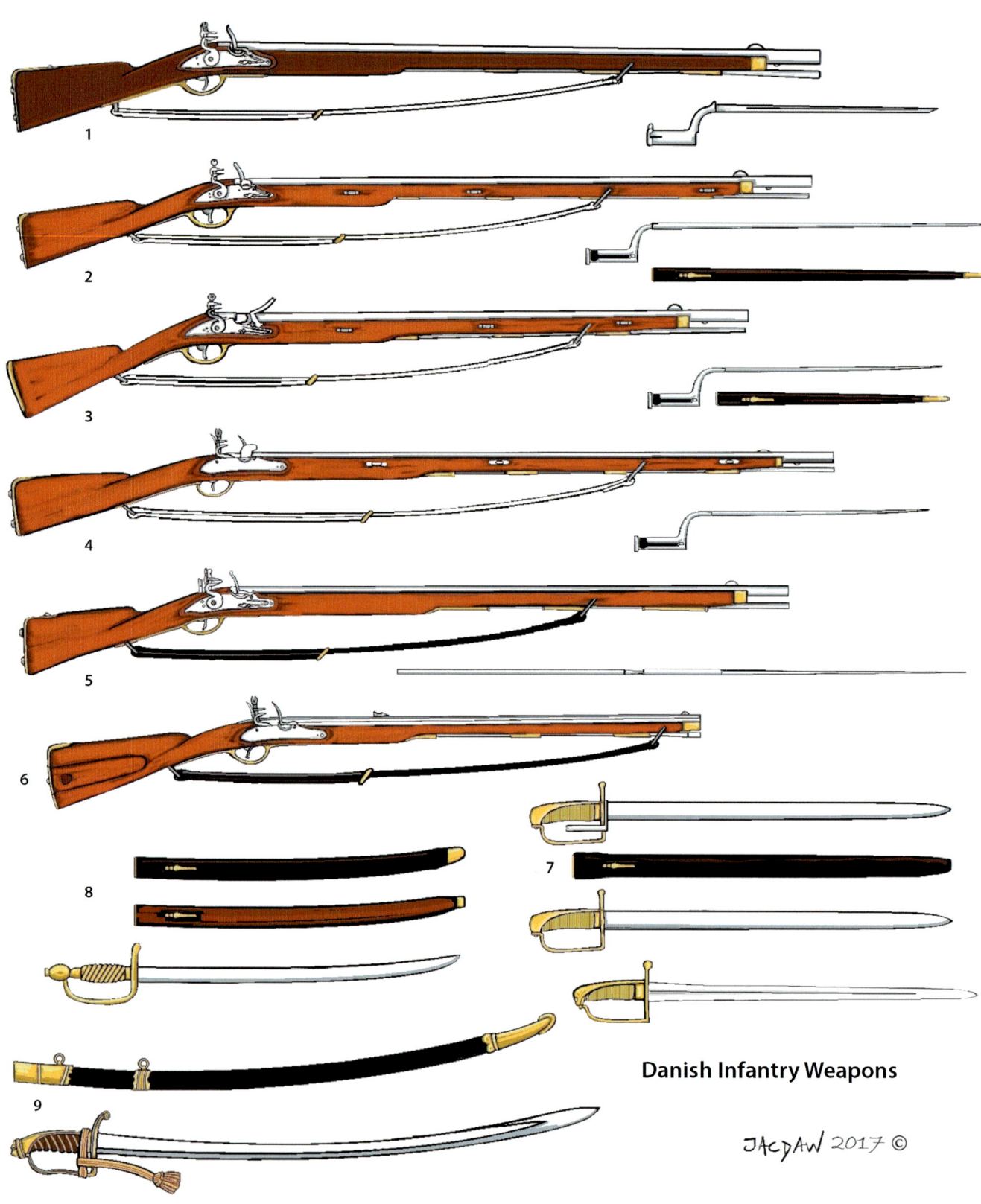

Danish Infantry Weapons

THE JÆGERKORPS AND THE LIGHT INFANTRY BATTALIONS

> ### Plate 21. Danish Infantry Weapons
>
> 1. The M1785 Infantry Musket, a slightly modified model based on the M1774 with the calibre reduced to 17.7mm. Some 1,435 of these muskets were produced.
> 2. The M1794 Infantry Musket was the basic musket used in Denmark during the war. It was a modified musket, based on the previous M1774 and its variations M1785/M1789/M1791. The M1794 was made on the direct wish of the Prince Regent, for a lighter musket with all the technical improvements found on Austrian and Prussian muskets. The M1794 was the principal musket used in Denmark until 1814, while the older Muskets M1774–1791 were used in Norway as well as by regional and volunteer militia formations in Denmark until 1814. The M1794 and M1807 were both much modernised. Note that the Danish reference to the calibres of their firearms usually refers to the ball and not to the bore.
> 3. From around 1808 a shortened version, with a new, steeper gun stock was made from the M1794 model. From 1808 this was used to arm all the new regimental Jægere of the newly formed 3rd and 4th Battalions of the line infantry as well as the new 2nd Battalions of the Skarpskytte Corps.
> 4. The M1807 Infantry Musket with the new 'inside lock': it was easier to maintain and was more resistant to dirt, damp, and rain than normal locks. By 1810–15 Denmark probably had the best muskets found in Europe at the time. Already the M1794 had both a cylindrical ramrod and a self-priming touch hole, both adding to speedier loading. It also had a flash screen, to protect the right-hand man. The 1807 model was further improved by its special easy to maintain and more water resistant inside lock.
> 5. The M 1789 *Skarpskyttegevær* (Sharpshooters' musket) with movable rear sights and with a combination ramrod/spike bayonet as used by the light infantry (*Skarpskytter*) and later by half of the jaegers (Jægerecorps). Again, very advanced for i's time.
> 6. The M1807 Light Infantry Rifle as used by the Jægerecorps and the regimental jægere.
> 7. Top, M1801 Light Infantry Sword *Hirschfänger* with the bayonet attachment. Middle, the *Hirschfänger* without the bayonet attachment. Bottom. M1791 Light Infantry Sword *Hirschfänger* as carried by the light infantry prior to 1801.
> 8. The M1756 Infantry Sabre, frequently misnamed as the M1753 Grenadier Sabre. Also used by artillerymen, grenadiers, Jaegere (often modified), NCOs and a number of other units.
> 9. The M1789 Officers' Sabre, this was the official model, but they were not the only models carried, as many officers bought their own swords/sabres they were often of a different model to those officially carried by the parent unit. The Jæger officers generally appear to have carried privately bought Hussar sabre models.
>
> Source: Drawn from photographs of the originals preserved in the private collection of Trond Wikborg in Norway and the collection in the Tøjhusmuseet, Copenhagen.

This practice continued long after the war when all the jægers were given the same belly-box, but now holding two extra loose balls, for use when the enemy stormed them, to be placed on top of the normal shot (thuds making the barrel hold three bullets!). This gave a devastating close-range blunderbuss style salvo. The use of this pouch was only officially confirmed in 1813, but was probably used much earlier and the resolution only officialised a current practice.

The Light Infantry Battalions (*Lette Infanteribataljoner*)

In 1789 three light infantry battalions (*lette infantribataljoner*) were formed. Their staff had the same strength and organisation as in the Jæger battalions. Each of the four companies of each battalion was composed of three officers, nine NCO's, 120 privates and two hornists. In 1808, all the three light infantry battalions were renamed Sharpshooter battalions (*Skarpskyttercorps*) and a reserve battalion was attached to each of them.

The Sharpshooters' Uniforms

Their shako had a green plume over a green cockade with a button coloured loop and it had green cords and tassel. The Sharpshooters wore the same style of uniform as the Jægere: however, their equipment was the same as the line infantry, but in black leather, including waist and shoulder belts with the cartridge box. This was possibly the most visible distinguishing mark between the Jægere and the light infantry. They had the same badger-skin 'shooting bag' (combined knapsack and ammunition pouch). From 1808 they used a square cow hide knapsack like the line

Danish Locks

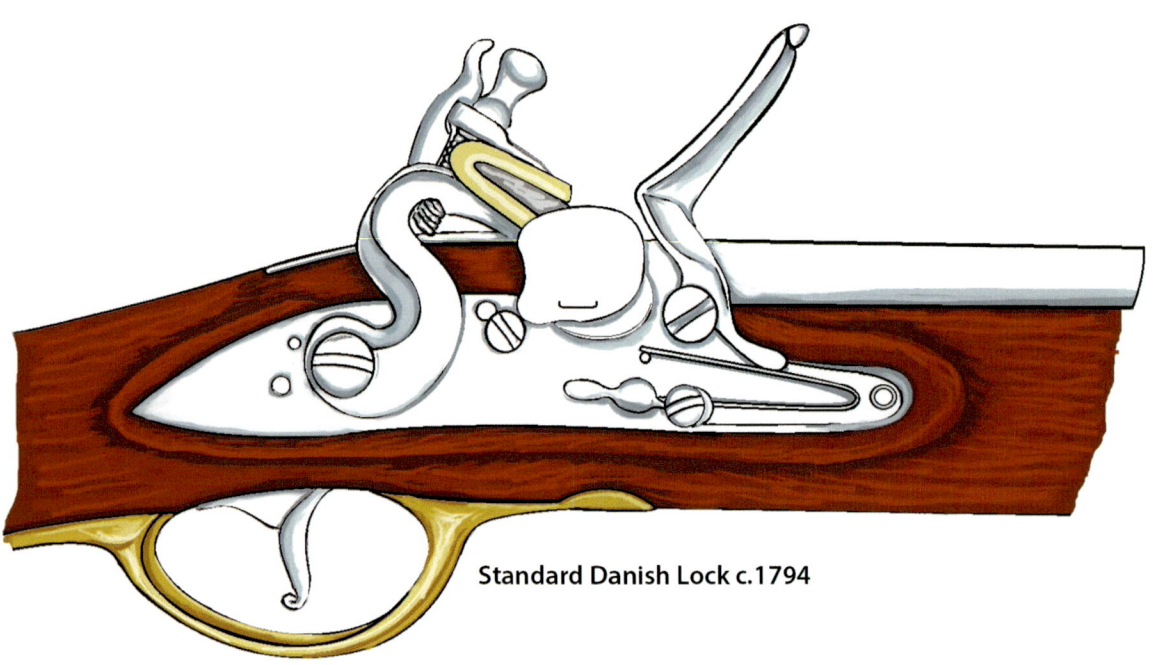

Standard Danish Lock c.1794

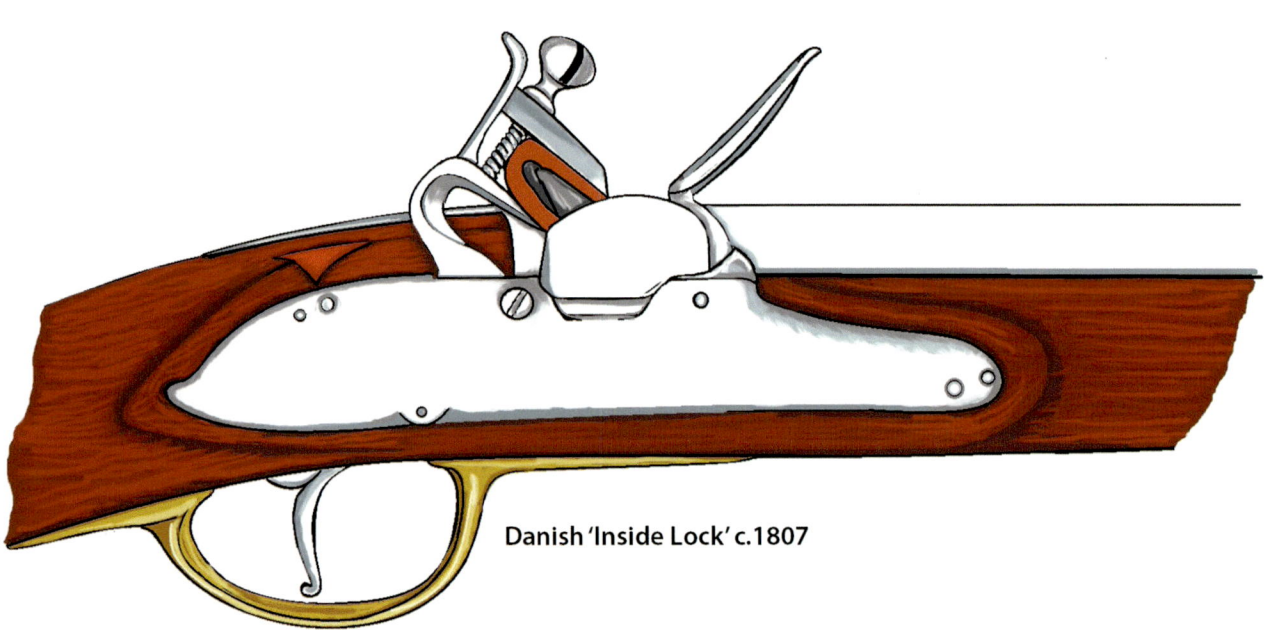

Danish 'Inside Lock' c.1807

> **Plate 22. Danish Firearm Locks**
>
> Top, Traditional Danish Musket Lock c.1794, showing flash guard.
> Botttom, Danish Khyl's 'Inside' Lock c.1807, this lock was also
> installed in the M1807 Rytter Carbines and Pistols.
> Source: Drawn from photographs of the originals preserved in the private collection
> of Trond Wikborg in Norway and the Tøjhusmuseet, Copenhagen.

infantry, but the shoulder straps and buckle fastening straps were of black leather.

They were armed with the light infantry musket (*Skarpskyttegevær*), not rifles which used the sharpened end of the ramrod as a bayonet. They would also carry hangers or *hirschfängers* without the bayonet attachment. Their uniforms followed the same evolution as the Jægere with shakos replacing the hats from 1808.

The NCOs wore the same uniform as the men and they used the same rank distinctions as those used by the Jægere. They were armed and equipped as the men

The officers of the light infantry battalions also had the same rank distinctions as the Jægere except that a number of their officers were said to have kept their bicorns, against regulations, as did some Jæger officers, all through the Napoleonic era. However, most of them wore the regulation round hats with red and gold cords and flounders, later they were replaced by shakos as in the rest of the army. The corps commander and his ADC were both mounted.

Their hornists had the same distinctions as the hornists in the Jæger regiments, with swallows' nests on their shoulders, and they tended to use the brass *Halvemåne* horn, carried on a black leather sling and green tassels. Until 1814, the *Stabs Waldhornist*/staff bugler was mounted.

Danish Officers' Shabraques

General's shabraque 1802–1808

ADC to Crown Prince Frederik 1802–1808

Shabraque for Officers 1808

Shabraque for Guide Officers

Shabraque for Livgarden til Fods and Infantry Officers

Shabraque for Jæger and Light Infantry Officers

THE JÆGERKORPS AND THE LIGHT INFANTRY BATTALIONS

Plate 23. Danish Officers' Shabraques

Top Left: general's housing and holster covers as used by a general without a regiment until 1808, after the Brockdorff collection. A general with a regiment would use a regimental shabraque with metallic lacing.
Top Right: shabraque as used by the ADCs to the Prince Regent. The generals' ADCs would use a similarly laced shabraque, but with blue covers. After the Brockdorff collection.
Middle Left, staff officer's shabraque from 1808.
Middle Right: shabraque for an officer of the Guides.
Bottom left: shabraques as used by the mounted officers of the Livgarde til Fods and the line infantry officers.
Bottom Right: Shabraque as used by the mounted officers of the Jægere and light infantry; the staff trumpeter used the same pattern, but with white woollen lace instead of silver lace. Based on a reconstruction made by Jørgen K. Larsen after the 1819 model.

7
The Infantry Colours

Firstly, a note on the sources for this chapter. We are rather lucky as both the Danes and the Norwegians have preserved a vast quantity of colours, the Danish colours are mostly stored in the reserves of the Tøjhusmuseet in Copenhagen, but very few are actually on display due to their fragility. Also in the Tøjhusmuseet there is an unpublished manuscript known as the *Fanebogen*, dated to the 1880s when a record was made of all the colours in the collection covering the reigns of Christian VII and Frederik VI, essentially the Napoleonic Wars.

The History of the Distribution of the Infantry Colours

Since the end of the Great Northern War both the Danish and the Norwegian colours had been in some disarray. The colours were of different ages and styles and some were in tatters. Up until then each company had a colour after the Prussian norm. The reforms following the 'War Scare' and following the confrontation with Russia in 1758–1762 meant that several different army reforms were made. Around 1762–1766 one major reform was carried out to reduce the number of colours to just one for each battalion including one Life Colour which was generally white and one Regimental Colour (which was not necessarily in the facing colours of the regiment, but more often followed regimental traditions). This was apparently inspired by the practices of Hannover, Brunswick and most of all Hessen-Cassel; this last country had a lasting influence on the future of the organisation of the Danish army. Nearly all the regiments in Denmark and Norway received new colours following the application of the regulation of one colour to each battalion, but with some differences in design as fashions changed. The importance of a stronger Danish nationalism, where Danish/Norwegian styles as opposed to the German influence were put forward, as the symbol of the state, beside the Royal rule, influenced this. The colours were still made of silk and hand embroidered with gold and silver: very elegant, but also very expensive.

In 1784–1785 Prince Karl of Hessen-Cassel, the commander of the army, instituted a major reorganisation of the army and, as a consequence, presented a plan for a totally new distribution and design of infantry colours. All the regiments in Denmark were to receive a completely new stand of colours. The Regulation of 23 July 1785 covered both the style and new distribution of the colours; it states:

> The new Colours shall be painted [Not embroidered, as previously, so much cheaper to produce]. The *Dannebrog* will be at topmost angle and the royal cypher in remaining angles, the shield of its province or the royal coat of arms in case of "a royal regiment" in the centre and the field in the regimental [Facing] Colour. This will also be the design of any further Colours.

The number, the distribution and importance, was now to be completely different to the preceding system:

> That in the future two companies of musketeers, were formed into a [so-called] "Division", it will receive one colour [instead of one to a company as before], so that each battalion, will now have two Colours, in the regimental [Facing] Colour, 4 to a regiment. At the same time the traditional "life colour" or "White Colour" will no longer be used. Instead each regiment, will be given a new [National] "*Dannebrog*" Colour, as the "first regimental Colour" ['*Livfane*'] It must then be carried by the Regiments grenadier division, or "Livbataljonen" as the Grenadier Division will also to be known as, when assembled.

Note: at this time the cross of the *Dannebrog* on Danish colours appears to have generally been straight sided, not a Cross Patée, but with one or two exceptions. Most are shown as square, occasionally rectangular.

All the previously used infantry colours were to be returned to the arsenals and be collected together, along with a number of now surplus cavalry standards, due to the reduction by half the numbers of standards in a squadron from two to one, and they were shipped to Norway in 1788 along with some even older colours. Norway should also follow the model of the Danish regiments, with two colours to each battalion. This was achieved firstly by giving both of the previously-used 'Norwegian Colours' to the first or regular battalion of the regiment. To the other mainly

THE INFANTRY COLOURS

'National' battalions, each would receive one set of the former 'Danish' colours. This way it was possible to double the number of colours without extra expenses. However, the Norwegian-enlisted Nordenfjeldske Regiment and Søndenfjeldske Regiment also received a new stand of painted colours of the 1785 model the following Norwegian army reform in 1789, which others probably should have done too, but most clung on to their 'Norwegian' colours for as long as possible.

Again in 1803 the army had yet another major reform. One result of this was, that one of the two grenadier companies was converted into a jæger company, and as a result all regiments had to return all of their 'Grenadier colours'/*Livfaner*. From then until 1811, no official *Livfane* was allowed in the regiments. Even with the exception of the Slesvigske Infanteri Regiment who kept their M1785 *Livfane*, it was still the 'Grenadier' colour which was the official *Livfane* until 1803.

Concerning the grenadier *Dannebrogs*, the eight which were returned to the Copenhagen arsena, were immediately transferred to the Marine Regiment and the five returned to the Rensburg Arsenal were not reissued, but stored.

Note that in total only 13 'grenadier colours' were ever issued in Denmark and another 10 were made and shipped to Norway.

The national *Dannebrog* was now only used by a number of special formations (the Livgarden til Fods, the Marine Regiment and the *Landeværnet*). Only in 1808, with the disbandment of the *Landeværnet* and their conversion into the reserve 3rd and 4th battalions of the line regiments, did its use become more widespread again. However, some regiments clearly found a need for one first colour in the regiment, therefore a *Livfanen*, and some apparently made one or used the old ones. So from around 1811, the use of white *Livfanen* was now allowed again, and used as basis for the distribution of new colours in the future, although very few, if any, received them before 1815–1819 or even later with the exception of the Dronningens Livregiment which had a new one made in 1811 when they received a new stand of colours.

This system continued until 1842, when the *Dannebrog*, became the standard colour, although in a new special army model with a so-called 'Mantowa-cross'. This became the model for all military colours used in Denmark until today.

The 'company' colours were referred to the as the ordinary or regimental colour and in the case of the grenadiers, a national colour. The small flames on the colour originally denoted their position in the army brigades. When the 3rd and 4th battalions were formed in 1808 from the militia, they were either presented with the old grenadier colours or used modified *Landerværn* colours.

So, from 1808 the distribution of the colours was the following: the 1st battalion had two regimental colours or, with two exceptions, a regimental colour and a *Livfane* (Dronningens, official, and Slesvige, unofficial). The 2nd battalion also had two regimental colours; the 3rd and 4th battalions each had two of their original militia *Dannebrogs*.

After 1808 there does not appear to have been much evolution in the design, except that all the new replacement colours would now bear the cypher of Frederik VI, the so-called the M1808 model, but although they were called the M1808, they were not necessarily issued in that year; in fact this model was retained long after 1815, a few of the older colours were modified with the addition of the new king's cypher. The finial (*Fanespyd*) was also changed for a model which now bore the cypher of Frederik VI. There do not appear to have been any regulations for the replacement of old colours, they would appear to have been used until they fell to bits or a new stand was made conforming to a new resolution. The only reason the majority have survived is that few were lost in action and they carefully stored the old colours from previous reigns (although some were reissued, particularly in Norway) and battalion fanions also replaced the colours as well. It was much the same situation in Sweden at the same time.

The regiments which are known to have been issued with new colours 1806–14 bearing the monogram of Frederik VI before 1815 were the following:

- The Dronningens Livregiment received new colours in 1811, including a white *Livfane*.
- The 3rd Battalion Holstenske Infanteri Regiment, two colours of the 1811 issue
- The Danske Livregiment between 1811 and 1814 (Precise date not known)
- The Norske Livregiment between 1811 and 1814 (Precise date not known)
- The Prins Christian Frederiks Regiment was issued with new green colours of the 1785 model in 1806 when the regiment changed their facings from buff to green. This regiment also had new colours of the 1811 model possibly issued in 1813.

No further regiments received colours of the 1811 issue before 1815 as far as is known.

Their Dimensions and Confection

Dimensions of colours varied from between 110cms to 180cms square, but 132cms square is fairly standard; sometimes they appear to be rectangular.

The colours were fixed to the stave by means of a strip of white or coloured silk and gilt nails. Sometimes they were nailed directly to the stave. The staves were painted black, red or white, although some of the staves appear to have been natural varnished wood as well, but as few have survived it is difficult to be dogmatic. They were between 220 to 250cms in length.

The finial (*Fanespyd*) was a gilt pointed pike head, generally in a triangular form, with the crowned monogram of Christian VII chiselled out in the centre. They had rather long red and gold cords with tassels, more or less the same length as the colour itself. From 1808 they made new finials with the cypher of Frederik VI on his accession to the throne. A fairly unique feature of Danish finials was that most of them had a D ring on one side of the shaft to tie the cords and tassels onto it; it appears to have been cast on.

The cloth was dyed in the facing colour and then painted with either the Royal Arms or the Arms of the province after which the regiment was named in the centre. In top hoist there was the national emblem of Denmark, the *Dannebrog* (red field with a white cross) and in the other three corners there was a gold crowned royal monogram, generally of Christian VII, surrounded by green laurels. When Frederik VI became king there is no proof that the colours were modified with his monogram, although when new colours were made it is logical to conclude that they had the new king's cypher. On each side of the colour there was a flame, red for the first regiment of the brigade and white for the second.

The militia and grenadier colours were made of four pieces of red silk and three pieces of white silk and stitched together in much the same way that French pre-revolutionary colours were made; the other decoration was painted on.

The colours were nailed on to the staves with gilt tacks over a strip of white or buff cloth, possibly even soft buff leather which served to reinforce the colour and avoid tearing, so all the colours would have this strip of cloth visible.

Note that the plates that accompany this chapter only show the obverse of the colours, unless the reverse was completely different.

Marker or Camp Flags

Most infantry and cavalry possessed marker flags for everyday use in camps and on the march to help the officers position their men. Normally two were issued to each company. Their approximate dimensions were 50 x 50cms. We do not possess much information on these flags, but if we assume the only existing line model is a standard model (probably dating to after 1815) then they resembled the company colour with the following differences: the field would generally be yellow and the flames were in the facing colour; in the top corner a *Dannebrog*, the provincial arms in the centre, with the company number painted around the base of the arms in gold lettering. Sometimes the name of the regiment was also inscribed on them as well. After the limited surviving documents, the staves were painted in the regimental facing colour.

Who Carried the Colours

The colours were usually carried by a junior officer called a *Fændrik* (ensign). When this rank was abolished in 1809 they were replaced with 'Well estimated or deserving NCOs' who would now normally carry the colours. On the march or in foul weather the colours would be rolled and carried in a protective canvas cover, this could be black, dark blue or grey. When the colour was being flown the canvas cover (called a 'condom') was commonly carried around the colour bearer's body as a bandoleer over the left shoulder. Even to this day it is carried in this way by the Kongelige Liv Garde Til Fods.

A regiment on the march would be led by its regimental band, followed by the commanding officer on horseback, followed by the colour party with the battalion's two colours. The rest of regiment would follow, headed by the sappers and the grenadiers. The two colours were usually carried side by side. Within the battalion the colours were carried in the centre of the line and they were always surrounded by a colour guard of four NCOs.

The Models

Firstly, one has to understand the use of The Danish Coat of Arms.

Until 1819, two types of Royal arms were used. The first of these were the so-called 'cabinet arms', which were the 'Pure' arms of the king (and state) with only the arms of Denmark (Or, three lions passant Azure, armed and langued gules crowned or and nine hearts Gules, set in three pals of three), of Norway (Gules, a lion rampant Or, crowned and bearing an axe Or with a blade Argent and Or) and of the Scandinavian union (Azure, three crowns Or). This last was because the kings of Denmark still felt that they had the right to use the arms of Sweden, according to the conditions of the Kalmar Union treaty. They were displayed on colours, shields, swords, etcetera, mainly in regiments with a royal connection. These were also the arms carried on various badges by ordinary guardsmen and NCOs of the Guard. They were also known as 'the lesser royal arms'.

The other coat of arms which was used, were known as 'the royal arms' or 'the greater arms'; these were the full set of arms showing all of the quarterings. It showed the arms of all of the provinces of the kingdom, with the *Dannebrog* overall. These arms were mainly displayed by the finer regiments or those with close royal connections, such as princes. These were the arms used by the Lifeguards, the Queen's Regiment and the Cadet Corps. These were on their colours and on their officers' belt buckles and on those of the Guards officers. See the descriptive below on the Livgarde til Fods colour.

Another difference was on the new Frederik VI colours the supporters, the 'wild men' now faced away from the arms as before under Christian VII they looked towards the royal arms. It has not been possible to discover why, but it was most certainly symbolic.

Where possible in the plates accompanying this chapter, the references for the colours have been noted on the text for each plate. These are the references by which they are known in the collection of the Tøjhusmuseet in Copenhagen, the collections in Norway and a number of which are preserved in Sweden. The two numbers correspond to the old serial number first followed by the new one in brackets.

The Foot Guards; Livgarde til Fods

The Livgarde til Fods had a parade colour or *Livfane*, which had a white field and dated back to Frederik V circa 1767. This colour was embroidered, not painted. It is preserved in the Tøjhusmuseet under the reference 105 (301). Note the finial with the monogram of Frederik V (1746–1766). The obverse and reverse were identical. This was reserved for parades and in use until 1842. The colour was charged with a trophy of arms and a knight holding a shield bearing the royal arms under a light blue scroll bearing the devise 'PRUDENTIA ET CONSTANTIA' (By prudence and steadfastness) in gold.

The Royal Arms were; A shield quartered by a cross patée Argent fimbriated Gules, which is the *Dannebrog*, Quarterly: in 1, Or, three lions passant regardant Azure, armed and langued gules crowned or, nine hearts Gules, set in three pals (which is Denmark). In 2, gules, a lion rampant or holding an axe argent, which is Norway. In 3, per fess: Azure, three crowns Or (which is Sweden) and or, two lions passant azure, armed and langued gules (which is Schleswig). In 4, per fess Or, a lion passant Azure supported nine hearts Gules (which is Jyske) and Gules a dragon Or (which is Funen or Fynske). Overall an escutcheon per fess, in chief, per party, sinister, Gules, a nettle leaf Argent charged with an escutcheon, per fess Argent and Gules (which is Holstein) and dexter, Gules, a swan Argent, beaked, armed, gorged and crown Or (which is Stormarn), in Gules an armed horseman Argent (which is Ditmarsie). Overall an escutcheon per party, which were or, two bars gules (which is Oldenburg) and azure, a cross patée, fitchée or (which is Delmenhorst). The shield had a supporter on either side, a wild man holding a club in natural colours standing upon a green ground. The obverse and reverse were identical. This colour was embroidered, not painted.

For ordinary revues they carried a *Dannebrog* painted with the arms of the kingdom in the centre. The obverse and reverse were identical. This was the ordinary or regimental colour from the time of Christian VII which was used for both daily parades and field exercises. It was first officially mentioned in the 1785 regulations, but was only issued in 1791 and was carried until 1840. The obverse and reverse were identical. No original colour has been preserved, but a full-sized drawing of the colours as approved by the king still exists.

The regiment also possessed four company pennons or fanions, probably used for drill, no doubt to preserve the standards, which were only carried for official state reviews. Each one was in the company colour. The 1st company had a pale-yellow pennon, the 2nd company had a red one, the 3rd a blue one and the 4th company had a white one. They all had a small *Dannebrog* in each angle, at the side of each *Dannebrog* there were was written 'L G 1/2/3/4 C', (Liv Garde 1st Company etc.) in the centre the cypher of Frederik VI, all the lettering was painted gold, not embroidered. The obverse and reverse were identical. The staves were painted red.

The Danish Cadets, Det Kongelige Landkadet Corps

Although this was a school unit and not a fighting unit, they were granted a colour to be used for parades. They had a M1785 regimental colour (*Dannebrogsfane*) which bore the arms of the kingdom complete with supporters and collars of the orders in the centre; in each corner there was a gold crown and the king's monogram 'C7' within green laurel wreaths. The obverse and reverse were identical.

The Danish Life Regiment on Foot, Danske Livregiment

They had a M1785 regimental colour which had a pale yellow field with in the centre a gold crown with a red bonnet over the arms of Denmark, which were, on a shield; Or, 3 lions passant Azure, crowned Or and langued Gules and 9 hearts Gules all within a gold frame, the shield had a supporter on either side, a wild man holding a club in natural colours standing on a green ground. There was a canton with a *Dannebrog* in the top hoist and a red flame on each side. In the other three corners there were a gold crown and monogram 'C7' within green laurel wreaths. They originally had a white *Livfane* with red flames; the rest was identical to the regimental colour. The obverse and reverse were identical. The regiment received a new stand of colours between 1811 and 1814 with the monograms of Frederik VI. This included a white *Livfane* and at least one pale straw yellow regimental colour.

Note that on the painting by Haffner of the Prince Regent of circa 1804, an infantry colour is shown which several historians have claimed that this colour was a 'Life Colour'. However, this is wrong; when one looks at the original painting: this is one of the buff regimental colours of the Danske Liv Regiment, also shown marching in the background of the painting.

The 3rd and 4th battalions carried the National colour Model 1801 made from the old *Landeværns* colour M1801,

Danish Infantry Colours I

Livgarde til Fods, Parade Colour M1767

Livgarde til Fods, Ordinary Colour

THE INFANTRY COLOURS

Danish Infantry Colours II

Landkadetkorps (Cadets) c.1787

Grenadier Co. M1787

Danish Infantry Colours III

Danske Livregiment til Fods, Regimental Colour M1785

Danske Livregiment til Fods, Regimental Colour M1811

THE INFANTRY COLOURS

Danish Infantry Colours IV

Norske Livregiment til Fods, Regimental Colour M1785

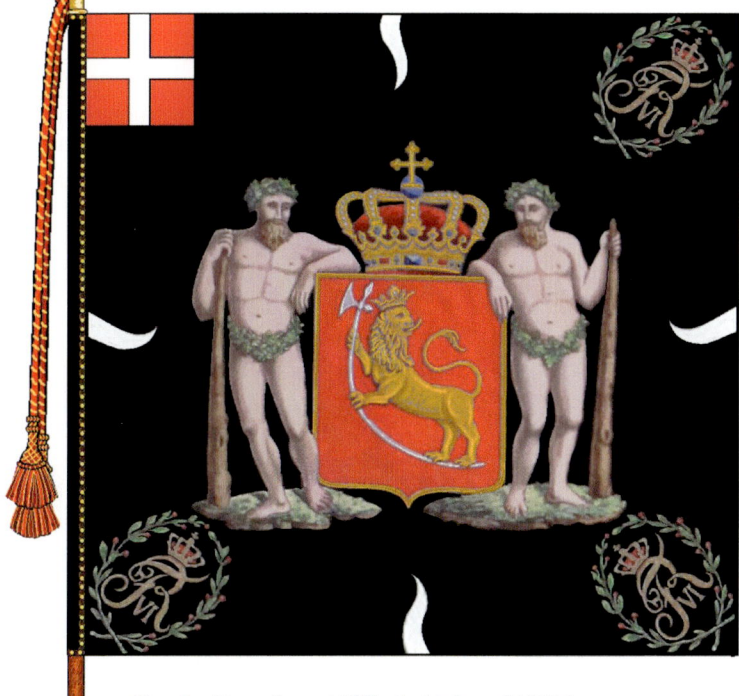

Norske Livregiment til Fods, Livfane M1811

minus the cartouche. From around 1811 when some of those regiments received new colours, it is also possible that these 3rd and 4th Battalions changed their Royal cypher as well.

The Norwegian Life Regiment on Foot, Norske Livregiment

The two M1785 life colours had black fields with in the centre a gold crown with a red bonnet over the arms of Norway, which were, on a shield; Gules, a lion rampant holding an axe all within a gold frame, the shield had a supporter on either side, a wild man holding a club in natural colours standing on a green ground. These had a special status, as the king decided that: 'since the siege of Copenhagen 1659 and as the regiment has had special relationship with the University, and for its bravery and as a special recognition of this fact, they were granted two black colours besides the two buff/pale yellow ones'. One of each was carried by the 1st and 2nd battalions

There was a canton with a *Dannebrog* in the top hoist and a red flame on each side. In the other three corners there was a gold crown and monogram 'C7' within green laurel wreaths. The obverse and reverse of both were identical, the lion in mirror image. As a special mark of honour the regiment was also allowed black shoulder straps and to carry infantry M1756 sabres. Probably all the Life Regiments were allowed to carry sabres as a sign of their status.

The regiment received a new stand of colours between 1811 and 1814 with the monograms of Frederik VI. This included two black colours as well as two pale straw yellow regimental colours and one of each colour was carried by the 1st battalion and 2nd battalions. The obverse and reverse were identical. They also had two ordinary (regimental) colours in buff yellow silk with the same motifs on them as the *Livfane*. The obverse and reverse were identical.

The 3rd and 4th battalions carried the national colour M1808, made from the old M1801 *Landeværn* colour. Some of them may have been repainted after 1808 with the monogram of Frederik VI.

The Crown Prince's Regiment, Kronprinsens Regiment; from 1808 The King's Regiment, Kongens Regiment

As this regiment was the Regiment of Crown Prince Frederik, he named it the King's Regiment when he ascended the throne.

The life colour had a white field with in the centre a gold crown with a red bonnet over the arms of Denmark, the simple version, which were, on a shield; Or, 3 lions passant regardant Azure langued Gules and crowned Or, and 9 hearts Gules all within a gold frame, the shield had a supporter on either side, a wild man holding a club in natural colours standing on a green ground, surrounded by a collar of the Order of the Elephant. There was a canton with a *Dannebrog* in the top hoist and a red flame on each side. In the other three corners there was a gold crown and monogram 'C7' within green laurel wreaths. They had the same motifs as the Danske Livregiment. The obverse and reverse were identical.

The regiment had an M1785 regimental colour which had a light blue field with in the centre a gold crown with a red bonnet over the full arms of Denmark, which were, on a shield; per fess, per party; Gules, a lion rampant Or, crowned and bearing an axe Or with a blade Argent and Or, three lions passant Azure langued Gules and crowned Or, and nine hearts Gules all within a gold frame, in base, azure three open crowns Or (Sweden), the shield had a supporter on either side, a wild man holding a club in natural colours standing on a green ground, surrounded by a collar of the Order of the Elephant. There was a canton with a *Dannebrog* in the top hoist and a red flame on each side. In the other three corners there was a gold crown and monogram 'C7' within green laurel wreaths. The obverse and reverse were identical.

When this regiment was renamed the Kongens Regiment in 1808, apparently no new colours were made, but the old 1785 colours continued to be carried until 1842. The 3rd and 4th battalions carried the national colour M1801, made from the old M1801 *Landeværn* colour.

The King's Regiment; became the Kronens Regiment in 1808

This was the old King's Regiment, it was renamed the Crown Regiment when Frederik VI succeeded his father on the throne.

The regiment had an M1785 regimental colour which had a light blue field, a canton with a *Dannebrog* in the top hoist and a red flame on each side. In the other three corners there was a gold crown and monogram 'C7' within green laurel wreaths. In the centre, they displayed the arms of Denmark as on the crown prince's colour. The obverse and reverse were identical. This regiment eventually received a new stand of the so called M1808 colours with the new king's cypher, but it was not before 1819. The field was still light blue and the flames were red.

When this regiment was renamed the Kronen or Crown regiment in 1808, apparently no new colours were made, but the old 1785 colours continued to be carried until 1842. Possibly out of respect for the late king.

The 3rd and 4th battalions carried the national colour M1801, made from the old M1801 *Landeværn* colour. As the Kings' personal regiment, the monograms on this regiment were modified with the cypher of the new King.

THE INFANTRY COLOURS

Danish Infantry Colours V

3rd and 4th Battalions' Colour c.1808
ex M1801 Landværns Colour

3rd and 4th Battalions Colour M1811

THE DANISH ARMY OF THE NAPOLEONIC WARS VOLUME 1

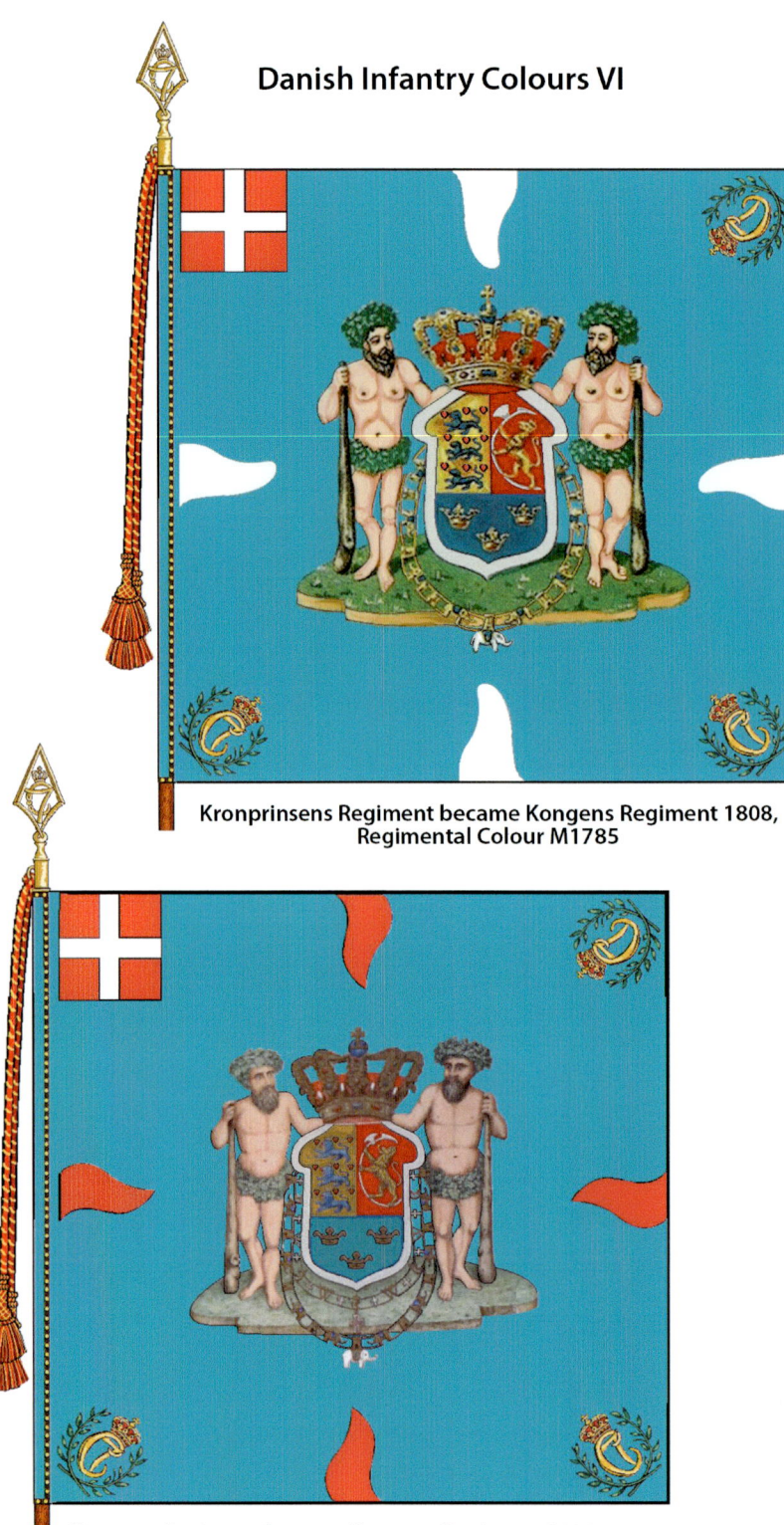

Danish Infantry Colours VI

Kronprinsens Regiment became Kongens Regiment 1808, Regimental Colour M1785

Kongens Regiment became Kongens Regiment 1808, Regimental Colour M1785

THE INFANTRY COLOURS

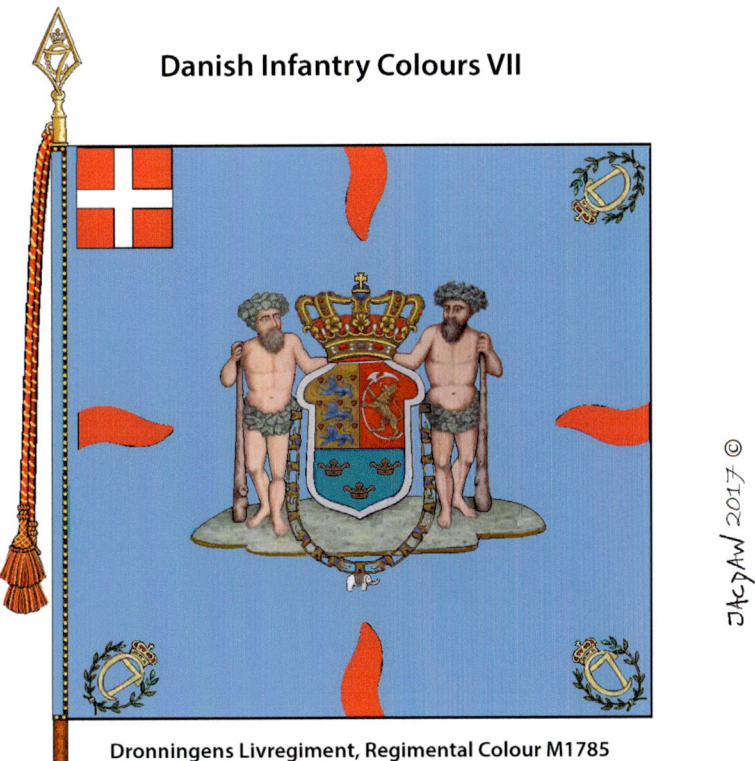

Dronningens Livregiment, Regimental Colour M1785

The Queen's Life Regiment of Foot, Dronningens Livregiment til Fods

As in other regiments they received four colours of the M1785 model, which were very similar to the model carried by the old Kongens Regiment and differed simply by only having the chain of the Order of the Elephant and not the *Dannebrog* around the shield.

Note that since the exile of the Queen Caroline Mathilde of Britain in 1772 and her subsequent death in 1775 in exile, there had not been an official Queen of Denmark. So between 1775 and 1808 Denmark had no queen, but the crown prince kept the regiment (and colours) out of respect of his mother. The colour is faded, and this is a reconstruction of original colours.

The regiment was issued with new colours which were made after Frederik VI ascended the throne for his wife Marie Sophie Frederikke, the new queen. As Frederik VI was very fond of his Queen, it was important for him that regiment should now have a splendid set of colours for her regiment. The first issue of this model of colours was in 1811. The *Livfane* colour (or Queen's colour) had a white field with the crowned royal arms in the centre, see above for the description, within a collar bearing the order of the elephant and supporters and a stand of colours on each side, there was a canton with a *Dannebrog* in top hoist, a red flame on each side, in each of the other thee corners there was gold crowned cypher 'MSF' (Marie Sophie Frederikke) within green laurel wreaths. The obverse and reverse were identical. The regimental colour had a light blue field and red flames. In fact, probably only the 1st battalion received them, as they were stationed near the regimental depot in Holstein. At this time the 2nd battalion was serving on the island of Bornholm, and only received its two new colours in 1814–15. Until this date, they probably simply kept on using the old ones.

The 3rd and 4th battalions received M1801 *Dannebrog* colours, made from the old M 1801 *Landeværn* colour with the addition of the new king's cypher.

The Hereditary Prince Frederik's Regiment, Arveprins Frederiks Regiment; from 1806 renamed the Prins Christian Frederiks Regiment

The regiment had an M1785 regimental colour which had a yellow buff field with red flames and in the centre the crowned arms of Denmark, which were, on a shield; per fess, per party; Gules, a lion rampant Or, crowned and bearing an axe Or with a blade Argent and Or, 3 lions passant regardant Azure langued Gules and crowned Or, and nine hearts Gules all within a gold frame, the shield had a supporter on either side, a wild man holding a club in natural colours standing on a green ground, surrounded by a collar of the Order of the Elephant. The crown was gold with a red bonnet. The obverse and reverse were identical.

The colour of the sheet changed to light green in 1807 when the regiment changed their facings and was

Danish Infantry Colours VIII

Dronningens Livregiment, Livfane M1811

Dronningens Livregiment, Regimental Colour M1811

THE INFANTRY COLOURS

Danish Infantry Colours IX

Arveprins Frederiks Regt. became Prins Christian Frederiks Regt. in 1806. Regimental Colour M1785

Arveprins Frederiks Regt. became Prins Christian-Frederiks Regt. in 1806. Regimental Colour M1806

Danish Infantry Colours X

Fynske Regiment, Regimental Colour M1785

renamed as the Prins Christian Frederiks Regiment and they received at least one new light green colour with red flames and the monogram 'C7'; note that the wild men look towards the shield.

There was a canton with a *Dannebrog* in the top hoist and a red flame on each side. In the other three corners there was a gold crowned monogram of 'C7' within green laurel wreaths. The obverse and reverse were identical.

Between 1813 and 1819 they were issued with a new stand of colours; the new colours also had a light green fieldand the cypher of the new king. Note that the wild men now look away from the shield. The 3rd and 4th battalions received M1808 *Dannebrog* colours, made from the old M 1801 *Landeværn* colours with the addition of the new king's cypher between 1808 and 1813.

The Regiment of Funen, Fynske Infanteri Regiment

The regimental colour had a white field with red flames, in the centre, the crowned arms of the province of Funen which were Gules, a Wyvern Or (known as a *Lindorm* in Danish) on a shield within a gold frame. The gold crown had a red bonnet. There was a canton with a *Dannebrog* in the top hoist, in the other three corners there was a gold crowned monogram of 'C7' within green laurel wreaths. There was a canton with the *Dannebrog* in the top hoist, and a red flame on each side. In the other 3 corners there was a gold crown and monogram 'C7' within green laurel wreaths. The obverse and reverse were identical.

A new stand of regimental colours M1808 were made, still with a white field and red flames, but with the crowned monograms of Frederik VI in the angles. The obverse and reverse were identical. These colours were probably not issued before 1810, possibly as late as 1814.

The 3rd and 4th battalions received the M1801 *Dannebrog* colours painted with the new king's cypher.

The 1st Jutland Infantry Regiment, 1st Jyske Infanteri Regiment

They had a M1785 Regimental colour which had a black field and red flames with, in the centre, a gold crown with a red bonnet over a shield bearing the arms of Jutland, which were, Or, a lion passant Azure over 9 hearts Gules, 4, 3, 2, within a gold frame. There was a canton with *Dannebrog* in top hoist, and a white flame on each side. In the other three angles there was a gold crowned monogram of 'C7' within green laurel wreaths. The obverse and reverse were identical. The new M1808 colours had the cypher of Frederik VI and the *Dannebrog* in the top hoist now appears to be a cross patée. The exact date of when they actually received the colours is unknown; probably after the end of the war.

THE INFANTRY COLOURS

Danish Infantry Colours XI

1st Jyske Regiment, Regimental Colour M1785

2nd Jyske Regiment, Regimental Colour M1785

Danish Infantry Colours XII

3rd Jyske Regiment, Regimental Colour M1785

The 1st and 2nd battalions each carried two regimental colours.

The 3rd and 4th battalions received M1808 *Dannebrog* colours, made from the old M1801 *Landeværn* colour with the addition of the new king's cypher.

The 2nd Jutland Infantry Regiment, 2nd Jyske Infanteri Regiment

The regiment had an M1785 regimental colour which had a white field with red flames, with in the center, a gold crown with a red bonnet over a shield bearing the arms of Jutland, which were, Or, a lion passant Azure over 9 hearts Gules, 4, 3, 2, within a gold frame. There was a canton with *Dannebrog* in top hoist, and a red flame on each side. In the other 3 corners there was a gold crown and monogram 'C7' within green laurel wreaths. The obverse and reverse were identical. The 1st battalion carried a regimental colour and a M1785 grenadier colour instead of a *Livfane*.

The 3rd and 4th battalions received M1808 *Dannebrog* colours, made from the old M1801 *Landeværn* colour with the addition of the new king's cypher.

The 3rd Jutland Infantry Regiment, 3rd Jyske Infanteri Regiment

The regiment had an M1785 Regimental colour which had a black field with red flames, with in the centre, a gold crown with a red bonnet over the arms of Jutland, on a shield, Or, a lion passant Azure over 9 hearts Gules, 4, 3, 2, within a gold frame. There was a canton with *Dannebrog* in top hoist, and a white flame on each side. In the other 3 corners there was a gold crown and monogram 'C7' within green laurel wreaths. The obverse and reverse were identical. The 1st battalion carried a regimental colour and a M1785 grenadier colour, gold and red cords, instead of a *Livfane*.

The 3rd and 4th battalions received M1808 *Dannebrog* colours, made from the old M1801 *Landeværn* colour with the addition of the new king's cypher.

Oldenburg Infantry Regiment, Oldenborgske Infanteriregiment

The regiment had an M1785 regimental colour which had a deep green field red flames, with in the centre a gold crown with a red bonnet over a shield bearing the arms of the province of Oldenburg which were, Or, two fesses Gules. The shield had a gold frame. There was a canton with the *Dannebrog* in the top hoist, and a red flame on each side. In the other three corners there was a gold crown and monogram 'C7' within green laurel wreaths. The obverse and reverse were identical.

The regiment changed their facings in 1802 from green to black and on that occasion they also changed their colours. The M1802 colours now had a black field with red flames. There was a canton with the *Dannebrog* in the top hoist, and a red flame on each side. In the other three corners there was a gold crown and a different version of the monogram 'C7' within green laurel wreaths. The

THE INFANTRY COLOURS

Danish Infantry Colours XIII

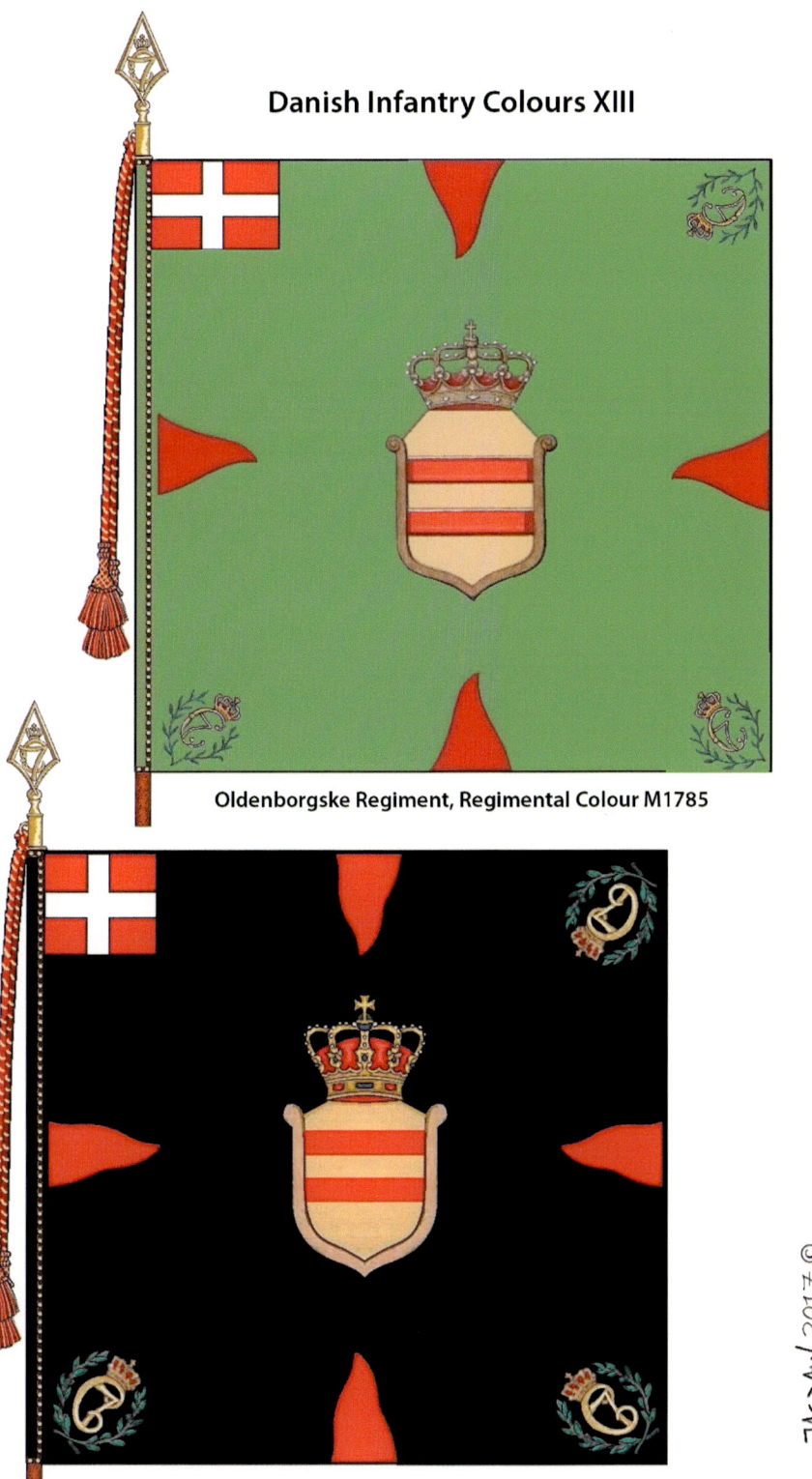

Oldenborgske Regiment, Regimental Colour M1785

Oldenborgske Regiment, Regimental Colour M1802

Danish Infantry Colours XIV

Slesvigske Regiment, Livfane M1785

Slesvigske Regiment, Regimental Colour M1785

1st battalion carried a regimental colour and an M1785 grenadier colour instead of a *Livfane* until 1803.

The 3rd and 4th battalions received M1808 *Dannebrog* colours, made from the old M1801 *Landeværn* colour with the addition of the new king's cypher. The 4th battalion of the Regiment of Oldenburg was exceptionally granted black regimental colours in 1813 as a reward for their conduct at the Battle of Sehested in replacement of their *Dannebrog* colours; these new colours would have had the new royal ciphers of Frederik VI.

A picture of a grenadier company marker flag/pennon of this regiment also exists; it follows the standard pattern, pale yellow with a *Dannebrog*, the provincial arms in the centre and the text 'Ob. I. R.' above the arms and 'Gren. Compagnie' painted below. This pennon probably dates to around 1815

The Schleswig Infantry Regiment, Slesvigske Infanteri Regiment

The Slesvigske Infanteri Regiment had a special status as it was the personal regiment of Prince Carl of Hessen, the formal commander of the army, and as such they were allowed far more elegant colours than any other line regiment; apparently they were even allowed to keep an unofficial white life colour in the 1785 issue, but the grenadier colour was still the official *Livfane* until 1803.

They had a M1785 regimental colour which had a pale blue field with a white flame on each side. In the centre there was a gold crown with a red bonnet over the arms of Schleswig, on a shield, were, Or, two lions Azure within a gold frame. There was a canton with *Dannebrog* in top hoist, and a white flame on each side. In the other three corners there was a gold crown and monogram 'C7' within green laurel wreaths with a darker blue back ground. The obverse and reverse were identical. The *Livfane* had the same design, but on a white field and the flames were red.

They later received the M1808 colours, which had a light blue field and medium blue flames; in the centre, a gold crown with a red bonnet above, on a shield, the arms of Schleswig which were Or, two lions Azure set within a gold frame. There was a canton with *Dannebrog* in top hoist, and a medium blue flame on each side. Exactly when it was issued is unknown, except it was obviously after 1808.

Traditionally the grenadier colour was carried at the Battle of Sehested in 1813, but this is yet another myth; however, the colour is still in existence, complete with finial and cords, and can be seen hanging in its regimental chapel.

The 3rd and 4th battalions received M1808 *Dannebrog* colours, made from the old M1801 *Landeværn* colour with the addition of the new king's cypher.

A marker flag/pennon of this regiment is in the Arsenal in Vienna, it follows the standard pattern, pale yellow with a *Dannebrog*, the provincial arms in the center and the text 'SLES. I. R.' above the arms and 'Musk Compagnie' below. This pennon probably dates to around 1815

The Holstein Infantry Regiment, Holstenske Infanteri Regiment

The M1785 Regimental colour had a pale yellow/buff field with white flames. In the centre there was a gold crown with a red bonnet, over the arms of Holstein, which were Gules, a nettle leaf Argent charged with an escutcheon, per fess Argent and Gules, all within a golden frame. An M1785 regimental colour is preserved in the Tøjhusmuseet under the reference 192 (189), partially damaged. The obverse and reverse were identical. There was a canton with *Dannebrog* in top hoist. In the other three corners there was a gold crown and monogram 'C7' within green laurel wreaths. The obverse and reverse were identical.

In 1802 the regiment changed their facings and the two battalions received new stand of colours. The M1802 regimental colour now had a black field with white flames, with in the center, a gold crown with a red bonnet, over the arms of Holstein, which were Gules, a nettle leaf Argent charged with an escutcheon, per fess Argent and Gules, within a golden frame. There was a canton with *Dannebrog* in top hoist. In the other three corners there was a gold crown and monogram 'C7' within green laurel wreaths. The obverse and reverse were identical.

From 1808 all the new 3rd and 4th Battalions should have carried the standard *Dannebrog* M1808 (ex *Landeværnet*) colours still with the previous king's cypher. However, as a reward for its conduct at the Battle of Stralsund in 1809, the 3rd battalion of the Regiment of Holstein was granted a new stand of regimental colours as was the 4th battalion for its conduct at the Battle of Sehested in 1813 (although they had to wait a little longer before receiving this model). The M1811 regimental colour had a black field with white flames as the 1st and 2nd battalions, with in the centre, a gold crown with a red bonnet, over the arms of Holstein, which were Gules, a nettle leaf Argent charged with an escutcheon, per fess Argent and Gules, within a golden frame. There was a canton with *Dannebrog* in top hoist. In the other three corners there was a gold crown and monogram 'C7' within green laurel wreaths. The obverse and reverse were identical. This was then the first regiment where all the battalions had the same regimental colours (although probably of two different 'Issues'). The remnants of one of the two Model 1811 colours are preserved in the Tøjhusmuseet.

The only surviving company marker flag from 1803–14 belonged to this regiment, it is light yellow with black flames like the regimental colour with the provincial coat of arms in the centre. Written around the arms is the inscription '1st musk comp' so we can safely assume that each company had one, each with the company's number

THE DANISH ARMY OF THE NAPOLEONIC WARS VOLUME 1

Danish Infantry Colours XV

Holstenske Regiment, Regimental Colour M1802

Holstenske Regiment, Regimental Colour M1811

THE INFANTRY COLOURS

Danish Infantry Colours XVIII
Livgarde til Fod, Company Fanions c.1808

1st Company

2nd Company

3rd Company

4th Company

THE DANISH ARMY OF THE NAPOLEONIC WARS VOLUME 1

Danish Infantry Colours XIX
Company Fanions

Holstenske Regiment, Company Fanion 1803–1814

Oldenborgske Regiment, Company Fanion c.1812

THE INFANTRY COLOURS

Danish Infantry Colours XVI

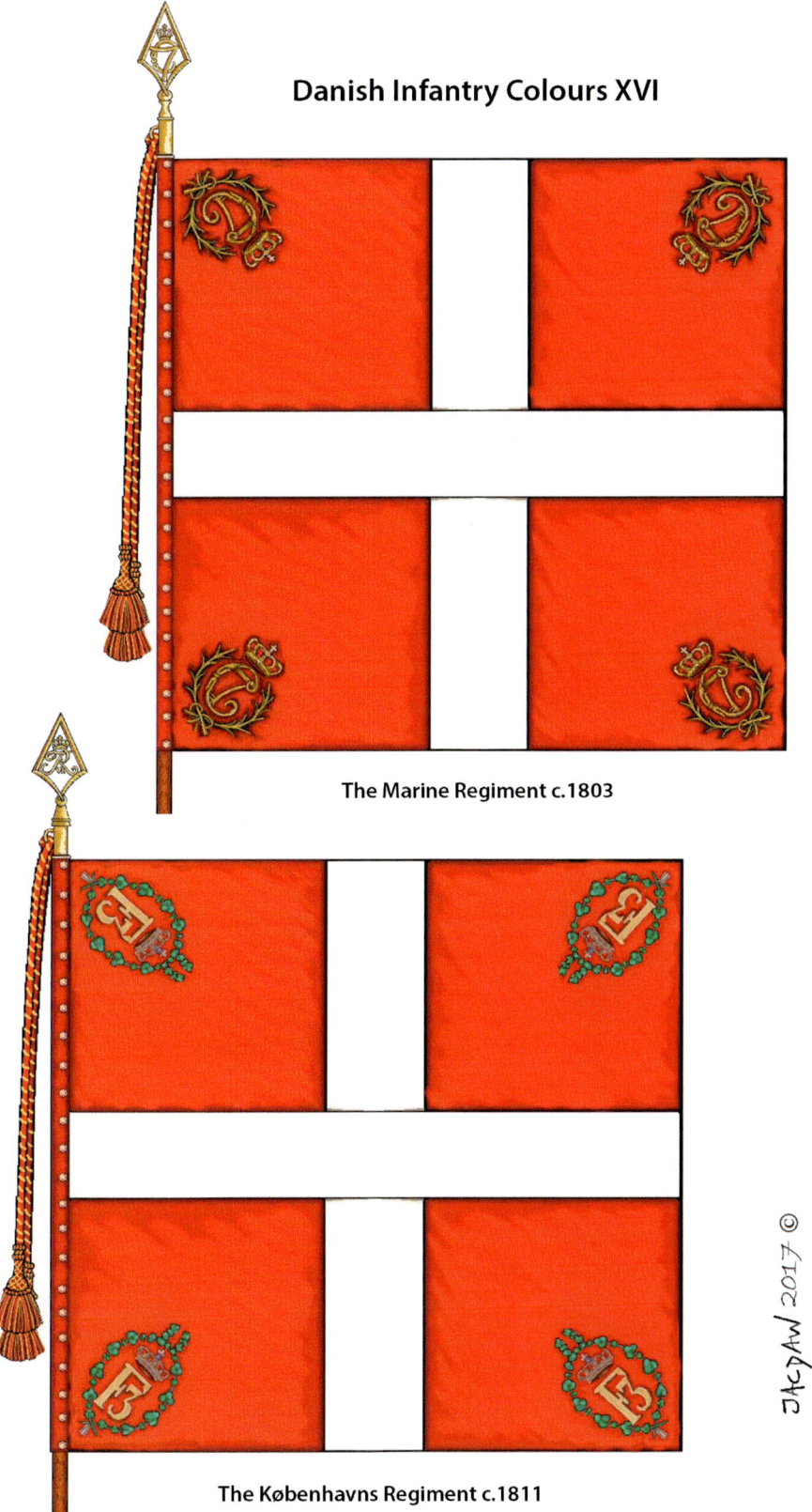

The Marine Regiment c.1803

The Københavns Regiment c.1811

Danish Infantry Colours XVII

Landeværnet Colour M1801

Landeværnet Colour M1801 for German Units (Holstein)

or designation. There is a written description of another company marker flag which, according to records in the Tøjhusmuseet, it 50x50 cms, it had a black field, the regimental colour; it had the provincial coat of arms in the centre and a *Dannebrog* in the top hoist. Traditionally this marker flag was carried at the Battle of Sehestedt in 1813.

The Marine Regiment

The regiment carried M1785 grenadier *Dannebrog* colours. In each corner there was a gold crown and the monogram 'C7' within green laurel wreaths. The obverse and reverse were identical. They were given one new colour M1803, which had a slightly different monogram, and seven old M1785 grenadier colours, some of which were probably transferred to the Copenhagen Regiment.

The Copenhagen Regiment, Københavns Infanteri Regiment

The newly-formed Københavns Infanteri Regiment also received national *Dannebrog* colours, like the Marine Regiment, when they were formed in 1808. Here apparently the 1st Battalion or possibly both battalions may have used a special monogram with 'F3' for the late King Frederik III. This was probably to commemorate his successful defence of Copenhagen during the siege of 1659. As their future role would be to defend Copenhagen, this was probably the reason. It may also have been a life colour. The obverse and reverse were identical.

The other battalions carried grenadier M1785 *Dannebrog*'s. In each corner there was a gold crown and monogram 'C7' within green laurel wreaths. The obverse and reverse were identical. The rest is unknown. In fact these colours were probably those of the old Marine Regiment inherited when they were disbanded. They were replaced with M1808 colours bearing the cypher of Frederik VI.

The Militia or Landevaern Regiments

These colours have been placed here due to the fact they were later reused and the men were transferred in a manner of speaking to the line.

These are the units were later re-formed and became the 3rd and 4th battalions of the line infantry regiments, originally they had simple national flags (*Dannebrogsfane*) which had the usual red field with a white cross, although the details for some of them are unknown, most of them had a either a white or medium blue coloured rectangle stitched in the centre of the cross with the inscription 'LANDEVÆRN FOR KONGEN OG FAEDRENELANDET' (Land Guard for King and Country) in gold lettering shaded black. The obverse and reverse were identical. The inscription was in written in German for the colours carried by the troops from the Germanic regions of Holstein, Schleswig and probably Oldenburg *Landeværn* units: 'Landeswehr für König und Vaterland'. These colours were first issued in 1801. In general, these squares of cloth bearing the inscriptions were removed when the *Landeværn* were transformed into reserve battalions.

Most if not all of the colours of the 3rd and 4th battalions bore in each corner, a gold crowned royal monogram of Christian VII, surrounded by green laurels; unfortunately we do not know which regiments had them. There appear to have been a number of variations in the design of the monograms used.

The light infantry units and most the volunteer units did not have or carry colours although there were a number of exceptions, Bornholm and Rensbourg amongst others carried a number of colours, and the smaller units may just have had company fanions or pennons. Other units known to have had a colour were Nyborg, Aalborg, Rønne, Borg, Westerstad, Østerstad, Nørrestads, Klædebo and Strand. These units will be covered fully in the chapters on the militia in Volume III.

Appendix I

The Soldier's Personal Equipment 1808–1814, the Official List

An infantry musketeer was issued a uniform, a musket and bayonet, a cartridge pouch (*kartouche*), calfskin backpack (*tornister*) and a bread bag. In addition, for a group of four men they had a tent, and their camp equipment which they could carry with them. The company also had an ammunition/supply wagon (*amunisjonsvogn*).

Armament
  Musket with ramrod, strap, lock plate and pan [but see note, below] and a tompion.
  Bayonet and scabbard, suspended from the waist belt.
  The grenadiers also had a grenadier sabre in a scabbard hung from the waist in a special frog.

Equipment
  A Cartridge pouch on a bandoleer (*skråbandolær*).
  30 packaged paper cartridges.
  Two flints and a worm (*krasser*), to draw musket balls from the barrel in the case of a misfire.

In the Back Pack
  Two good shirts.
  One pair of stockings.
  One pair of shoes.
  One fine and one coarse comb.
  One clothes brush, which was also used to pipe clay the belt and bandoleer.
  One shoe brush.
  One fatigue cap.
  Tallow to dress sore feet.
  One hymn book.
  A sewing needle and thread.
  A bread bag marked with red numbers on it, and a brown belt.
  A wooden butter box.
  A knife and a wooden spoon.
  Their bread ration.

In the Company Wagon (per Man)
  Six flints.
  90 cartridges dispensed 30 at a time.

Camping equipment. (For four men, who took turns to carry it)
  One copper kettle, carried in a sack with brown straps.
  Two tin canteens with a brown strap.
  One small axe.

The mention of 'lock plate and pan' may also describe the new flash guard on the M1794 and M1807 'inside-lock' muskets. The M1794 was the answer for the request for a lighter modern musket which was faster to reload. The armourer of the Copenhagen Arsenal, C.W. Kyhl, designed this all-new musket with many new features compared to the previous models. The musket really was quite ingenious, as it featured a number of important improvements on earlier models. Faster loading was permitted by introducing a conical touch-hole enabling gunpowder from the barrel to 'leak' on to the flash pan. A new bayonet attachment with a spring enabled faster bayonet mounting and dismounting. The pan had a vertical flash guard protecting the eyes of the soldier to the right of the shooter, where sparks could hit his eyes and disrupt his aim. This was further improved on the M1807 model. These models were not used much in Norway

Appendix II

Danish Ranks and British equivalents

Non-Commissioned Ranks in Different Branches of the Army 1803–14

Infantry	Jæger	Cavalry	Artillery	English Equivalent
Menig	*Jæger*	*Rytter/Menig*	*Menig*	Private
Gefreiter	*Underjæger*	*Underkorporal*	*Overkonstabel*	Lance Corporal
Korporal	*Overjæger*	*Korporal*	*Bombarder*	Corporal
Sergent	*Sergent*	*Vagtmester*	*Sergent*	Sergeant
Fourer	*Fourer*	*Kvatermester*	*Fourer*	Quartermaster
Kommandersergent	*Kommandersergent*	*Overvagtmester*	*Kommandersergent*	Sergeant Major/Colour Sergeant
			Fyrværker	Sergeant Major
			Overfyrværker	Regimental Sergeant Major

Commissioned Ranks 1803–14
    Sekondløjtant Ensign
    Løjtant Second Lieutenant
    Premier Løjtant Lieutenant
    Kaptajn Captain
    Major Major
    Oberstløjtant Lieutenant-Colonel
    Oberst Colonel

Specialist Ranks 1803–14
    Feltskærer Surgeon
    Berider Riding Instructor
    Våbenmester Master of Arms
    Bøssesmed Armourer
    Fanesmed Blacksmith
    Sadelmager Saddler

Appendix III

Danish Military Music

Unfortunately, we know very little about Danish military music before 1820 when the regiments and authorities began to keep records of regimental music and marches, so most of the music played today is no older than circa 1820. What little is known is of the older tunes and marches related to regiments during 1803–1815 is noted here.

The Danish army of the period had two standard marches, which was to be used by all regiments for Trooping the Colour, official parades, and as a common 'battle march' when the army fought in battle order.

The 'Old Danish March' used until 1808, was the official march of the Danish army. It was originally used for field exercise with all commands being given in German, from the time when the army was more 'Foreign' than Danish. This all changed when Frederik VI became king and a new set of regulations was introduced for the army. An order 18 June 1808 stated:

> I have the principle, that the simple shall be combined with the practical, in all military exercises, and in all drill. I therefore order that the now used [common] march is to be replaced by this new more easy to march to melody, and this can also be beaten quickly. It can be beaten to a Marching step of 90 paces a minute [a quick march version also to be used from this date]. From tomorrow this shall be beaten by all regiments in Copenhagen, as those tambours have already learned it. The Regiments outside Copenhagen will receive notes and will learn the same [as quick as possible].
>
> Frederik Rex

The march was officially composed by the drum major of the Life Guards, one G.F. Kittler, but a persistent myth tells us that he had this march from a note found in the old English siege camp from 1807, and that it was originally from a highland regiment. This has never been confirmed, but it is possible. More likely it was notes from one of the several bandsmen who deserted from the English regiments, some of whom took service with Danish regiments.

Appendix IV

The Development of Danish Muskets and Locks

By Jørgen Kofoed Larsen

The history of the Danish muskets are quite more interesting than one would think, and Denmark had from around 1798 some of the most modern muskets in use in the world at this period of time.

Muskets in their principal forms 1700–1815
During this period of time very little happened, except for some small basic changes in design and methods of production. Three basic types of musket thus evolved:

1. The British 'Brown Bess' or long land pattern musket
The 'Brown Bess' was a sturdy style of musket and was easy to mass produce. No significant improvements to either improve quicker firing or making it easier to fire in a close rank formation were made during this period. Variants of this musket were used from 1722 until 1838. Until the invention of the 'Forsyth Lock' percussion system in the 1820–1830s, this was a gun that could not eb used in damp or rainy weather and only the regimental gunsmiths could maintain and repair their locks.

2. The French 'Charleville' musket
Regarding the 'Charleville', apart from having bands to hold the barrel in place instead of inside lock-pins, and a slightly smaller calibre and tighter bore, nothing made this musket technically better, nor easier to fire quickly than the 'Brown Bess'. Another disadvantage was the lighter ball which lessened the range and hitting power.

Most of the armies in Europe adopted models based on one of these two muskets sooner or later. However, there was one musket type which was slightly different:

3. The Prussian infantry musket
The Prussian musket appeared to be very similar in appearance to the 'Brown Bess' (this was probably because the 'Brown Bess' was originally made after early Dutch and German muskets), based on a model first made in 1723. During the Seven Years War, with its mass battles in strict closed lines and controlled salvo fire, the Prussians needed a weapon better suited for this style of warfare. The Model 1740 was one of the first to use iron ramrods which did not break in action. The musket was further improved in 1773 with a cylindrical iron ramrod, now both ends could be used and it did not need not to be turned around, which aided faster loading by cutting down the number of movements necessary to load and requiring less room to move when in closed ranks. It was further improved in 1780 by adding a self-priming touchhole, so the powder was not only added on the pan first, but would run from the inside to the pan, when musket was turned on its side and tapped. Again this favoured speedier loading and easier and secure priming. The only drawback of this musket was that the Prussians persisted in continuing to use a rather crude and heavy rear-stock, which hampered accuracy.

The same improvements were used in Saxony and Austria, but the rest of the major belligerents persisted in using their own older more traditional designs. Austria, in an even more conservative reform around 1800 returned to a pure 'Brown Bess'-style design. Different tactics were experimented with to try to counteract the defects of the muskets design. Britain adopted the two deep line, more by necessity than by design as nearly all units in the field only had a depth of two or three lines anyhow, so they were already using this formation to maintain the correct width of the line. The 'about face' position was adopted, and the tactic of close-range rolling platoon salvoes and finishing with a bayonet charge once the enemy was sufficiently shaken was used to avoid prolonged fire fights. France adopted a tactic involving a massive use of skirmishers and concentrated artillery fire, and tried to avoid protracted line firefights and instead adopted massive attacking column bayonet attacks; with the obvious drawback that very few of the men could fire back. The Russians, Austrians, and the Prussians (partially from 1808) adopted different versions of the French tactical model including its drawbacks. Prussia then conceived a more flexible version of the same tactic. Their defeat in 1806 was not due to inferior weapons, but to bad leadership and tactics. Most of Europe adopted one or the other of these fighting tactics.

Denmark was not so conservative. The Prussian model musket was closely studied and used as a base for improvements by a number of the very able gun makers in the Danish Service (of whom Kyhl was by far the most inventive) already the M1774 musket (56,000 were made) had adopted the cylindrical ramrod, and M1791 (11,000 made) adopted the self-priming touch-hole. However, both were still rather heavy (over five kilos) and could in weight and ergonomy be compared with 'Brown Bess'.

The Prince Regent, ever to the forefront of military trends and technology, had always felt that his army should have a lighter musket and of the most modern design. This job he gave to Kyhl and this led to the M1794 Musket. This was lighter (4.3kg) and had all the improvements of its predecessors. Kyhl also made other improvements of his own. First of all, a screen or flash guard was added to the pan to protect the right-hand man in the firing line, again making it easier to fire in closed ranks. The stock now had a chinrest and a form to aid easier aiming. It had a new quick-lock bayonet attachment, with a spring added; making it possible to fix a bayonet in seconds, so that firing could be carried out without the bayonet weighing the musket down and the bayonet was only to be fitted when it was needed. This musket was taken into full service from 1798. Some 50,000 of this model had been made by 1808.

Kyhl still wanted to add one more improvement to his gun, but to do this he had to wait until 1807 to present the special 'Kyhls Inside lock'. As a young regimental gunsmith Kyhl had followed the Norwegian army during the war of 1788. His unit had carried out a flanking manoeuvre around the Swedish line of retreat and take up a position that would cut off the Swedish retreat. Both sides formed up for battle, but suddenly a heavy downpour made all the powder damp and the Norwegian unit was forced to retire as they were unable to fire and cede the way to the retreating Swedish army. This made Kyhl swear that this should never happen again! Norwegian powder already had a reputation for poor quality and whenever they could they preferred to use captured Swedish powder. He conducted a number of experiments, concentrating on an improved lock. In 1807 he was ready and the new lock was added to the M1807 pistol, carbine and the M1807 muskets (some 20,000 of these were made). The inside lock was by its design highly protected and combined with the self-priming pan much more waterproof than any lock before it. However, the lock was also so simple in design that it was very easy to clean and maintain by the soldiers themselves, and as it had few working parts it was easy to repair in general.

Until the adoption of the percussion cap this was probably one of the worlds most advanced locks, and one of the world's most advanced army muskets. Denmark could therefore use a three-deep line, combined with advanced light infantry tactics, with success, and loaded and fired their muskets with ease from closed ranks, even in wet and damp winter conditions as during the winter campaign in Northern Germany in 1813 and the Battle of Sehestedt.

When production started of the M1807 musket, stocks of the M1794 musket (and some M1791 muskets with some of the same improvements) were shipped to Norway to equip several of the new light formations created in 1810–11. In Denmark a large number of M1794 (and 1807) muskets were shortened, first for the use of all the new Jaeger companies raised with the *Annekterede battaljoner* in 1808. In 1811 it was decided that from now on, that in all the line jæger companies, half should be armed with rifles (M1803 and M1807) and the other half with the *Jægermusket* M1794/1808, so that all the companies were armed with compatible weapons and had the same firepower.

In 1815 the same arms were ordered for the different Jæger Corps and the former Skarpskytte Corps replacing the by then rather old and worn M1789 *Skarpskyttegeværer* (9,000 had been made) which had armed half of their strength until then. As with M1794/08, it is unclear if any of that M1794/08 so converted also received back sights, most probably did as this would have been an easy conversion.

The Danish rifles in this period were of the 'German type' as was the British Baker Rifle. They all received cylindrical iron ramrods, which enabled them to fire and to load when kneeling or when lying down. They all had in their stock a built-in toolbox. They did not receive self-priming touch holes, as they had their priming powder in protected powder horns. They did not have flash guards either as normally they would never fire in closed ranks but in looser open order two rank formations. The 1807 Rifle had a Kyhl's lock as well, with same improvements in maintenances and resistance to damp and water.

Appendix V

Danish Food and Rations

By Jørgen Kofoed Larsen

The best which could be said of Danish rations was that one could live off them, if and when one actually received any.

The 10-man copper cooking pot with lid, was so large that it was too heavy for a man to carry in the field, so it either was placed on the regimental supply wagons or left in the field camp. This often led to the soldiers marching for days on end without warm food, and only living off of the so-called field ration. Ten men shared a pot as *Korperalskab* (corporals' group) and either he, or a soldier with some knowledge of cooking, took turns to prepare the food.

Frederik both as prince regent and as king tried to formalise food and rations and ensure that a soldier had at least one hot a meal a day, but in practice, often because of economy or neglect, they were not of good quality. In barracks food was prepared in common, but in field camps the rations were shared out in unprepared portions, which the soldiers then had to cook themselves. Normally the dried peas or grain had to be soaked in water for some time. Then it was cooked, normally with a portion of salted, smoked or fresh meat or dried fish in same pot. Then the soup or porridge was kept in the pot, while meat or fish was placed on the lid. Each soldier had a wooden spoon and a knife, and all then 'dig in' sharing the pot and the contents on the lid. The drinking cup was the top of their water bottle or canteen. A soldier would normally carry a small glass flask in his back pack for his Schnapps ration.

King Frederik exclaimed in 1814 'If only we had been able to give all our soldiers one man cooking pots like the French, now our soldiers starve and freeze, how can we continue fighting effectively'(this was observed during the winter campaign).

Regarding rations, the contents were basically the same as they had been from the beginning of the 17th century, and this was more or less the same in both the army and the navy. Because of the limited methods of storage, most foodstuffs would be dried, smoked or salted. Also, some emphasis on the distribution of some fresh meat was carried out (meat in the army, fish in the navy). The poor quality of the water meant that in barracks or on-board ship, (thin) beer was the main drink.

Black bread was the basic foodstuff given to the individual soldier. It was either distributed as a 1.5kg kilo loaf every two days or as a 3.5 kg loaf every five days (both sizes are mentioned). This was used as breakfast and to eat when needed. Some times hardtack (like the British version a hard wheat biscuit) was also distributed as a alternative. Many soldiers also made bread soup as a warm breakfast dish. To make this the bread was broken in bits, beer if at hand or water was added and cooked to a brown soup. If some milk could be found this could be poured on top. This was also Frederik VI's preferred breakfast dish all his life – it was said to taste much better than it looked!

Each day 1/8 of a litre of schnapps (*akvavit*) was given to each soldier, nearly always of poor quality, but the strong (and probably foul!) taste was seen by the common soldier as a sign that it was good! This helped soldiers to withstand the hardships of the cold and the hunger and as such, and they were probably slightly inebriated most of the time. Soldiers normally drank their schnapps from the lid of their water canteen or directly from small private aquirred bottles kept in their backpacks, in which all soldiers were expected to carrry their daily ration. Only officers drank from glasses.

The Basic Rations (to be distributed in camp and to be cooked by the men themselves)
There were three basic types of ration:

1.
250g (heavily) salted pork/bacon.
One large cup of dried peas.
This was made into yellow pea soup and the cooked pork eaten as a side dish often with slices of black bread.

2.
250g fresh ox meat.
One large cup of pearl barley.
Some salt.

This was made into porridge and the meat cooked and eaten as side dish with black bread.

3.
250g dried fish.
Either one cup of pearl barley or later ½ cup of rice.
Some butter if available.

Note:
These basic rations could be mixed when distributed or mixed by the soldiers themselves. Also, as nearly all soldiers were from farms of some kind, they often brought extras with them or were sent by family. Further extras could be had or bought on farms as they passed, and sutlers also followed the army. Nearly all the soldiers and officers also smoked pipes, mainly clay ones.

Field Ration
When away from camp or on field service, a special field ration was distributed

1/8 liters of schnapps
500g of hardtack (*Beskøjte*)
260g of smoked bacon

It was expected that any leftovers of the black bread were carried in the bread bag. The smoked bacon was sliced and used as a 'cold cut' between two pieces of hardtack.

If not too old, the hardtacks are not so hard, but more like a biscuit and taste rather fine. If the men were in camp or had a pot at hand, the hardtack was often crumbled in water, heated and eaten as porridge.

Appendix VI

The Battle of Køge, 29 August 1807

An account of the battle from Danish sources, text supplied by Lars Kjær, *Arkivar og Arkivkoordinator*, Køge Town History Archive, Køge Museum, and Bruno Juul.

5:00 a.m. The British troops were approaching the town of Køge. Wellesley's main force was marching directly towards Køge. A small force under his second in command Colonel von Linsingen had left from Copenhagen in the middle of the night to carry out a pincer movement and attack to the south of Køge, to attack from behind and prevent the *Landeværn* from escaping.

9.00 a.m. The battle began in the fields to the north of Køge. The main British force was in position and ready just south of the Skilling inn. The Danish militia, commanded by *Generalløjtnant* Castenschiold, was positioned approximately 1,200 meters further south. The battle began with an artillery duel. The Danish artillery quickly ran out of ammunition, since they had not brought sufficient supplies with them – the rest was still locked in gunpowder depot in St. Nikolai's church).

10.00 a.m. Wellesley opens the battle and decided to attack, and the Danish line quickly broke. The Danes fled, but formed a new defense line along the current Zoffmannsvej.

11.00 a.m. The Danish forces made a few fragmented attempts of resistance. The new line of defense now came under attack; the assault was led by the Scottish 92nd Regiment of Foot, The Gordon Highlanders. Some of the Danish soldiers continued to hold out for a short while, then the militia collapsed and they fled back towards the town of Køge. After some disorganised resistance and scattered fighting in the town which continued from house to house until around 1:00 p.m. when some Danish soldiers entrenched themselves in the Town Hall, and continued to fight against superior forces.

4:00 p.m. A last defense was attempted in the Herfølge Cemetery and the battle was over. Some of the fleeing soldiers had been reorganised by *Generalmajor* Oxholm around the Church of Herfølge, A total of about 120 men had managed to gather at the cemetery. The Herfølge Church is a tall church with thick high cemetery walls and was therefore a good defense point and they entrenched themselves behind the church walls. As both the priest and deacon had disappeared and with them also the keys to the church the door had to be broken down. At first the militia succeeded in keeping the vanguard at bay, but eventually more British troops arrived and also some guns from the horse artillery were deployed on Mill hill to the east of the town, and a short struggle ensued. When Oxholm realised that continued opposition was useless he decided to surrender. The battle was over.

The battle in the church and cemetery cost two people their lives and 13 more were injured in the cemetery and more outside. Five officers, one drummer and about 120 rank and file were also taken prisoner and fell into the hands of the British soldiers. The prisoners were taken away and put on barges in the Sound. On the way they were prevented from escaping and returning to the battle by the soldiers guarding them. The wounded were transported to Herfølge rectory where inside 34-year-old Helen Margrethe Tønnesen took care of the wounded. The Dean of Højelse, M.P. Kruse came later in the day and wrote about her: 'She had great wisdom and a determined spirit, supported by her language skills she dealt with the victorious enemies; she was present everywhere and with heartfelt tenderness refreshed and nursed the wounded'.

The British troops settled then down in the empty village of Herfolge as almost everybody had fled. A soldier from the British army wrote in his memoirs that the women and children hid in chimneys in fireplaces since they did not expect anything other than death from the British troops. The Church wafer box was stolen by British troops on this occasion.

Wellesley wrote in his report:

> That although the Danish had fled with consternation and hastily and partly discarded their weapons and clothing, the new militia did exhibit a brave spirit. Some of these raw recruits fired out of the windows in Køge on our cavalry and continued to shoot down on our infantry. Others hid behind the rows of sheaves of corn standing in the fields and shot at their pursuers, not without loss for us.

During this phase of the combat some survivors of the Danish *Landeværn* soldiers managed to flee to the south. Many threw away their clogs so they could run faster –this is why it became known as the 'Battle of the Clogs'!

The Danish Order of Battle:
Commanding Officer: *Generalløjtnant* Joachim Castenschiold.
Second in Command *Generalmajor* Oxholm

7,000 infantry in 11 battalions, 150 cavalry in two squadrons and 120 artillerymen serving nine guns, calibre unknown, but probably 3-pdrs. The foot consisted of the 5th, 6th and 7th Battalions of the Nordre Sjællandske Landeværn Regiment, the 1st, 2nd, 4th, 5th, 7th, 8th, 9th and 10th Battalions of the Sønrdre Sjællandske Landeværn Regiment. There were 70 horsemen from the Sjællandske Ryttre Regiment, the only regular troops present, and 80 troopers from an unidentified *Landevaern* cavalry unit.

However, another list records 100 regular cavalry (About 70 men from Sjællandske Rytter Regiment and 30 men from other regiments, mostly from the Hussars depot and recruits' school in Køge), about 60 mounted foresters (*Herregårdsskytter*), 50–60 'lance riders', and around 300 mounted 'Landevaern ryttere'. The lance armed cavalry was a squadron raised privately by a local landowner in Roskilde (Grandjean) who brought 120 riders mounted on farm horses with him to Castenskiolds force. They arrived unarmed, but as there were no cavalry arms available they were given spears made by a local smith instead. Arriving in the evening, they were sent out on outpost duty the next morning, where they were duly surprised by the KGL Light Dragoons and were chased back to town. The KGL were only stopped by infantry fire (by which they lost about four men). The would-be lancers lost about three men, dead/wounded or prisoner, but by the evening only 60 riders could still be mustered, the rest having gone home for good! No uniform of any kind was recorded.

The Danes lost two officers killed and four wounded, while the rank and file sustained 150 men killed and 200 wounded. Their greatest loss was in prisoners. The British captured over 1,700 men including *Generalmajor* Oxholm, 9 majors, 19 captains, and 28 lieutenants. Anglo-German trophies included all nine artillery pieces, one colour, and 68 wagons.

Appendix VII

The Orders of Battle and Actions of the Danish Auxiliary Corps of the Grande Armée

Order of Battle of the Danish Auxiliary Corps in 1812
Commander in Chief 1813: Prince Frederick of Hesse
Divisional General: Ewald
Chief of Staff: Prince of Holstein-Beck, Adjutant-commandant
Chief of Staff in second: *Major* de Muck
Aides de camps: de Bardenfleth; Heilmcrone; Lilienkron

1st Brigade – *Generalmajor* Wegener
    Oldenburg Infantrieregiment (4 battalions)
    Schleswig Jægercorps (1 battalion)
    Jyske Lette Dragons (2 squadrons) *Oberst* Engelsted.
    Holstein Hussars (2 squadrons)
    A battery of Foot Artillery and a battery of Horse Artillery

2nd Brigade – *Generalmajor* Dorrien
    Dronningens Infantrieregiment (1 battalion).
    Fynske Infantrieregiment (1 battalion)
    Holstein Infantrieregiment (1 battalion)
    Schleswig Infantrieregiment (1 battalion)
    Holstenske Skarpskyttekorps (1 battalion)
    Holstein Rytter Regiment (2 squadrons)
    A battery of Foot Artillery and a battery of Horse Artillery

As part of the French XIII Corps, commanded by Marshal Davout, 1814
Commander in Chief: Prince Frederick of Hesse
Chief of Staff: *Major* de Bardenfleck.
Artillery Commander *Major* de Muck

Vanguard Brigade, *Oberst* Waldech
    Slesvsigske Jægercorps (2nd Battalion and the 3rd company)
    Holstenske Skarpskyttekorps (2 battalions)
    Jutland Hussars (2nd and 6th Squadrons)
    Battery Gerstenberg (a 6-pounder horse artillery battery, 10 guns)

1st Brigade, *Generalmajor* von Schulemburg
    Oldenburg Infantrieregiment (1st, 2nd and 4th Battalions and the Light Company from the 3rd Battalion)
    Dronningens Infantrieregiment (1st Battalion with the light company from the 2nd Battalion)
    Holstein Rytter Regiment (4 squadrons; later fell to 2 squadrons)
    Battery Koye (a 6-pounder Foot battery of 10 guns)

2nd Brigade, *Generalmajor* Lasson
    Fynske Infantrieregiment (1 Battalion)
    Holstein Infantrieregiment (3rd and 4th Battalions)
    Slesvsigske Infantrieregiment (1st and 2nd Battalions)
    Jydske Lette Dragons Regiment (4 squadrons)
    Battery Friis (a 6-pounder battery of foot of 10 guns)
    Korende Battery Gönner (a 3-pounder mobile battery of 10 guns)

In Reserve?
    Fynske Infantrieregiment (1st and 2nd Battalions)
    3rd Jydske Infantrieregiment (1st Battalion)
    3rd Company of Slesvsigske Jaegercorps
    Fynske Lette Dragons Regiment (4 squadrons)

The artillery was assisted by men of the Matros Company
Strength was around 10,200 men.

The Principal Actions
Cavalry skirmish at Gudow, 18 September 1813 in Mecklenburg
A squadron of Jyske Lette Dragons on a reconnaissance mission ran into a regiment of Cossacks.

Cavalry skirmish at Gudow, 26 September 1813 in Mecklenburg
One squadron of Jyske Lette Dragons under *Rittmester* Wittrog ambushed a large force of some 300 marauding Cossacks whom they repulsed and put to flight, leaving a number of dead and wounded Cossacks behind them.

Skirmish at Weisser Hirsch, 7 October 1813 in Mecklenburg.
An advance guard of Lutzow's Frei-corps and a number of Cossacks attacked a fortified Danish camp. Whilst attacking the camp the enemy was hit in the flank by the hussars: the Cossacks broke and the infantry fled losing a large number of dead and wounded. The Danes also took 54 prisoners.
>Schlesvigske Infantry Regiment.
>2 or 3 companies of Jægers
>*Sekondløjtant* von Ewald
>2 squadrons of the Husarregiment (the 2nd and 6th squadrons?)

Battle of Rosengarten, 12 October 1813
A running cavalry battle between a Danish light dragoon regiment and at least one regiment of hussars of the German-Russian Legion. The hussars were beaten losing 60 dead and wounded as well as 47 prisoners.
>*Oberst* Engelsted
>Jydske Lette Dragons regiment, they lost two dead and three wounded

The Battle of Boden, 4 December 1813
A important Danish victory against a numerically vastly superior vanguard of the Prussian, Russian and Swedish corps led by Lieutenant General Walmoden
>2nd Brigade, *Generalmajor* Lasson
>Fynske Infantrieregiment (1st and 2nd battalions)
>Slevsigske Infantrieregiment (1st and 2nd battalions)
>Jæger company of Dronningens Infantrieregiment (2nd Battalion)
>Jæger company of Holstein Infantrieregiment (3rd Battalion)
>Jæger company of Oldenborg Infantrieregiment (3rd Battalion)
>Fynske Lette Dragonregiment (60 men, one squadron)
>Regiment of Hussars (squadron of 50 men)

Note: at this battle the Danes fought in winter dress, greatcoats etc.

Battle of Alt-Rahlstedt, 6 December 1813
A mixed force of Danish light dragoons and a regiment of French chasseurs struck and routed a large force of Cossacks at the village of Tonnendorf and chased them to Rahlstedt. Here a regiment Russian-German Legion hussars and other Cossacks counter-attacked them, after which the dragoons and the French Chasseurs made a fighting withdrawal executing a number of counter attacks to keeping the enemy at bay.
>*Oberst* Angel Place
>Jyske Lette Dragonregiment
>One regiment of Chasseurs à Cheval

Skirmish at Bornhøved, 7 December 1813.
A Swedish Cavalry brigade under *Generallöjtnant* Sköldebrand made a surprise cavalry attack on the Danish rearguard. A rather confused affair, the Swedish cavalry charged a village which had walls and hedges all around it. Some of the Danes were caught out in the open before they could form square; their artillery fired too high and units were bumping into each other, friend and foe alike. However, as the Danes got themselves sorted out the Swedish started taking some casualties. It was regarded as a Danish victory, just, with both sides withdrawing.

Franco-Danish Forces
Commander: *Général de Brigade* Lallemand
>2 (?) Squadrons 17th Polish/Lithuanian Line Lancers
>Holstein Rytter Regiment
>Hussar Squadron
>Holstein Infanteriregiment (1st and 2nd battalions)
>Holstenske Skarpskyttekorps (1st and 2nd battalions)
>3rd Jydske Infanteriregiment (1st battalion)
>A company of Schleswig Jægers
>Jæger Company 4th Battalion Oldenborgske Infanteriregiment
>Korende Battery Gonner, 2 guns
>Battery Gerstenberg

Swedish Forces
>4 squadrons of Scanian (Skånske) Hussars
>2 squadrons of Mörner Hussars
>2 squadrons of von Schill's Hussars (Prussians), commanded by the brother of the von Schill killed fighting the Danes at Stralsund in 1809.
>4 squadrons of Scanian (Skånske) Carabineers
>A force of 1,300 men.

Battle of Sehested, 10 December 1813
The Danish army of 10,000 men (*Auxiliærkorpset*) under Prince Frederik of Hessen were withdrawing from northern Germany, but the road to Rendsburg was blocked by a force of 10,000 men of the Prussian-Russian-Swedish army corps men under Lieutenant General Walmoden. The Danes lanced a series of brilliantly executed attacks which threw the allies back over the Eider. Wallmoden's main force was destroyed and he lost about 2,000 men, including 654 prisoners and two guns, while the Danish suffered 549 wounded of which only 66 died.

Commander: Prince Frederick of Hesse
Under his direct command
>Korende Battery Gonner
>17th Polish/Lithuanian Line Lancers
Avant-garde *Général de Brigade* Lallemand
>Schleswig Jægercorps (2 battalions)
>Oldenborgske Infanteriregiment

Jutland Husaren Division (2nd and 6th squadrons)
  Battery Gerstenberg
1st Brigade *Generalmajor* Schulenburg
  Slevigske Infanteriregiment
  Fynske Lettedragoner Regiment, *Oberstløjtant* Høgh-Guldberg.
  Battery Friis
2nd Brigade *Generalmajor* Lasson
  Fynske Infanteriregiment
  Holstenske Ryttere Regiment
  Battery Koye
Strength 9,500

Note: at this battle the Danes fought in winter dress, greatcoats etc. The artillery was assisted by men of the Matros Company. One company of the Hertuginde Lovise Augustas Liv Jæger Corps was also present.

Appendix VIII

Known Military paintings by C.A. Lorentzen 1749–1828

Circa 1789. Carl af Hessens, general in command at the Battle at Quistrum Bridge in Sweden 27–28 September 1788 (Frederiksborg Nationalhistorisk Museum).

Circa 1790. Painting attributed to C.A. Lorentzen. Cavalry parade with Crown Prince Frederik.

C.1800. the town of Bergen, seen from a Battery called Hæggrénsset (It is possibly as early as 1790 as the Prince Regent bought '15 Norwegian Scenes' from him that year).

Circa 1801. Battle of Copenhagen (Panorama).

Circa 1802. Slaget Paa Reden, where he infers that it was the British who called for a truce.

Circa 1803. Portrait Major F.C.C. Friboe, the Hussar Regiment.

Circa 1804. The Prince Regent on horseback in uniform as a general (Attributed).

Circa 1807. The terrible Bombardment of Copenhagen by the British Army (one of several).

Circa 1807. The shameful conduct of the British nation at the Nyholm on 17 October.

Circa 1807. Gunboats off Kastellet and Danish artillery in Action.

C.1807/1808. A painting titled erroneously 'English artillery in action at Copenhagen 1807', but in fact it shows a Danish foot artillery battery coming in to action against British warships. Present location unknown, possibly in the United Kingdom.

Circa 1810 street scene (Kongens Lyngby, Frilandsmuseet)

Circa 1811/1812 His Royal majesty in cortège to the appointment of knights at Rosenborg

Circa 1811/1812. Konglige Livgarde til Hest and Hussars escorting King Frederik VI to the theatre (Kongens Nytorv, Castle Rosenborg, Copenhagen)

Circa 1812–13. Painting attributed to C.A. Lorentzen. Uhlans in camp.

A little-known fact about this artist is that he frequently slipped a cameo of himself into the picture, either as an artist, as in painting of Frederik going to the theatre, or holding a horse in, 'English Artillery in action'.

Bibliography and Sources

Original Sources I: Iconographical Sources

Brockdorff, Schack von, *Den Danske Armées Uniformer* c.1806 (Copenhagen: Tøjhusmuseet)

Köller, Frederick Ludwig von, a series of watercolours (Kiel: Darmstadt University and Federal State Library)

Ljunggren, Carl Johann, *Minnes-Anteckningar under 1813 och 1814 årens kampagner uti Tyskland och Norge* (Stockholm: 1855)

Lorentzen, Christian August, *Uhlans in camp 1812-13* (private collection)

Lorentzen, Christian August, *Frederik den 6. kørende til det kongelige teater* c.1811/1813 Kongernes Samling (Castle Rosenborg Copenhagen: With the kind permission of Peter Kristiansen, Curator)

Möller, *Fuldstændige Tabeller over alle den Kongelige Danske og Norske Armee tilhørende, regimenters, corpers, batailloners, borgervæbningers og frivillige etc, corpers Corpser Uniform* (Kiöbenhavn: C. Steen forlag, 1810) not to be confused with Waldemar Moller of c.1892

Senn, Johs, Eckersberg C.W. Wilhelm Heuer & J. Reiter, *Danske Klædedragter* (København c. 1808-1812)

Suhr Brothers, *Abbildung der Uniformen aller in Hamburg seit den Jahren 1806 bis 1815 einquartiert gewesener Truppen.* (Berlin: Staatlicher Museum Kunstbibliothek). These illustrations were published in the 1820s in a book called *The Danish Army in Hamburg (1812 – 1814) Uniform Plates*. They were drawn and painted by Christoph and Cornelius Suhr. Only four copies are known to be in existence.

Von Prangen, series of 19 watercolors of Danish soldiers, Glückstadt c. 1809-1810 (Hamburg-Altona Das Altonaer Museum,)

Original Sources II: Manuscripts

Kierulf, Herman, *Kalender over samtlige officerer.ved den kongelige Danske og Norske Armée ansatte Officeerer og øvrige Beetiente, saavelsom over Borgervæbninger og frivillige corps No. IV.* (København: Kongelig og Universitets Bogtrytter, 1811)

Printed Sources

Aagaard, Erik, *Den Norske Hær I Dansketiden-et billedheft* (Oslo Norway: Forsvarsmuseet Småskrift nr. 10, 1992)

Aagaard, Erik, *Det Norske kavaleris standarter* (Oslo: Norsk Våpenhistorisk Selskap Årbok, 2016)

Aagaard, Erik, *Det Norske infanteri faner.* (Oslo: Norsk Våpenhistorisk Selskap Årbok, 2017)

Aagaard, Erik, *Tilføyelser og debat: Krigsskolens faner* (Oslo: Norsk Våpenhistorisk Selskap Årbok, 2018)

Bellander, Erik, *Dräkt och Uniform* (Stockholm: P A Norstedt & Söner 1973)

Blom, Otto, *Ældre danske metal og jern stykker* [Older Danish Metal and Cast Iron Cannons] (København: Krigsministeriet, 1891)

Bruhn, Helge, *Dannebrog og danske faner gennem tiderne* (København: Jespersen og Pios Forlag, 1949)

Carman, W.Y. *A Dictionary of Military Uniforms* (London: B. T. Batsford, 1977)

Cassin-Scott, Jack, *Scandinavian Armies in the Napoleonic Wars* (London: Osprey, 1976)

Eriksen, E. & Frantzen, O. L., *Dansk Artilleri I Napoleonstiden* (København: Tøjhusmuseets, 1988)

Funcken, Liliane & Fred, *L'Uniforms et les Armes des Soldats du Premier Empire* (Tournai: Casterman,1969)

Johansen Hauerbach, M.W, *Fanekatalog over Hærmuseets samling* (Oslo: Utg. Hærmuseet, 1956)

Johansen, Oberstløjtnant Jens, *Frederik VI's Hær 1784-1814* (København: Udgivet af Generalstaben, Heydes Bogtrykkeri,1948)

Jonsgaard, Moen Ola *Regimental Distinctions of Norwegian regiments 1807-14* (Oslo: Elverumske Skieløber Compagnie, 2014)

Kannik, Preuben, *Military Uniforms of the World in Colour* (London: Blandford, 1968).

Knötel, Richard, Knötel H. & Sieg, H, *Uniforms of the World* [Handbuch der Uniformkunde] (London: re-print, Arms & Armour Press, 1980)

Lange P.H.W., *Den danske generalstabs historie* (København: Unknown Publisher, 1889)

Liebe. Poul Ib, *Napoleons Danske Hjælpetropper "Auxiliærkorpset 1813"* (Copenhagen: Forlaghet Zac, 1968)

Lienhart, Dr. & Humbert, R, *Les Uniformes de l'Armée Française de 1690 à 1894* (Saint Aignan: Edition de Leipzig, 1897)

Lars Lindeberg, *De så det ske – Englandskrigene 1801-14* (Copenhagen:Lademann Forlagsaktieselskab,1974)

Nielsen, Kay S, *Danske blankvåben* (Copenhagen: Forlaghet Sixtus, 1978)

Over, Keith, *Flags and Standards of the Napoleonic Wars* (London: Bivouac Books, 1976)

Petersen Karsten Skjold, *Kongens klaeder. Hærens uniformer og udrustning I Danmark- Norge* (Copenhagen: Tøjhusmuseet, 2014).

Petersen, Karsten Skjold, *Faner og Estandarter I den Danske Haer* (Copenhagen: Tøjhusmuseet, 2016)

Richter, V., *Den danske landmilitærestat 1801-1894* (København: bd. 1-2, 1934-1935)

Sandstedt, Fred, *Between the Imperial Eagles, Sweden's Armed Forces during the Revolutionary and the Napoleonic Wars 1780-1820* (Stockholm; Armémuseum, 2000)

Scheel, Heinrich Otto von, *Mémoires D'artillerie, Contenant L'artillerie Nouvelle Ou Les faits Dans L'artillerie Françoise en 1765* (Paris: chez Magimel, 1765). This was the book used as a guide for modernising the Danish artillery.

Strøm, Knut Erik, *Norske Borgervæpingsuniformer et Billedhefte* (Oslo: Forsvarsmuseet Akershus, 1992)

Thaulow, Th. *Samsø i krigsårene 1801-14* (Samsø: Boghandler Henri Neble, 1934)

Thaulow, Th., Mentze, Ernst, & Møller, M. Friis, *Livgarden gennem 300aar* (Copenhagen: Martins Forlag, 1974)

Vaupell, Otto, *Den danske Hærs Historie til Nutiden og den norske Hærs Historie indtil 1814* (København: Forlagt af den Gyldendalske Boghandel, 1872-76)

Walberg, Erik, *Vapenlexikon Artilleri 1350-1880* (Stockholm: Sveriges militähistorika arv SMHA 2017)

Walbom-Pramvig, B, *Uniformer, Faner og Väben I Den Danske Hær fra 1659 til 1980* (Frederikssund: Forlaghet Thorsgaard ApS, 1988)

Wise, Terry, *Flags of the Napoleonic Wars (3)* (London: Osprey,1981)

Wise, Terry, *Military Flags of the World 1618-1900* (New York: Blandford/Arco, 1978)

Wolter, Hans Christian, *Den Danske Hær I Napoleonstiden 1801-1814. Håndbog om uniformer, faner, udrustning og krigshistorie* (Copenhagen: Tøjhusmuseets skrifter 12. Tøjhusmuseet, 1992)

Magazines and Periodicals

Bruun, Daniel, 'En ung Rytterofficers Erindringer fra felttoget 1813' *Militært Tidsskrift*, 43.årg. (1914) pp.1-30

Hoff, An, 'Ridende og kørende artillery', *Danske Artilleri Tidsskrift*, 1970, p.185-194

Hoff, An., 'Det ridende artilleri i Danmark', *Danske Artilleri Tidsskrift*, 1970, p.222-227

Snorrason, Torstein, & Wügler, Hansen, 'The Assault on Stralsund 1809, Part I', *Tradition Magazine* (English), No. 52, pp.22-25, 36-37

Snorrason, Torstein, & Wügler, Hansen, 'The Assault on Stralsund 1809, Part II,' *Tradition Magazine* (English), No. 53, pp.2-7

Snorrason, Torstein, & Wügler, Hansen, 'The Light Dragoon Regiment of Jutland 1813-1814', *Tradition Magazine* (English), No.56, p.33

Snorrason, Torstein, & Wügler, Hansen, 'The Battle of Boden 4th December 1813', *Tradition Magazine* (English), No. 64, p.20

Wolter, Hans Christian, 'Danish Infantry of the Line and Light Infantry 1803-1814, the Perry Achievement', *Chakoten*, December 2016, No. 71 årgang nr.4, pp.10-17.

Thureholm, Ole & Larsen, Jørgen, & Wolter, Hans Christian, 'Danish and Norwegian Cavalry and Artillery 1803-1814, the Perry Achievement', *Chakoten*, September 2018, No. 73 årgang nr.3, pp.4-10.

Uniform Prints

Dr. Peter Bunde. Brigade Uniformtafeln, *Tafel 16 KGR DÄNEMARK REITER- LIEBREGIMENT*, Herzogenrath, Germany 1999.

Dr. Peter Bunde. Brigade Uniformtafeln, *Tafel 17 KGR DÄNEMARK REITER-REGIMENT SEELAND*, Herzogenrath, Germany1999.

Dr. Peter Bunde. Brigade Uniformtafeln. *Tafel 18 KGR DÄNEMARK REITER-REGIMENT SCHESWIG*, Herzogenrath, Germany1999.

Dr. Peter Bunde. Brigade Uniformtafeln, *Tafel 19 KGR DÄNEMARK REITER-REGIMENT HOLSTEIN*, Herzogenrath, Germany1999.

Dr. Peter Bunde. Brigade Uniformtafeln, *Tafel 22 KGR DÄNEMARK; DIE INFANTERIE REGIMENTER 1808-13*, Herzogenrath, Germany 2005.

Dr. Peter Bunde. Brigade Uniformtafeln, *Tafel 23 KGR DÄNEMARK; LIEBGARDE ZU FUSS 1806-15*. Herzogenrath, Germany1999.

Dr. Peter Bunde. Brigade Uniformtafeln, *Tafel 26 KGR DÄNEMARK LIEBREGIMENT DER LIETCHEN DRAGONER*, Herzogenrath, Germany 2015.

Dr. Peter Bunde. Brigade Uniformtafeln, *Tafel 27 KGR DÄNEMARK LEICHTES-DRAGONER REGIMENT FUNEN*, Herzogenrath, Germany 2015.

Dr. Peter Bunde. Brigade Uniformtafeln, *Tafel 28 KGR DÄNEMARK LEICHTES-DRAGONER REGIMENT JUTLAND*, Herzogenrath, Germany 2015.

Dr. Peter Bunde. Brigade Uniformtafeln, *Tafel 29 KGR DÄNEMARK PRINZ FRIEDRICH FERDINAND DRAGONER REGIMENT*, Herzogenrath, Germany 2015.

Dr. Peter Bunde. Brigade Uniformtafeln, *Tafel 33 KGR DÄNEMARK LIEBREGIMENT ZU FUSS DER KÖNIGIN*, Herzogenrath, Germany 2009.

Dr. Peter Bunde. Brigade Uniformtafeln, *Tafel 41 KGR DÄNEMARK; INFANTERIE REGIMENT HOLSTEIN* , Herzogenrath, Germany 2009.

BIBLIOGRAPHY AND SOURCES

Dr. Peter Bunde. Brigade Uniformtafeln, *Tafel 258 KGR DÄNEMARK; FUSS-ARTILLERIE*, Herzogenrath, Germany 2012.

Dr. Peter Bunde. Brigade Uniformtafeln, *Tafel 259 KGR DÄNEMARK; REITENDE ARTILLERIE,* Herzogenrath, Germany 2012.

Web Sources

'Uniformserie Suhr' < http://napoleon-online.de/suhr.html> (accessed 9 January 2020) for the plates by Suhr.

'Arma-Dania. The Virtual Museum of Danish Arms and Armour' <https://www.arma-dania.dk/public/timeline/_ad_blankvaben_list.php> (accessed 9 January 2020); site containing details and photographs of Danish weapons.